TILL DEATH US DO PART

PHILIP VERNON NICHOLLS

cc|p
CARIBBEAN CHAPTERS

First Edition, December 2018.

 Caribbean Chapters Publishing Ltd.

Book cover designed by Jahred Corbin

ISBN (paperback): 978-179-1884-69-7

ACKNOWLEDGEMENTS

IT IS difficult to accurately acknowledge all those who have contributed in a meaningful way to the publication of this book. This is because attempting to include persons by mention of name runs the risk of leaving out equally meritorious persons whose help has contributed in several ways, be it by word or deed, to the telling of this tale which is not fictional because it relates what has transpired. To everyone who offered a kind word of support, be it by a chance meeting or by deliberately getting in contact from places near and far to pass on their best wishes or to give constructive criticism for the relating of events in my first book, a forerunner to this one, their actions are much appreciated.

Over the last two years that I have been working on the manuscript I have had much help from Glynne Murray with the editing and correction of my written thoughts. Several friends unknowingly contributed by being sounding boards for my thoughts, thereby turning my thoughts into words and often by their advice and support helping me immensely.

Unfortunately, I am precluded not only by protocol, but so as not to bring them into the hurly burly fray of what my legal troubles have become, from naming the several judicial persons, again from near and far, who not only directed me to where I would find answers to questions of law that would assist me with the challenges I was facing, but challenged me to put my thoughts in writing. My appreciation knows no bounds.

Shatara Ramsey, Maxine Babb, Juel Holder and Shernell Cole, all of whom at one time or another endured being my Legal Secretary, assisted me with turning my writings into transcripts, often tempering my rich language by striking same from the final version. They have assisted me tremendously.

Finally, my God-daughter Erica Hinkson has been a tower of strength in marketing this and my previous book, and has teamed up with my daughter Carissa to bring me into the modern world of Social Media. Not to mention Anya and Edaynah, who keep reminding of what should not be commented on lest I should embarrass them.

AUTHOR'S NOTE

WHEN I was called to the Bar in 1986, I never envisaged that within a decade I would be embroiled in circumstances that would eventually lead to me spending more time on other matters than the practice of law. The last five years, during which time I have written two books—even though the books have arisen from events of a legal nature—are evidence that the direction of my life had completely changed from my chosen calling to one where I now view the legal system with contempt rather than as a host for honourable men to display their learning and more importantly their character.

Over this time I have spent more time on questions and dealing with issues that I was not trained for ironically because of the misuse of law by persons who were sworn to uphold it. The breach of trust by two of the closest attorneys-at-law to me as I started out in practice now pales in comparison with what has been done not only by others in the profession, but the dysfunction within the judicial system.

I never envisaged it and to be fair I really do not have any answers to solving the problem or even suggesting measures to mitigate against future problems despite having spent long sleepless nights pondering the subject. Sadly, I have concluded that the problem is not simply with the Law but with humanity, which has used the Law in ways not intended to be used, and exploited the conservatism in the profession of not wanting to call a spade a spade and rock the boat.

My first book was written with a burning sense of anger at what had transpired. I felt a compelling need to get matters off my chest partly because of the failure of the police/DPP to lead any evidence against me which meant that I had no chance to dispute same and offer another narrative to the one put forward by the charges filed. When I look back at the drafts of the manuscript, they contain a level of vitriol that at the time surprised me, but on reflection was not surprising.

This second book has been written not so much with the continuing sense of anger that is still very much there, but out of a sense of incredulity that despite clear facts as to what has transpired there has been absolutely no effort to help me out of the malaise that has been inflicted on me. In fact, quite the opposite, there has been a deliberate attempt to ensure that my life continues to be held hostage by others who bear me clear ill will.

Such help I was hoping would have been forthcoming not for my personal benefit, but so that the remaining several clients affected by what has gone could be relieved of their misery. The refusal by many to simply do what is right, not to mention those who have continued to deliberately obstruct my efforts at recovery, is symptomatic of the worst traits of human beings, not just lawyers.

Much of this second book is a continuation of what went before, although it is possible to read one book without the other. As I was exhausted after I finished the first I had no immediate plans to write a second, but the reactions to it with continued questions about whether it has made a difference were just the spur I needed. As ever I take full responsibility for what is published in case a certain idiot, as he has done before, threatens to sue persons who type the manuscript.

But perhaps the heartfelt note that I received from Anya, one of my 16-year-old twin daughters, which brought tears to my eyes, sums up best what the last five years have been about. And as she has so poignantly expressed her thoughts it has become the foreword to this my second book.

FOREWORD

I HAVEN'T read my father's book yet. I know it sounds terrible, it sounds like I don't care about what has happened to him or what's going on in his life. But honestly, I'm just scared. I'm so scared. I've seen firsthand what his job has done to him, what his fellow colleagues have done to him and it makes me so sad. I remember the day my father was arrested like it was yesterday.

I was eleven years old, just started my 6th week of 1st form at Combermere and I was having a good day at school with my friends, completely oblivious to what was happening to my father at the time. I remember he was supposed to pick me up that day and take me and my sister to get some books from Cloisters. So imagine my surprise and complete happiness at seeing my old nanny, who I love dearly, drive in and say she was here for me and not for Tyeisha, her granddaughter who is in the same year as me. I didn't realize what was going on just yet, I just assumed that Daddy had got caught up with work and he asked Auntie Lucy to come and pick us up.

I never in my wildest dreams would've imagined that he was in a jail cell. Never. I was expecting to see him when I walked through the door, but he wasn't there. My first thought was: ...*is Daddy dead? Is that why everyone's acting so strange?* "No he's not dead," my older sister informed me, but she still wouldn't tell me where he was; apparently she knew and I didn't. I wasn't happy about that.

Eventually after a lot of begging and non-stop asking she

told me where he was. "Dad's been arrested" she said. My heart literally stopped. I couldn't breathe, I couldn't believe it. I honestly couldn't. Tears welled up in my eyes and I fought so hard to hold them back, but I couldn't. "Why?" I asked in my heartbroken, 11 year old voice. "What did he do?" I don't remember what she told me, I honestly don't... but I do know what he was wrongfully accused for and since that day, everything has been worse than before.

With regard to my father's financial situation, I am so worried about him. I want to read his book, I really do, but I can't. I will try to though. I will honestly try. I always keep saying I'm gonna do it in the summer or the Christmas vacation, but it never happens.

Anya Nicholls

To my family and friends,
both those still with me
and those already departed,
who by their support and encouragement
have been with me along this tortious journey;

Not to forget my detractors;

Hope springs eternal.

Hope has kept me going through it all.

TABLE OF CONTENTS

This book is a memoir.
The events are portrayed to the
best of the author's memory.

Events, locales and conversations come
from the author's recollection of them.

In order to maintain anonymity, in some
instances names of individuals, and some
identifying characteristics and details such
as physical properties, occupations, email
addresses and places of residence, have
been changed or omitted.

CHAPTER 1

Forget the Lotto... Lucky to be Alive

ON TUESDAY December 6th 2016 I was at home resting and listening to music as I often do before drifting off to sleep. This was one of many normal days when the children were not with me. Suddenly I began to feel generally unwell—hot, clammy and disoriented. I sat up in bed with my head spinning and wondered what was happening, as the fan was on despite the relatively chilly time of year. Despite this I felt as if I was roasting up.

I reached for the phone to call my brother Christopher who is a doctor and was prepared to weather the riot act that he usually reads me when we discuss my health. I remember picking up the phone but not making the call. It later turned out that I did not call him. The next thing I knew the phone was on the ground, and I was in somewhat of a daze. I picked the phone up from the ground, looked at my watch and noticed that while only a minute or two had passed I no longer had the feelings of illness that had so prompted me to try to contact Christopher. I shrugged my shoulders and thought to myself: *Philip, you are getting old now having these hot flashes...* and I went to sleep.

On Friday December 9th I travelled to Jamaica to obtain a Police Certificate of Character, which was needed to process my

Application for a Pre-Boarding Clearance from Immigration Canada. One was required for each country I had lived in for over three months as an adult. The expletives that came out of my mouth when I was made aware of the requirement cannot be printed here. I was seething at the continued fall-out from the events of October 2013.

While in Jamaica I received a call from the office of Dr. Jeff Massay on December 12th asking whether I could come in the next day for what Dr. Massay termed was an end of year chat. I replied that I was not in the island and would not be back until the day after, but would come in on December 15th. I chuckled as I thought that this invitation to a chat with Dr. Massay, while not uncommon, was a polite way of inviting me to be read the riot act.

Dr. Massay has been more than simply my cardiac specialist for nearly the last thirty years. During this time he has not only provided wise counsel on a variety of subjects, but allowed me to sound off to get things of my chest and hence I would usually be given the last appointment. He had on many occasions spoken to me about how stress had and would continue to be a factor in my health challenges. Arising out of these discussions I had written a chapter on the subject in my previous book and was touched that he took the trouble out of his busy schedule to come to its launch.

He always seemed to be there when he was needed most. I recall the Saturday of the 1995 Test Match against Australia at Kensington Oval as a case in point. He had called me in something of a panic to say that despite his best efforts he had been unable to acquire a ticket for the game. I promised to get him one as I would have been at the ground early as part of my duties on the Grounds Committee. I had no luck. All the tickets were sold, with not even any complimentary ones remaining.

For the only time that I can remember during my eighteen year sojourn on the Board of the Barbados Cricket Association I thought *to hell with that, I have been down here* (by then nearly ten years) *too long not getting any benefit and expending my energy without getting nor expecting any compensation...* so I was going to get a ticket by hell or high water. I went into the Oval's office and informed Mrs. Mahy that since I had not requested all manner of complimentary tickets like others and now all were gone, I wanted a Medical Pass issued to Dr. Massay so he could view the game. I coopted him to the Medical Committee of doctors on duty at the ground on match days right then and there.

This drew the inevitable comments that I was skirting the rules, which I denied, although I admitted I may have been bending same but it was for a good cause and so the pass was issued. During the day's play I got an urgent call from the same Oval's office that the Australian coach, Bobby Simpson, had suffered a heart attack in the dressing room and the whereabouts of Dr. Massay was needed urgently. I chuckled, not at Simpson's misfortune but at what fate had decreed and indicated where he was sitting in the Three W's Stand just upstairs of the office. Simpson survived, thanks in no small part to Dr. Massay, but the relaxation I had hoped he would have gotten from a day at cricket had come to a sudden end.

As scheduled I went to see Dr. Massay on December 15th. During the chat, much of which was about the need for me to lose more weight and get more exercise, I casually explained to him the episode that had occurred just over a week ago. It was so far from my mind by then that I could not even be sure of the day it happened. As I described what had occurred, he started to frown. So, I asked:

"What's wrong?"

He said, "Philip, I feel you either suffered a minor stroke or the defibrillator that Dr. Greene implanted in you had shocked you. I will have to interrogate it."

"Interrogate? What ever do you mean?"

He replied "I will get the technicians here to download the data from the device, so we can check what occurred."

That afternoon I returned to his office to be hooked up to various electronic paraphernalia to allow for the interrogation of the monitor inside of me. This was done by two young technicians, Ian and Katrina, and as I was to learn that since it was implanted it records every beat that my heart has taken.

As the paper with all the squiggly lines was being churned out they appeared to be getting increasingly excited as they read the data. I asked: "What's going on?" to which they responded "The machine shocked you, so it is working and did its job. See the printout." Of course the 'printout' was unintelligible to me. But then they added "in fact that was not the first time... it shocked you a couple of months earlier but you were sleeping as it was about 3:00 am. Your heart stopped, and it restarted it."

The next day it was back to Dr. Massay. He had the printouts in front of him and said:

"Philip, look. Your heart started to go into arrhythmia, meaning it started beating uncontrollably. What the machine did was to monitor it for about thirty seconds and when it realised that it was not slowing naturally, it shocked you, stopped your heart and then restarted it within the parameters that Dr. Greene set when he inserted it. That was when the phone would have dropped from your hand and you didn't know why."

He continued "Well, my boy, the machine has now done its job twice and all I can tell you is that you have had your luck, so don't waste time playing the Lotto. It has more than paid for itself." He then mused: "I suspect that something similar is the cause of sudden death among young persons who die suddenly of a heart attack." I thought immediately of Stephen Alleyne because as Dr. Massay said it happens suddenly without warning.

"No use worrying," he continued "there is nothing you can do about it… the device is a safeguard."

As he and several others have suggested to me, the intolerable stress that I have been under these last two decades has contributed in no small measure to my present predicament. As in all things I have to accept that some of my lifestyle choices over the years may well have contributed to this, but as I think back over the last twenty-five years not a day has passed when I have not worried about some aspect of the Cottle predicament, how I am going to make life enjoyable again, or as my pharmacist Allison Hutson Daniel says, how I am going to start smiling again.

Not for the first time I find myself writing at 4:00 am as I put pen to paper to start my second book. This is not only because it is quiet and the phone doesn't ring, but it is the result of tossing and turning for a couple of hours in an unfruitful attempt to fall asleep. As I was later to find out my sleep pattern was a contributory cause to the immediate problems, but like in all aspects of my life it is a vicious cycle of interconnected events.

As I look back on events that have transpired since I finished writing my first book *More Binding Than Marriage* towards the end of 2015, nearly two years later the sense of foreboding that I have felt has often turned to depression as the stark realization of the path that my life has followed envelops me, so in a sense writing gives some relief.

The quip by Dr. Massay about the Lotto resonated with me more and more, as I had long felt that my best chance of getting out of the financial quagmire that I am in would be to win the Lotto. Or perhaps I should now join a political party and submit an invoice for payment of millions. Neither is likely to happen, but as Jeff has said I have my luck in other ways and for that I am thankful, especially as I watch my three daughters grow into fine young ladies.

CHAPTER 2

Nothing Much Has Changed

AS I struggled to end my first book I recalled a similar feeling that I last experienced towards the end of 1986. Then I was trying to finish my dissertation as part of my requirement for the award of the degree of Master of Laws from the University of Manchester. Despite many a sleepless night while studying, it appeared as if I was simply treading water, going nowhere but just becoming more and more frustrated. The similarity did not end there, for there was a cost to my health then as well. Pulling eighteen-hour days hunched over research papers (no computers or smart phones to assist you in those days) inevitably meant unsociable hours and eating food from anywhere open at 2:00 in the morning.

From one of those late-night purchases I was to contract food poisoning that led to the development of a sero negative arthritis that attacked my hip joint and has left me with a permanent limp. Fast forward to today and the growing connection between the stress I have been under and the cardiac issues that I am currently facing precipitated in part by a lack of sleep.

Just as I did in 1986, I was to do in 2015 and just start writing otherwise I would still be collecting information. One difference is that I don't know where my copy of the 1986 dissertation is, unlike my first book. It is at times like this that I regret my failings to adopt the much appreciated traits of the late F. St.C. Hutchinson Q.C with respect to record keeping. Today I can refer to books that he started keeping long before I joined Cottle Catford in his familiar neat handwriting to confirm what happened to title deeds of much older vintage, so locating a lengthy treatise should not have been difficult.

This time around it has been somewhat different, because it is not so much getting started but ending that is now the problem. To start this second book was easy, and for that I must thank many of the readers of the first book—family, friends, colleagues, students and total strangers who have come up to me, introducing themselves if they were strangers, but all making very positive comments about the book while commiserating with me about the underlying events which formed the basis for my writing.

Unlike my first book, the title for this book was not in my mind when I started writing. This did not hamper the pace of my writings, but what I found was that almost daily I was off on another tangent as another problem, all connected to the original problem of Cottle Catford, reared its head. So my problem was not so much when to start, but when or how to end, as the more things changed the more they remained the same.

That saying is French in origin, traced to a 19th century novelist by the name of Alphonse Karr. To my mind, it perfectly illustrated where I am as I write more than two years after the publication of my first book, for nothing has changed—or to be more accurate nothing positive has emerged while the horrors associated with my personal situation have not only continued, but have gotten worse.

My role as a parent had now brought me into close contact

with Combermere School and it was there that the impact of what I was facing was brought home forcibly to me.

For some time there had been complaints about an environmental problem at the school—a pungent odour that was making children and staff sick. Whatever the cause of these smells and whoever was responsible for failing to deal with the issue is now a moot point, but at the time it led to severe disruption in the school on more than one occasion.

The school was forced to relocate for a term on one occasion, and on the other when an alternative site could not be located at short notice to house most of the school together, it simply closed. During the closure a myriad of environmental tests were carried out to determine the cause of the smells and in the end the cause was traced to bad maintenance of a tired plant which to be fair was not unique to Combermere.

Difficult as it was for Beverley and I to deal with the unexpected burden of ensuring that minors who if left alone would fall prey to that well-known saying that the devil finds work for idle hands, it was nothing compared to what the majority of parents were facing as school was closed. It was not just a question of supervision, but as time wore on and on, valuable teaching time was being lost which would never be regained for students facing career-changing exams.

As the situation at Combermere dragged on with no apparent resolution in sight as the children had been out of school for more than six weeks, I attended what I initially thought was a Parent Teacher's Meeting to discuss the situation held at Harrison College. As persons arrived at the meeting it became clearer and clearer to me that the meeting participants were not only parents with children at school judging from the age of many.

I soon learned that many of the attendees were not parents,

as they informed me that they had come to attend a meeting of the Combermere Old Scholars Association (CSOSA) and challenged why I was there. I on the other hand thought I was there for a Parent Teachers Meeting but was soon to understand that the two had become combined.

My chief interrogator as to the reasons why a person who clearly was not an Alumni of the University of Waterford was at the meeting was one Alex Macdonald who suggested (ironically, as we were at Harrison College) that I had no right to be there. By this time the meeting was very charged, so in attempting to bring some order to the chaotic proceedings so that I could leave at a reasonable hour I advised Alex and others present who may not have known, that as I had two children at the school and as this was a PTA meeting to discuss the current state of affairs, I had *locus standi*. I was not as the late national hero Errol Barrow was to famously say in another forum 'loitering on the premises' of Harrison College.

I continued that it would be remiss of me not to welcome the body of CSOSA into the hallowed halls of Harrison College as a former Head boy of the school. The fact that Combermere (especially the old scholars) would stoop so low as to enter these premises albeit for a meeting dealing with Combermere, clearly illustrated that there was a serious problem at the school to be addressed and we should proceed to that without the long talk being engaged in.

I continued that Kolij was a situation that I was sure my learned friend who is no longer with us but was looking down over me (I was referring to the picture of David Thompson that was hanging amongst those of former Prime Ministers over my left shoulder) must have him turning in his grave at the thought of the site of the meeting to discuss the way forward for Combermere.

Alex followed me to the mike and formally proposed the establishment of a Committee to represent the combined bodies and the first two names nominated to serve were his and mine.

So there I was, an interloper among a group of Combermerians trying to ascertain whether there was a problem in the first place, and if so how to address it so that the children could get back to school. We had several meetings and through it all I had to listen to old stories of the events of a time past at the school, which as we grow older we are all fond of indulging in. Of course I could contribute little, only knowing some of the characters but not living it.

One of the fond characters to the members of the Committee was one Joe Physics aka Aurie Smith, which immediately brought to mind his deranged brother Vernon, and I made my usual caustic comments about him.

The talk turned to my book, which most of them had read, and it saddened me to hear them say "Philip if you had gone to Combermere this could not have happened to you" as most of the people causing me misery ironically went to Kolij. It was so true as I said sadly "yes nothing has changed" and as I thought I reflected that perhaps only when death intervened would something change, and that is how the title for this book evolved.

Shortly after that meeting, I had a chance meeting that reinforced to me how death can impact on the course of future events. I had gone into the bank to do a transaction. It was not urgent and as the line was long, I was minded to leave and return another time, but something made me stay. Shortly after I joined the line a lady joined and asked if I was Mr. Nicholls. I had a moment's hesitation before I replied while I tried to place her face, as I feared at first another Cottle problem. She continued: "I am Reuben Bayley's mother. Saturday gone was 24 years that he died."

I will readily admit that I became tearful and greeted her with a hug, for here was a lady that I had not met often and in fact the last time I had seen her was at the funeral of her son.

Reuben and I had journeyed through Kolij together. Not only was he a scholar, but he was a good footballer and an even better athlete, winning more than one gold in Middle Distance Events at the Carifta Games. In our last year at school he was Deputy Head Boy to me in 1979-80. His death after collapsing while playing football from an apparent aneurism shocked us all, as he was a fit young man and the last person one would have thought to have succumbed at an early age from natural causes.

His mother continued: "I have read your book." I was mildly surprised, and she said, "I saw it in town and you and Reuben were friends, so I needed to." At that moment I started to feel guilty, as it was only Reuben that I knew in the family and so had lost touch with her. She said he would be turning in his grave at what has transpired. I knew that while the good die young, some never leave you, so while there is a physical parting where that parting is with someone who you really have no use for. Reuben, like my other friends who died young such as Barenda and Stephen, is often in my thoughts. They may have left physically, but they like many are watching over me.

Ms. Bailey will not have to buy this book, but as I simply said to her asking of how it was going: "No change... no change."

CHAPTER 3

Keeping the Faith

AS TIME has passed and I reflect on my situation, I would describe my feeling now not as self-pity, but one of burning anger towards a profession that I not only readily embraced but was excited to enter as I did in 1987. I think of the teachings and encouragements of my father's friends, many of whom were stellar luminaries of this profession and men and women who I would wish to emulate. Sadly, many of them have gone to the great beyond, but all have taught me innumerable lessons which guided and shaped my vision for what an Attorney-at-Law should be.

In some respects their advice and words of wisdom, welcome though they were, had not prepared me for the deviousness of some of my later colleagues. This was not surprising, as many of these men and women in my father's close circle did not possess the ruthless streak nor the unbridled greed that has afflicted many in this noble profession. It was stressed to me that I should not view the profession as a means to riches but one of service, and so early in my career I offered myself to be elected to the Bar Council and served for many years on the Disciplinary Committee, eventually becoming its Chair.

It is with sadness now that I find myself with little use for the Bar, as I have found it a virtually toothless organization driven by the agenda, by and large, of whoever is President and, in my view not assisting the members in the critical areas affecting the profession. I would name these as the non-functioning Judicial system and the interaction between members of the bar. For these reasons as long as Justice Beckles' recent decision on the question of having to be a member of the Bar remains in effect, I for one will not be minded to pay my dues.

I determined that I would not make the mistake of believing that all persons were honourable. While I try to sorround my children with positive individuals, I make sure they are exposed to some of the perils of life that as young ladies they must be aware of. Contemporaries of my era were not faced with many of the perils that they face, as this digital age records everything and the internet makes a nonsense of any expectation of privacy, especially when you yourself post the information. My favorite mantra to them, just as I have told all my students, is: do not take any picture that you cannot show your father as it is bound to come back to haunt you in the future as many young people seem oblivious to the fact that your social media postings make the job of Human Resource Departments easier when whittling down applications for a job.

The legal profession is no different from any other even if there is an unfounded belief that all Attorneys are up to no good. It is a perception that President after President of the Bar has had to address and one that I know from firsthand experience has afflicted me. No one other than our maker can know what is in our hearts, but I have found my faith and indeed my belief in the profession sorely tested by the actions of some others that have caused me not only distress but harm.

I am well aware that all professions will have charlatans—

persons who pretend they are one thing to John Public, but are nothing more than schemers engaging in the type of subterfuge that one would expect of any cheap hustler; a wolf in sheep's clothing in other words. These persons have no conscience because their only thought is of 'Number One'. It should be clear to everybody that such persons now occupy not only one of the noblest professions but the highest office that one can be elected to anywhere in the world.

As one directly affected in my chosen profession, that is of little comfort as I ask myself how a man can, in a sworn Affidavit, assert that a false charge of money laundering against me can have no effect on me as an individual or my career, yet state in another forum that clients of his who were also charged with money laundering suffered so much trauma that they must be compensated for their loss after the charges were conveniently dropped?

The insomnia that has afflicted me over the last few years is part of a vicious cycle. My inability to sleep is due in no small part to the fact that my conscience makes me worry not only about my predicament, but also about the predicament that some clients are still facing because of the Cottle meltdown which has resulted in millions of dollars still owing.

It is a conscience that, I have discovered to my peril and detriment, several of my 'colleagues' unashamedly do not possess. I have learnt at my cost that one should not ask for any quarter nor expect one, as this profession has degenerated into a dog-eat-dog spectacle, whereby your desires trump (is that word not now appropriate?) any concept of doing what is right.

Last year my eldest daughter Carissa celebrated her twentieth birthday and I can honestly say that the issues surrounding Cottle Catford & Co. have been on my mind since before her birth. Even when I was technically on holiday there was always thought about when the next problem was going to rear its ugly head. As the smart phone has become as indispensable a part of your ensemble, akin to an undergarment, the convenience that this device has brought has to be counterbalanced by the fact that you are always on call. One can never really use the excuse of old that the mail has not arrived.

Despite it all I must be thankful that I am alive and for that I must thank the Almighty first, as a couple of trusted friends have more than once reminded me: "He has a purpose for you, otherwise He would not have guided Dr. Massay to diagnose you and Dr. Trevor Greene to complete your successful surgery." He clearly does, for as another friend related in a dream he had of me, he saw me chasing away two of our classmates who had already gone to the great beyond when they came seeking my company.

I will be the first to admit that I am not overtly religious (Dean Jeffrey, my apologies, but I know you have heard worse on the field of play when representing Pickwick) but I am *au fait* with the teachings of the traditional Anglican church, and thus when I see how younger and fitter persons than me have been 'called home' then I must accept that indeed He has a purpose for me. Who then am I to question the will of the Almighty? I hope simply to embrace it, as my work clearly is not finished. As is often said 'the good die young' and as I can no longer be classified as 'young' it behooves me to try and see what good I can do.

As I talk about this aspect of my existence, it would be remiss of me not to express my appreciation to two former secretaries of mine, Juel Holder, Shatara Ramsey and to my current secretary Maxine Babb, who have always plied me over the years with uplifting messages of support. Shatara especially has been a tower of strength for me in her encouragement and willingness to assist me with any task when I ask for help. For me, it was a sad day when I had to say to her "If an opportunity comes your way feel free to leave because I don't know where I will be in the future." Her help has in no small part been the reason I still have something of a practice.

I have specifically spoken about my gratitude to Dr. Massay and Dr. Greene, but I also need to make mention of Dr. Collette George who has been readily available to offer advice about the control of my diet and to help me manage my diabetes which I was diagnosed with twenty years ago by Dr. Michael Wharton, who shared many a dressing room with me while at Kolij.

There is however one other person that I must credit at the outset of this book for playing a pivotal role in my existence and that is my long-suffering trainer, Kim Cordice.

For reasons that left me totally embarrassed, my description of our relationship was omitted from my first book. I know I wrote it, but through a printer's devil it's not there, a fact I only realised when Kim called me after reading the book to say, "I thought you said I was in your book. I can't find it." The next morning I rushed to the gym to prove her wrong and could not find it, so I had to suffer at the hands of 'Barracuda' Kim while she took her revenge in a particularly punishing schedule.

Kim has been my trainer now for nearly twenty-five years. I must, however, disavow all responsibility that she might bear from those who would chirp that she has not done a good job. I like to think that she did the best she could under the circumstances of one who would face a grumpy old me at all hours of the morning with the same complaint "You not tired of making me do this?"

One thing that Kim is not proficient in is counting reps, because her count of reps differs significantly from not only mine, but many others. As far as I know three follows two, and four follows three, and that one must reach ten in some sequence. Who tell me think that? I hear all types of excuses like: "I only count reps that I consider satisfactory" and that there is no right of appeal from her decision. And she wants to know why I am "cursing" her and threatens to complain to her mother? It is ironic because I was first under the hand of her 'Partner in Cruelty' in the gym, Joe Bourne, who decided that he would transfer me to Kim because he did not think I would use the language I used with him when he requested that certain weights be lifted.

While the language has mellowed, the sentiment has stayed the same and as many have said, we have had a love-hate relationship over this time that they "were not getting into." Kim has tried, but says I am very disobedient and would not do as told. I will not say what my response was, but want to publicly acknowledge that she has assisted in prolonging my life through constant harassment to get me in the gym, even calling at 5:00 am to make sure I am up.

It is only now that at the age of 40 (no one would believe it looking at her) that she has acquired her own bundle of joy who keeps her too busy, as she says, with similar tantrums, that she does not have any time for me. But Kim, I will be back, you cannot get away so easily.

So with their help and of course the guidance of the Almighty I have now cheated death not once, but twice, according to the goodly doctor. Before my latest episode occurred I was to feel cheated myself, as I felt that death had robbed me of the opportunity to simply ask 'why'. That is how I felt when I learned of the death of Allan Watson.

I am sure that I would be forgiven for doing far less than simply thinking of the many fantasies that floated around in my head with respect to the type of purgatory I wished to inflict on my former Partners over the decade that ensued after the end of the Partnership.

Why did I feel this way? In my mind I had suffered personal humiliation because of the meltdown of Cottle Catford & Co. I had been thrown in jail. I had lost face to countless others and was forced to eek out a living day by day. All my hard work had been ripped asunder by this man who, totally oblivious to his fiduciary responsibilities, had absconded from the island since 2010 with his loot. Never once was there a consideration for the misery that he had caused me, not to mention many others who had been caused financial misery because of his actions.

I had wanted the opportunity to confront the bastard and let him know how I had suffered; to get it off my chest; and dreamt of the day I saw him returned to the island in handcuffs to face what the Americans call the 'Perp Walk'. These primal thoughts were countered with my feeling that there really wasn't any satisfaction in seeing a man the age of my father incarcerated or hauled off a plane in chains. As I reflected, however, many of my friends suggested to me that I should just accept that the Lord knows best, and as Dean Jeffrey Gibson, said to me: "… just hope that he made peace with his Lord, as we all have to do." At the same time many others would often repeat to me the Bajan saying that 'God Don't Like Ugly' and that he would have to reckon with what he had done.

In the seven years between the end of the Partnership on December 31st 2002 and when he exited Barbados in or around January 2010, I doubt that I spoke more than a few dozen words to him either in or outside of Court, and it perplexed me how in Court he repeated more than once that he was hurt by the harsh verbal and written vilification I had inflicted on him since the problems began. Excuse me? Maybe one day someone will publish all the letters I have written to my former Partners about the Firm. Suffice it to say that persons who have read them have come away with the impression that I had bent over backwards in my attempts to arrive at a solution, but sadly I have had to accept that both he and the cohorts who have assisted him and his wife have determined that the loss must fall on my shoulders alone.

Did he ever care? I don't think so, and just as the world is getting a lesson in what the narcissistic behavior of some persons can cause, as I reflected on our meetings or lack of communication in the last two years of the Partnership, I often felt that while he may have been embarrassed by what had happened, he did not have the spine to admit his errors and responsibilities and try to rectify things.

More than once people have told me that while I toss and turn at night worrying about this and that, he is probably fast asleep under the spell of Lady Macbeth, his wife, who during all my attempts to recover some of the funds sat impassively in Court with not an ounce of compassion or remorse for what their actions have caused me and countless others. Maybe her punishment now is that she will have to rely on Vernon Smith for her guidance. But as my friend Andrew Sealy said recently, "I doubt Vernon is losing any sleep over you," a statement that I know is true. I myself hope, however, that he has one eye open for when Marcelle Smith comes back for him.

It was ironic that shortly before I heard of Watson's death I had written another letter to the authorities asking what had become of the Arrest Warrant issued in April of 2015 by Justice Sonia Richards for failing to attend a Judgment Summons hearing to indicate how he was going to repay the debt to me. That is now irrelevant, and my attention will now have to turn to claims on his Estate to attempt to satisfy the Judgments awarded.

I was just wasting my breath, as it clearly went in one ear

and out the other; absolutely nothing was done about it. I later learnt through the grapevine that as the Warrant arose in civil proceedings, the DPP was not minded to seek extradition. How convenient. It's amazing how certain persons avoid charges and others charged have same dropped in circumstances that leave some people perplexed. Imagine that the entire criminal charge brought against me was based on civil proceedings, yet now he is using the excuse of the Warrant being issued because of civil proceedings not to seek extradition—hypocrisy at the highest.

But my attempts at bringing Watson back did not rest with the DPP. I had a copy of the Court Order issuing the Arrest Warrant served by the Police Force's Fraud Squad for the attention of Sergeant Howard, the officer who had arrested me. I had previously advised him where Watson was, providing a copy of the report issued by G4S in the United States as to his whereabouts. Despite this, no action ensued and for the last few years Watson could live a life untroubled since he took flight from Barbados, while I who stayed and tried to clean up the mess was condemned by the dishonest actions of others including the former DPP to a living purgatory.

The long road that I have travelled still appears to have several more stops on it. It is no doubt a long and torturous road, and taking a cue from the late Dr. Martin Luther King in the speech he made the night before his assassination, "I may not get there but I am determined to leave the ground work for my children to recover."

I must keep the faith. Several times I was told that it is a futile battle, and while I have accepted that I will never recover all the amounts due to me, I cannot give up and concede victory to the forces of evil over the forces of good.

Shortly after the first rumor of Watson's death, I had occasion to go to Kensington Oval to pay tribute to Tony Cozier who had recently passed. I arrived and found Prime Minister Stuart there, and after we had both paid tribute he said to me: "Philip, I know you have been dealt a bad hand and it has gotten even worse now with the death of Watson."

"Yes, it has, Prime Minister," I said.

This time it was his words to me that were prophetic.

As I would have advised anyone in the position of Watson's family, it would be pointless to make any formal Application for Probate of his Estate, as it would only attract a stream of claims. Mine may have been the most public or well-known, but I am aware professionally of several other claims. I am sure however that he had so structured his affairs in the end that it would not be necessary for any relative to seek probate of his Estate and be subject to a deluge of claims.

But true to form, those two charlatan Attorneys who have been assisting Watson and his wife as conspirators after the fact filed an Application in Court seeking not only to discharge the Injunction I had been granted against the disposing of their property, but the discharge of the Judgement debts obtained by me on the grounds that his family needed to be able to access funds to pay the Estate debts which includes their legal fees.

It is at times like those that your faith is mostly tested.

APPENDIX 3A

Filing Attorney:
PHILIP NICHOLLS & ASSOCIATES
Attorneys-at-Law
No 8 Pine Gardens off Pine Plantation
Road St. Michael
T: (246) 826-0054   F: (246) 425-9394
Email: info.nichollslaw@gmail.com

CLAIM FORM

Form 1

(Rules 8.14(a))

SUPREME COURT OF BARBADOS
IN THE HIGH COURT OF JUSTICE

CLAIM NO. | Cv47 | of 2017

BETWEEN:

PHILIP VERNON NICHOLLS   **CLAIMANT**

AND

BARRY LOUIS VALENCE GALE   **FIRST DEFENDANT**
COMMISSIONER OF POLICE   **SECOND DEFENDANT**
DIRECTOR OF PUBLIC PROSECUTIONS   **THIRD DEFENDANT**
THE ATTORNEY GENERAL OF BARBADOS   **FOURTH DEFENDANT**

The Claimant, **PHILIP VERNON NICHOLLS** of No. 8 Pine Gardens, off Pine Plantation Road in the parish of Saint Michael in this Island claims against **BARRY LOUIS VALENCE GALE,** First Defendant of Hastings Attorneys-at-Law situate at Trident Financial Centre, Cnr. St. Matthias Gap and Highway 7 in the parish of Christ Church in this Island; **THE COMMISSIONER OF POLICE,** the Second Defendant of Police Headquarters Royal Barbados Police, Lower Roebuck Street in the City of Bridgetown in this Island; **THE DIRECTOR OF PUBLIC PROSECUTIONS**, the Third Defendant of Frank Walcott Building, Culloden Road in the parish of Saint Michael in this Island; and **THE ATTORNEY GENERAL**

23

OF BARBADOS, the Fourth Defendant of Webster's Business Park in the parish of Saint Michael in this Island.

The Claimant seeks:

1. Damages against the First Defendant for defamation for false written allegations of theft by the Claimant made by him to the Second Defendant as a result of which the Second Defendant wrongfully arrested the Claimant causing him to suffer false imprisonment, malicious prosecution and loss of income as a result of the disintegration of his legal practice.

2. Damages against the Second Defendant for wrongful arrest and false imprisonment.

3. Damages against the First Second and Third Defendant for malicious prosecution.

4. Damages against the Third Defendant for defamation by allegations that the Claimant was involved in money laundering by instituting charges against him without any supporting factual or legal basis for doing so and having done so failing to prosecute same in a timely manner as a result of which the Claimant has suffered loss to his reputation and financial loss due to the disintegration of his legal practice.

5. Damages against the Fourth Defendant for the actions of the Second and Third Defendants.

6. Damages to be awarded as considered just and equitable in the cause.

7. Such other remedy that the Court deems fit.

8. Costs to be agreed or assessed.

9. Interest pursuant to Section 35 of the Supreme Court of the Judicature Act, Cap. 117A of the Laws of Barbados.

I certify that all facts set out in this Claim Form are true to the best of my knowledge, information and belief.

Dated the 16th day of January 2017

_____

Claimant's Signature

STATEMENT OF CLAIM

1. The Claimant is an Attorney- at-Law presently residing and practicing at No. 8 Pine Gardens, off Pine Plantation Road in the parish of Saint Michael in this Island. At the material times when the grounds for this action arose he was residing at No. 14 Dover Mews, 3rd Avenue Dover in the parish of Christ Church in this Island.

2. The First Defendant is an Attorney-at-Law who has been accorded the designation of Queens Counsel and is resident at Graeme Hall Terrace in the parish of Christ Church in this Island. He currently is and was at the relevant times carrying on the practice of Law under the style of Hastings Attorneys-at-Law from offices at Trident Financial Centre, Cnr. St. Matthias Gap and Highway 7 in the parish of Christ Church in this Island and was at the time of the events central to this matter the President of the Barbados Bar Association.

3. The Second Defendant is the Head of the Royal Barbados Police Force in this Island and charged with the responsibility for the actions of the members of the Royal Barbados Force including those tasked with instituting and having conduct of prosecutions in the Magistrates Courts of this Island.

4. The Third Defendant holds the office of Director of Public Prosecutions and under the Constitution has responsibility for initiating and discontinuing where appropriate criminal prosecutions in this Island whether brought in the name of the State or the Commissioner of Police.

5. The Fourth Defendant is the holder of the office of Attorney General under the Constitution as a member of the political electorate with the responsibility for the administration of justice in this Island and as such is the representative of the Government with legal responsibility for the operation function and errors of the Second and Third Defendants.

THE CLAIM AGAINST THE FIRST DEFENDANT

6. On the 22nd day of October 2013 the First Defendant wrote a letter to the Second Defendant containing false and defamatory allegations in relation to the Claimant that the First Defendant knew were untrue to wit that the Claimant had **"appropriated funds placed in trust with the Firm of Cottle Catford & Co. for a client that the Firm then represented for his personal use."** This letter when contrasted with a letter dated the 5th day of March 2008 from the First Defendant to the Firm of Cottle Catford & Co. confirms that the First Defendant was aware that the words highlighted were false.

7. The First Defendant wrote this letter to the Second Defendant with the false allegation as highlighted at a time when he was the President of the Bar Association and had stated publicly it was his intention to weed out the bad apples from the Bar. It was done with malice aforethought and actuated by spite, the culmination of several years of threats made verbally and in writing of and to the Claimant by the First Defendant as to the Claimant's character and integrity as an Attorney-at-Law.

8. The natural inference of the words of the First Defendant taken in conjunction with his previous public statements were that the Claimant was one of the bad apples in the legal profession that needed weeding out.

9. The actions of the First Defendant were calculated to not only defame and disparage the Claimant but to cause the Claimant to suffer arrest, the deprivation of his liberty, embarrassment as a result of same and the loss of reputation, both locally and internationally as is evident by the fact that the news of his arrest was reported prominently on local radio, T.V and written press and it also spread across the internet like wildfire. The Claimant to this day continues to suffer the consequences of his arrest even though the charges were dismissed for want of prosecution for which the First Defendant must be held partially liable, if not totally, for the Claimant's losses.

10. At the time of writing of the letters of March 5, 2008 and October 22, 2013 the First Defendant was aware or should reasonably have been

aware that the shortfall in the funds of the client's account of Cottle Catford & Co. that he alleged that the Claimant had misappropriated were the responsibility of two of his former Partners, Allan Watson and Joyce Griffith. The said Allan Watson was for some time prior to the writing of the letter and at the time of writing the letter being represented by Leslie F. Haynes Q.C., one of the legal partners of the First Defendant at the time, in a law suit instituted by the Claimant against his former Partners to recover the funds due to the client's account of Cottle Catford & Co.

11. In the premises the actions of the First Defendant were not only defamatory of the Claimant but were designed to and did lead to the wrongful arrest, false imprisonment and malicious prosecution of the Claimant for which the First Defendant is liable in part if not solely to the Claimant in damages for his actual and foreseeable losses as a result of the First Defendant's actions.

THE CLAIM AGAINST THE FIRST DEFENDANT FOR WRONGFUL ARREST AND AGAINST THE SECOND DEFENDANT FOR WRONGFUL ARREST AND FALSE IMPRISONMENT

12. The Second Defendant as Commissioner of Police is responsible for the actions of the officers under his command and is therefore liable for the unlawful actions of Sergeant Terrence Howard, Police Constable Troy Mason and two (2) other constables including a female officer dressed in plain clothes whose names are not known to the Claimant, who were involved in the arrest of the Claimant on the 29th day of October 2013 at the Claimant's then residence at No. 14 Dover Mews, 3rd Avenue Dover in the parish of Christ Church in this Island.

13. On the 29th day of October 2013 the said Sergeant Howard and the abovementioned officers in his company, presented the Claimant with a warrant to search the premises he occupied for **"receipts, bank statements, cheque books, invoices and other documents which would attend evidence as to the commission of an offence to wit theft."** Given the wide ambit of the warrant the Claimant requested of Sergeant Howard what specifically they were seeking, to which he

responded that they were seeking items pertaining to the sale of land by John Connor a former client of Cottle Catford & Co. in 2008.

14. The Claimant indicated that the firm of Cottle Catford & Co. no longer existed and that all of its records were in storage at places not mentioned in the warrant. He indicated that the premises for which the warrant was obtained was primarily his residence and that the items stated in the warrant were not on the premises. The Claimant indicated to Sergeant Howard that he had in his possession at the premises a file pertaining to the affairs of John Connor with respect to the sale of land and a civil suit that arose as a result of the said sale and that he was prepared to hand over the said file to Sergeant Howard and the other officers to assist with their investigation to avoid any disturbance to his household.

15. This was accepted by Sergeant Howard and the Claimant handed over the file in his possession relating to John Connor whereupon the agents of the Second Defendant asked him to accompany them to District A Police Station to answer some questions. The Claimant indicated he was perfectly capable of answering any questions on the matter at the premises where he was and refused to accompany them. As a result the Claimant was advised by Sergeant Howard that he would be placing him under arrest at about 10 a.m.

16. In the circumstances the arrest by the agents of the Second Defendant was unreasonable and unlawful the following reasons:

(i) The agents of the Second Defendant had on their own accord not searched the premises for which the search warrant was issued and as a result had not found any items as indicated in the warrant as evidence of theft.

(ii) The agents of the Second Defendant had not examined the file handed over by the Claimant prior to his arrest and as such could not have determined whether there was any evidence therein of the theft they were investigating.

(iii) The questioning of the Claimant with respect to theft of money due to John Connor was solely related to the civil suit file handed over by the Claimant to the Second Defendant and from prior copies of documents already in their possession and did not in of themselves indicate that a criminal offence of theft had occurred.

(iv) The Second Defendant acted with respect to a complaint by the First Defendant to who no money was owed by the Claimant with respect to an allegation of theft in a letter which itemizes repayment of a civil judgment as evidence of theft by the Claimant.

(v) The Claimant was advised after arrest that he was being charged with money laundering on the instructions of the Third Defendant but at no time prior to his arrest or after his arrest was he questioned about any allegations that he had engaged in said money laundering nor did the search warrant indicate that it was seeking any evidence for same.

17. In the premises the Claimant's arrest was wrongful and as such illegal and the subsequent charges that were instituted by the Second Defendant were made without the proper evaluation of the facts of the matter. In the premises the charges levelled by the Second Defendant were made because of a predisposed reliance on an unsubstantiated allegation of the First Defendant supported by a civil judgment against the Complainant as the basis for a criminal charge and subsequent prosecution as a result of which the Claimant suffered wrongful arrest and false imprisonment.

18. The Claimant was detained firstly at District A Police Station from around 10:15 a.m. on the 29th day of October 2013 until about 5:00 p.m. when he was transferred to the Central Police Station for processing, after which he was kept in a lock up from 9 p.m. until about 10:30 a.m. on the 30th day of October 2013 when he appeared in the District A Magistrates Court. The Claimant was released on Bail by the Court around 11 a.m. that same day after surrendering his Passport. The Claimant as a result suffered false imprisonment at the hands of the Second Defendant as a result of the actions of the First Defendant indicated in paragraph 6.

19. The Claimant was denied his liberty from between 10:15 a.m. on the 29th day of October 2013 until 11 a.m. on the 30th day of October 2013 despite being only interrogated for 90 minutes. The false imprisonment

of the Claimant was all the more egregious as the Complaint had advised the Second Defendant as follows:

(i)   The need for him to make arrangements for the care and control of his minor children after completion of their attendance at school for the day which request was initially refused causing the Claimant much distress as he was threatened with being stripped search for 'being disruptive' when he demanded that he be allowed to make the necessary arrangements for the welfare of his minor children.

(ii)   Requested of the Second Defendant through his agents on more than one occasion including requests by his Attorney-at-Law that he be granted Police Bail. On each occasion he was told that there was no officer with the level of seniority present at Central Police Station to grant same between approximately 6 p.m. and 9 p.m. when the Claimant was taken to the Cells. The Claimant was also informed that Inspector Jefferson Clarke who was in charge of his case and who had spoken to the Complainant earlier that day at District A could not be located to authorize same.

(iii)   The Claimant was forced to sleep in conditions that were dangerous to his declared health needs having been diagnosed with Sleep Apnea that required him to use an electric sleep aid despite same being brought to the attention of the Second Defendant. At no time to the Claimant's knowledge was the Claimant's doctor and or any medical practitioner contacted about the Claimant's chronic condition.

20. As a result the Claimant suffered false imprisonment at the hands of the Second Defendant and claims damages against the Second Defendant and the First Defendant for same.

THE CLAIM AGAINST THE SECOND DEFENDANT FOR MALICIOUS PROSECUTION

21. For a period spanning twenty-two (22) months, from the 30th day of October 2013 until the charges were dismissed for want of prosecution on the 13th day of August 2015, the Claimant was required to attend Court proceedings on no fewer than nine (9) occasions to answer to the

charges for an offence allegedly committed in 2008. On each occasion the Second Defendant through his agents Sergeant Neville Watson and others unknown to the Claimant requested that the hearing of charges against the Claimant be adjourned for a number of reasons outlined below:

(i)   On the 19th February 2014 the Complainant appeared to apply for and was returned his passport for travel overseas.

(ii)   On the 10th March and 6th June 2014 the Second Defendant requested an adjournment on the ground that 'the file had not come down from the office of the Director of Public Prosecutions (DPP) as a result of which the Second Defendant was not in a position to proceed.

(iii)   On the 9th September 2014 the Second Defendant indicated that was not in a position to lead evidence pertaining to a matter that allegedly occurred in 2008 because investigations were still continuing.

(iv)   At the fourth court appearance on December 16th 2014 the matter was adjourned because the substantive Magistrate was on holiday.

(v)   On January 12th 2015 at the fifth hearing of the matter fifteen (15) months after the arrest of the Claimant the agents of Second Defendant intimated that the delay in its ability to proceed with the prosecution was because of the need to get orders for discovery of documents in the hands of Banks from the High Court who were unwilling to produce same, the same documents for which the search warrant was issued in October of 2013.

(vi)   At the sixth and seventh hearings of the charges on the 12th March and 22nd May 2015 the Second Defendant indicated that a request had been made for the office of the Director of Public Prosecutions to take over the prosecution because of its complexity due to the fact that it had recently learned of a judgment the Claimant had obtained against his Former Partners in 2009. As a result the Second Defendant was waiting on a legal officer from the office of the DPP to assist with the prosecution. The Second Defendant assured the presiding Magistrate that the promised discovery of documents supporting the charge would soon be handed over to the Claimant.

(vii)   Despite this realization and despite an order of the High Court in April of 2015 for the arrest of Allan Watson with respect to funds owing to Cottle Catford & Co. a certified copy of which was served on the Second Defendant along with evidence of his address in the United States of America the Second Defendant has refused and or neglected to institute proceedings to extradite the said Allan Watson to Barbados while continuing the prosecution of the Claimant.

(viii)   Partial discovery was handed over to the Claimant on the 15th July 2015 at the eighth hearing of the matter after Sergeant Howard was summoned to Court. The Second Defendant indicated that it was still not in a position to proceed as no one had come from the office of the DPP to take over the prosecution.

(ix)   The matter was dismissed for want of prosecution on the 13th day of August 2015 on the ninth occasion that the Claimant attended Court when the Second Defendant failed to complete the previously ordered discovery by the Magistrate for District A. At that time no one from the office of the DPP had appeared to take over the prosecution as stated previously as a ground for adjournment.

22. As a result of the aforementioned delays in the prosecution of the matter the Claimant suffered embarrassment, opprobrium and the loss of business in his professional practice which has continued until today especially as news of his arrest was placed in the news by the Second Defendant and appeared prominently over both radio and television and in the print media. By comparison to date no news of his acquittal has been given by the Second Defendant. From the chronology of events outlined it was clear that the Second Defendant was stalling at all times with the prosecution in breach of the Claimant's Constitutional rights by seeking to obtain evidence after the arrest that it did not have two years prior when it arrested the Claimant as a means to justify the charges.

23. In the circumstances the Claimant alleges that the Second Defendant is guilty of malicious prosecution because it knew or must have reasonably known for many months prior to the dismissal of the charges against the Claimant that it was not in a position to prosecute the charges and as a

result is liable in damages to the Claimant for the tort of malicious prosecution and for the loss he suffered resulting therefrom.

THE CLAIM AGAINST THE THIRD DEFENDANT

24. Towards the end of his interrogation on the 29th day of October 2013 at District A Police Station the Claimant was advised by Sergeant Howard that in addition to theft he was being charged with money laundering on the specific instructions of the Third Defendant. At no time prior to his arrest was this information conveyed to the Claimant or was he after his arrest and prior to his being charged questioned about any aspect of the offence of money laundering.

25. The Claimant was thereafter charged in addition to theft with "money laundering" in accordance with section 5 subsection (1) clause b and Section 6 of the Money Laundering and Financing of Terrorism (Prevention and Control) Act 2011-23 and though the charge was subsequently dismissed for want of prosecution he continues to suffer the stigma associated with this charge and has been deemed if not a terrorist then a Persona Non Grata by both the U.S.A and Canada.

26. The Third Defendant as part of his duties represents the island of Barbados at regional and international conferences dealing with the question of money laundering held by agencies such as the Financial Action Task Force and the Caribbean Action Task Force. The purpose of these agencies is to develop policies and inform countries as to the perils of money laundering and to recommend and encourage countries to aggressively prosecute same. Severe penalties have been enacted in legislation around the world to combat same and countries risk being excluded from the International Financial system if they do not enact legislation guarding against these practices.

27. As such the Third Defendant must be presumed to be aware of the history of these institutions derived from decisions by the Organization of Economic and Development to stymie first the profits made by drug barons and then later expand its outreach to crimes of a monetary nature arising from any criminal enterprise utilizing the International Financial System and the severe penalties that arise from conviction.

28. The Third Defendant who is charged with the responsibility of prosecuting in Barbados crimes associated with money laundering must be presumed to know or appreciate that such charges internationally have been made with respect to activities of a criminal enterprise and that such a charge never mind a conviction would lead to stigmatization of individuals charged especially in a small society.

29. The Third Defendant given that the title of the Act dealing with money laundering speaks not only of money laundering but of "Financing Terrorism" and with the knowledge of prevailing world concerns of which he would be aware, as a reasonable person, would have a duty as the DPP not to charge anyone with an offence that he did not believe or could not reasonably believe would lead to a conviction as it would be reasonably foreseeable that such a charge would have repercussions especially on a professional person such as the Claimant who the Third Defendant has knowledge practiced in the Offshore Financial sector.

30. The Third Defendant by instigating the charges of money laundering against the Complainant, in circumstances that clearly fell outside of the parameters mentioned in sections 28 and 29, failed in his duty to the Claimant as a person to whom he owes a duty of care to exercise the functions of his office in a fair and impartial manner and thus committed the Tort of malicious prosecution by:

   (i)   First authorizing a charge of money laundering against the Complainant that the Third Defendant had little realistic chance of obtaining a conviction.

   (ii)   Failing for over twenty-two (22) months to prosecute said charge or by presenting any evidence on discovery as to the charge of money laundering.

   (iii)   Failing to comply with the requirements of criminal law by laying a charge of money laundering that was merely speculative in nature which of necessity would have failed to meet the standard of criminal prosecutions of beyond all reasonable doubt.

(iv)   Charging the Claimant with the offence for a transaction that he was not the Attorney acting in the specific transaction that was the subject of the allegation.

(v)   Alleging that the transaction in question for the sale of land which was not in itself an illegal transaction or part of a criminal enterprise could be the basis for alleging money laundering could have occurred since the funds in the transaction were deposited in a legitimately approved account.

(vi)   Alleging that the Claimant engaged in money laundering by use of funds that at no time were placed in his personal account or used for personal gain.

(vii)   Alleging that the funds in question were laundered by introducing same into the legitimate banking system at a time after the funds were placed in the said system.

(viii)   Failing to disclose prior to prosecution as required under the Constitution the discovery of documents specifying the alleged money laundering that the Claimant engaged in.

(ix)   Failing to prosecute the charges having insisted on the charges being laid, by refusing to take over the prosecution in the Magistrate's Court despite being requested by the Second Defendant to do so or in the alternative entering a dismissal of the charge as he has done in other cases.

31.   As a consequence of the actions of the First Defendant, the actions of the Second and Third Defendants for which the Fourth Defendant is liable the Claimant has suffered the near total destruction of his legal practice especially in the Offshore Financial sector with the result that he has suffered financial and personal loss, has suffered loss in general and expense associated with having to pay for increased medical care which loss includes but is not limited to the following:

(i)   The Claimant has not received any enquires in over three (3) years from persons interested in retaining his services as an Attorney in the Offshore Financial sector. The Claimant has also had his services terminated by clients of his operating in the said sector as a result of the charges. The Claimant had been an active participant in this sector from around 1993. The loss of this business has severely impacted on the Claimant's ability to make a living as his practice has been dealt a devastating blow by the unsubstantiated allegations contained in the charges brought against him by the Second Defendant at the instigation of the Third Defendant to wit that he had engaged in money laundering.

(ii)   The Claimant's U.S. Visa that he had held unbroken since around 1965 was revoked on or about the 30th day of October 2013 the day after he was charged with the offences at a time when the U.S. authorities could not have known of the allegations against the Claimant unless they had received prior notification of same from the Third Defendant.

(iii)   With the dismissal of the charges for want of prosecution the Claimant as required by U.S. Law applied for the issuance of a U.S. Visa on June 23rd 2016. To date it has not been granted pending receipt of notification from the authorities in Barbados that the Claimant faces no further charges which notification the Second and Third Defendants have refused and or failed to provide a reason for not doing so which has resulted in the continued suffering of the Claimant namely financial loss and increased health concerns because of his inability to travel to the United States of America.

(iv)   The Claimant has suffered the indignity of being required to produce Police Certificates of Character for an application for an Electronic Travel Authorization to Canada, which authorization can be approved within minutes because of his wrongful arrest. Further, the Claimant has had to expend time and expense in trying to secure the needed Certificates from three (3) countries to obtain this Certificate and has been hindered in doing so by the archaic and ridiculous rules of the Royal Barbados Police Force as a result of which he has not been granted the necessary certificate.

(v)   The Claimant has been subjected to additional scrutiny while conducting routine financial transactions with in the local banking sector subsequent to his false arrest and allegation that he has engaged in money laundering.

(vi)   The Claimant suffered loss while he tried to board a flight to the U.S.A. on the 25th December 2014 having not known that his U.S. Visa had been revoked and as a result suffered the loss occasioned by missing that flight connecting flights he had booked on the 25th December 2014.

32. The Claimant seeks the following:

(i)   Damages for wrongful arrest and malicious prosecution against the First Defendant.

(ii)   Damages for wrongful arrest, false imprisonment and malicious prosecution against the Second and Fourth Defendants.

(iii)   Damages for malicious prosecution against the Third Defendant.

(iv)   Damages for loss of fees in particular for work in the Offshore Financial sector as a result of the money laundering charge due to the actions of the Third Defendant.

(v)   Damages for Defamation against the First and Third Defendant.

(vi)   Special Damages for losses incurred by the Claimant as a result of the charges.

(vii)   Such other remedy as the Court deems fit.

(viii) Costs to be agreed or assessed.

(ix)   Interest pursuant to Section 35 of the Supreme Court of the Judicature Act, Cap. 117A of the Laws of Barbados.

Dated this 11th day of January 2017.

PHILIP NICHOLLS & ASSOCIATES
Attorneys-at-Law for the Claimant

37

CHAPTER 4

Travelling

I HAVE on occasions made references to events that have occurred while I have been away from Barbados. One of the regrets of this saga is that it has impacted on my ability to travel, not least because of the revocation of my visa but because the loss of work has impacted on this ability which was the main reason for my travelling.

Travelling not only broadens one's horizon but in my case it provided a welcome break—the ability just to turn off even for a weekend away from the stress associated with what was going on. That was now not possible for the reason I stated above and also because of the contraction in my practice which meant the ability to finance such travel was not there. In many respects it was catch 22: don't travel and drop off the merry go round which was the promotion of the island's offshore sector.

My brothers and I were fortunate that our parents held to a similar belief that travelling was beneficial to your upbringing and that they had the wherewithal to do so. Being exposed to the way others lived helped me understand not only how they lived, but it also gave me an insight into the thinking, perspective and traditions of other persons. Having been exposed to this aspect of life from early, I in turn believed that it was important for my children to be exposed wherever possible to similar experiences.

As my mother is a Trinidadian, it was only logical that many summers were spent meeting her side of the family. The memories of those visits have lingered long and as I look back there is a realization that those experiences were grooming me to face and deal with future challenges in life.

One such visit more than forty years ago gave me an early recollection that in some circumstances the Law can and should be broken for a good cause. While the events then were not a forerunner to later debate as to whether an immoral law should be obeyed, it drove home to me that one's actions could have consequences. After a day out, we were returning to Port of Spain over the mountain pass from Diego Martin when it soon became clear that one of my uncles who was driving had enjoyed the family gathering to such an extent that it was impairing his ability to keep a straight line. His driving could have been described as at best erratic and downright scary at worst.

My aunt Flora, a back-seat driver *par excellence,* having never held a license or driven herself, suddenly shouted "Stop this car!" She instructed me to take over the wheel—I being the eldest child—despite my protestations that I had no experience driving. Her reply was that she had seen me move the cars on my parents' property on more than one occasion and though I was only sixteen she preferred her chances with me than with her brother.

Fortunately for me the car was an automatic and all that was needed was to steer and follow her directions, albeit in the middle of the night and having never driven outside of my parents' property before. My being here to tell the story suggests that she made the right call. Ironically, I have never driven or had the desire to drive in Trinidad since then, perhaps the result of the traumatic shock that I recall my psyche suffered because of the episode.

I took away two things from that incident. One was that the perils of driving under the influence of alcohol can have severe consequences. It is something that has stayed with me all my life and today I can proudly say I have never gotten behind the wheel of a car while inebriated. In fact, I can widen that statement to stipulate that I cannot recall ever being inebriated to the extent that I was unable to remain responsible for my actions. Tipsy, yes, but drunk, no.

The second takeaway was that one must always be brave enough to make that difficult call and be prepared to offend rather than later think 'if only I had'. I can still hear my aunt's words "what would I tell Yvonne if something happened to you children under my watch?" It has stayed with me all my life and is something I have remembered when I found myself facing an unpleasant decision.

Trinidad was not the only island that we visited as children. St. Vincent, Bequia, and of course Jamaica where my father's sister Marina lived with her husband Harold and daughters Nickie and Jackie. That 1977 visit to Jamaica introduced me to a country that I have always looked forward to returning to and which I now consider to be my second home. My initial impression as we were introduced by Auntie Marina, who was to later become my surrogate mother when I was studying at Norman Manley Law School (NMLS), ensured that we were introduced to the various experiences that Jamaica had to offer—Devon House, King's House, Mo Bay jerk chicken, Jamaican patties, the Blue Mountains and of course Bob Marley and the Wailers.

I was later to return to Jamaica in October 1983, having graduated from University of the West Indies to enter the Norman Manley Law School (NMLS). This was my first extended trip from home and I was now not a visitor, but a resident in a different country. The experiences learned and friendships made were invaluable to my outlook on life, and I must stress that these friendships have remained strong and the support I have received from these friends has been of enormous help in maintaining my sanity.

Jamaica is the largest of the English-speaking islands that make up the West Indies and has a rich cultural history. Each island has its own identity, but in my view the Jamaicans are the most nationalistic of all territories in the Caribbean that I have visited. It has angered many other West Indians when the average person in the wider world, especially in countries with no cricketing background, identify all West Indians as Jamaicans. This has no doubt been influenced first by the spread of the gospel of reggae music courtesy of Bob Marley and other legends, and latterly the explosion associated with their exploits on the international athletic scene lead by the indomitable Usain Bolt.

Many academics, whether sociologists or historians, posit how there are only two regional institutions binding us in the West Indies: the University of the West Indies and the West Indies cricket team. I would like to add a third, namely the individuals who ferry persons around for a living, whether they are known as minibus men, ZR men or maxi-taxi operators. As a student in Jamaica I relied a lot on public transport much more than in Barbados. On my several visits to Trinidad I had also experienced the phenomenon of a ride in a West Indies public vehicle. In Jamaica, as I used their services more and more, I was struck at the commonality of behavior among these operators. They all have a common bond, namely a total disrespect for the lives and limbs of the passengers that they carry all in a chase of that additional dollar, and the traffic laws in the country in which they operate.

While in Jamaica I joined the Kensington Cricket Club and the two years that I was there helped me gain a fascinating insight into various aspects of Jamaican society that prior to then or after I have never experienced in Barbados. Because of the calling of elections, the club was left scrambling to field a team for a particular game, as some members of the team lived in a stronghold of the Jamaica Labour Party and the game was being played in a stronghold of the People's National Party. They simply were not playing, and it drove home to me that the passion and danger of politics in that country was taken to a new height when compared to events at home. Not only did we play in Barbados, but the dressing room was seen as the ideal place to settle arguments about who was best to run the country.

In Manchester, England where I lived immediately after Jamaica while reading for my LLM, my experiences of public transportation there were completely different from those of the Caribbean. Buses and trains ran to a strict schedule, and you did not have enough money to bribe a bus driver to open a door to allow you to disembark at a place other than a designated bus stop. When compared to the Caribbean where bus stops are created at the whims of drivers and passengers it made a surreal experience to be seated in a traffic jam while the bus inched along to the bus stop in plain view, and the driver saying to those asked to be let off "at the stop, only at the stop." It is mind-boggling that our local operators either are oblivious to the reasons why the stops are placed in certain places, or simply are certainly immune to the danger they are creating for all concerned by stopping indiscriminately.

In Manchester I came across what after a while I realized was my first experience with subtle racism on the buses. If one were to use the public bus transport between 10 am and 4 pm, outside of rush hour, by and large the buses would be utilized by pensioners. After a while it became evident that no matter if you were seated in the front of the bus, many of these persons upon boarding would struggle for some time to walk to the back of the bus to find an unoccupied row rather than sit next to you.

This was in stark contrast to when a student boarded, as they would simply drop down in the seat next to you. Discussing the situation with some friends, we all related the same experiences, so we decided to put our theory to the test. One day four of us took up seats separately in rows one behind the other at the front of the bus when we boarded first at the commencement of the journey in the city centre. We watched with quiet amusement how persons, obviously pensioners from their age, upon boarding would walk past the empty seat next to us or climb the stairs to the top tier to avoid sitting next to us.

What else was there to do but laugh at the thought of some of these people, many of whom had difficulty in reading other than the most banal tabloid newspaper, believing they were superior to us? It often reminded me of the reported story I read once of a man who was trying to explain to his young son what apartheid was, and simplified it by saying to him it was a belief among certain white people that they were part of a superior race to blacks. His young son thought of this, paused for a moment, and simply said "Obviously they have never seen Viv Richards bat." The simple logic of a child.

Several other instances of this subtle discrimination come to mind, but one I found the most strange was when my fellow candidates for the LLM and I were invited to dinner by one of our lecturers. She was a single middle-aged white lady and was also a priest at a local church. She always wore her collar. It was I and my colleagues from Uganda and Angola, three men and one woman, a petite girl from Australia. There we were, three black men and one white girl, who having got off the bus, were trying to locate her house on foot. We walked through a residential neighborhood trying to find her address, but strangely no one was in sight to give directions. All of a sudden we saw our lecturer driving towards us. When she reached us she said "I came for you because a couple of neighbors called to warn me that there were three suspicious looking black men walking about." We did not know whether to laugh or cry, only for Peters from Uganda to break the ice by saying to our Australian colleague "You mean Bridget you so tiny they could not see you?"

More than 20 years after the bus incident, while travelling from Barbados to Vancouver in Canada, I encountered something similar. I had been routed via Miami and Dallas not simply because by travelling on American Airlines I was adding to my Frequent Flyer Status, but often it would have been quicker than flying through Toronto which would have required either an overnight stay or a lengthy lay over before catching a red eye flight.

It was very noticeable that the further west you go in the United States, many of the check-in desks are manned by only white folks, more reflective of the population there than say in Miami or New York, where many African-Americans or Hispanics hold these posts. About eight of us were travelling to a conference in Vancouver. We all had different connecting flights into Dallas, a major hub where those of you who have visited would know that the airport had its own internal train service between terminals long before Miami did.

Upon reaching my gate for my connecting flight, a youthful-looking girl, after I had presented my ticket and passport, looked at me and said: "Good gosh this is about the sixth passport I have seen from Barbados in the last fifteen minutes and to think before that I had never heard of the place." She seemed totally incredulous to the ignorance she was displaying made all the more by the fact that she was working for American Airlines which had been flying to Barbados for years. I did not see the need to try and educate her, so I just smiled, but it drove home to me not for the first time how people in many cases do not venture far out of the surrounds they live in. This was ten years before the Trump era, but it clearly shows how his message could resonate in those areas.

Upon entering the plane I found my seat in business class and was begging to store my hand luggage and coat, as it was winter. As I was doing so one of the flight attendants moved towards me and my initial thought was that she was coming to collect my coat. I was therefore somewhat taken aback when she said "Let me help you... you can't leave this hand luggage here..." and proceeded to take it towards the back of the plane. I just stood there and after a minute or so she returned and I asked her why I could not keep the bag there as this was my seat, and I offered her my boarding pass.

She became very red-faced and went for my bag and returned it without the offer to help stow it. After taking my seat, a middle-aged American couple behind me said "You are obviously not an American." I said: "No. Why do you ask?" and they said "… because an almighty noise with threats of suits would have erupted at the slight if it had been done to an African-American." I simply said "Some ingrained ideas are hard to change. I think she got my point by my look."

Traveling often brings home to you that a majority of people in the world have not heard of your country. Having quizzical looks at your passport was not an uncommon occurrence. It happened to me with my university cricket team while returning to the port at Kent from our tour of Denmark. It took the assurance of 15 others that the country did exist for me to be admitted and that as a member of the Commonwealth I did not need a visa.

If that happened in England I should not have been surprised at the similar experiences I had in Argentina and Uruguay. In the latter the immigration officer refused to believe that a country he never heard of did not require special visas for its citizens, and I spent upwards of two hours at the airport while he awaited confirmation from his head even after he had been shown by me where we appeared on the list in his booklet of countries not needing a visa. He was polite nevertheless, and did advise of the do's and don'ts of the city while we chatted.

By contrast I must say that on entering India and South Africa the immigration officers immediately started conversations about Sir Garfield Sobers and other West Indian cricketing greats. These travels were not for holidays, but were all either for attending promotions with entities like the Canada-Barbados Business Association or the Barbados Industrial Development Corporation, or usually conferences put on by the International Bar Association.

Despite some of these happenings, travelling by and large was a pleasure with one caveat needing to be added if before 9/11. My travelling had become more extensive as I tried to build the offshore portfolio at Cottle. I still recall my first trip on such a mission—I think it was in 1993—to Vancouver to attend a function put on I think by the Canada-Barbados Business Association, seeking to promote Barbados as a first class destination to Canadians seeking to establish businesses overseas. Peter Boos was one of the architects behind the promotion. The late David Thompson, then a minister in the Erskine Sandiford administration, was on that trip and I vividly recall him giving me some advice I always found useful, namely that while it may be comfortable to stay within the circle of persons you know, it was only by networking that you were likely to make yourself known.

Over the next eight years I travelled extensively in this endeavor. I have often said that you seldom saw many of the sights of the cities you visited, and in my case with a young family at home I tended to return home as soon as possible after a meeting ended without taking any time for myself.

On the actual day that has become etched in memory forever—9/11—I was due to travel from Ottawa, the capital of Canada, to Montreal. I was there as the President of the CBBA for our annual promotion, which had run every year from 1993. During this time I lost count of the number of cities in Canada that I visited as part of these promotions. The irony that despite this because of my arrest Canada now wanted Police Certificates of Character before I could board a plane was not lost on me.

I was checking out of my hotel when the concierge sent a bell boy to help me with my bags. On arriving at my room, he asked where I was going because there had been a crash in New York at Kennedy Airport into one of the twin towers. I asked "Are you sure? There are no tall buildings in the immediate surrounds of Kennedy." By the time we reached the lobby it was mass confusion. Every TV in the lobby, the restaurants, any place that had one was on, and several airline crews who use the airport were gathered around. By this time the second tower had been struck.

In a typical human reaction I decided I did not want to fly at the moment, and therefore enquired as to whether I could get a taxi to Montreal. I was informed that there was a regular limousine service and therefore I booked a pick up. The fare was reasonable and the ride was about three hours, during which my driver and I listened in bewilderment to what was going on. During that time I made several calls home as rumours were beginning to abound. Suffice it to say that as I pulled up at my hotel in Montreal around the time my flight was to depart

Ottawa, it was announced that all flights in Canada had been cancelled. But for that decision I would have been stranded, but was early enough to still get my hotel room before they became a scarce commodity. Later when Air Canada refunded me the unused portion of my ticket I did fleetingly wonder whether it was justified as I had determined to miss the flight.

After 9/11 the world of travel changed. Not only what you could pack, but what your actual hand luggage would be, changed forever. I experienced it immediately when leaving Montreal, as the hand luggage I travelled up with was now deemed outside of regulations and could not be carried on board. In fact such luggage, a hanging folding bag for one's business suits, had disappeared or had to be refined. Searches of checked and hand luggage became more intrusive and the frequent traveler had to really plot and determine what they could take with them and what they could not. It took some time, but I think I have mastered it now. But even when you do a trip through Miami airport, especially transiting from Jamaica, it makes you wonder as you are patted down, sniffed, x-rayed or researched again.

One thing that is important is to have a reliable and easily accessible travel agent and Anne Marie Benjamin from Going Places has given me excellent service over the years, no more so than when I was leaving South Africa from a Sports Law Conference. My flight to London was not direct, but connecting out of another city. I had misunderstood how to claim your VAT refund on some jewelry I had purchased and was told that as I was in a domestic departure lounge I could not get it done, as it was done at the international departure. It was clear I would not have the time at my in-transit destination, so it was suggested that I have customs on arrival in Barbados certify that I had brought it in and they would send the refund.

As anyone knows, our customs duty would have eroded any

savings, so I determined to stay the extra night at the airport hotel that would cost me far less than the refund. Having already checked in it was the only way I could leave the terminal by not boarding. I announced to the BA staff that I was not feeling well and didn't think I could travel. As I was not travelling, my luggage had to be off-loaded, and 'presto'.

It didn't take long for the staff to realise what I had done, or why I did it, and they said to me "How are you so sure you can get a seat on the flight tomorrow?" whereupon I told her "My travel agent has already booked it. Check your system," which they did, smiled and said: "She is good." So once again Thanks Anne Marie!

It has been distressing for me that the events since 2013 have curtailed my ability to travel unrestricted. I can think of only two instances in the last twenty years when my travels did not incorporate some form of work and therefore contrary to an allegation that I have heard made I was not flying around the world joy riding. I have seen only too well what this inability has done to my practice. I derive no income now from the offshore sector and that investment both monetarily and from a time perspective has now been ruined by the antics of persons who not only should know better, but were sworn to uphold the Law independently and without favour.

CHAPTER 5

Living Under Suspicion

FOR ME it was the Money Laundering Charge that was more problematical to deal with. This was not to trivialize the theft charge but because of the era we are living in and not to mention the location, the spectre of money laundering raised separate distinct considerations. One of these was the cancellation of my United States visa contemporaneous with the charge in October 2013.

More than a year was to pass after my arrest before I learned of this cancellation. I was totally unaware at the time, but as I was to realise, a realization that today is still at the forefront of all that I do, the stigma of this charge despite it having been dismissed makes it clear that the maxim 'innocent until proven guilty' means little in some circumstances. Mine was one of them, because having been accused it was to some extent irrelevant whether I was guilty or not because of my profession. I do not need to comment on my ongoing anger at what I perceived was unfair treatment because of the accusations of others.

The issues that I was facing were made clear in two articles in the *Nation* penned by my former sixth form history teacher Ralph Jemmott on March 24th 2016, and another by the former Senator Francis Chandler on May 18th that year, both of which

I reproduce here with their permission.

In the immediate aftermath of my arrest I found myself withdrawing from appearances in public. I had an acute complex about what people would be saying about me. I often thought that though they may have been engaging me in conversation, this may have been more out of politeness, as deep down they may be thinking 'he is nothing but a scamp'.

As time passed I came to realize that many persons not only did not know the day-to-day happenings of what went on at Cottle, but because of their knowledge of me and to a great extent my family, simply wanted to say 'keep fighting, keep your head up, and God does not like ugly'. I lost count of the number of people who have said that or sent a message of support with that underlying meaning.

Unfortunately for me this was only good for persons in my orbit. For others the ease with which the internet can disseminate news meant that the accusation was prominently available whenever any potential client did their basic due diligence on me. I was not afforded the benefit of the doubt.

The saga concerning my USA visa which continues to this day is perhaps the clearest example of this. While I fully appreciate and accept that any country has the right to determine whether or not it wants to welcome a person within its borders, one's perspective of the exercise of this right can be coloured by what circumstances affect you. In my case as I knew that the charges levelled were totally unjustified it did not help me in coming to terms with the decision. To later learn that there was clear evidence that the decision of the Embassy was made upon information provided by a fellow Attorney who was clearly abusing their positions made matters worse.

At the time of my arrest I had no idea of the troubles that would lie ahead as I tried to clear my name. My ability to do so was to a certain extent impeded not only by the system, but by those who were so cloaked in its tentacles that they were oblivious to the effect it was having. I can still see the puzzled look on the face of a certain Police prosecutor who felt that I was engaging in an unseemly rant when after a year of attending Court I stated this was abject nonsense when all I am hearing is request after request for adjournment rather than proceeding with the matter. He appeared not to appreciate my point of the effect it was having on me as he muttered that I was on bail, unlike some that were remanded.

I have lost count of the number of individuals both in and outside of the legal profession who have approached me to question with a degree of bewilderment why I was charged with money laundering. I too have failed after hours and hours of searching to uncover any similar charges brought against an Attorney anywhere in the world based on the facts that arose out of the Cottle debacle. As I was to find out, the mere allegation was bad enough.

An examination of the letter dated May 16th 2016 sent to me by the Embassy in response to my letter querying the reasons for the revocation of my visa made it clear that more was at play. The only logical conclusion that I could reach was that the action was as a result of deliberate misinformation provided to the Embassy.

The allegation that I might abscond was to me so laughable, as though I have visited the States more times than I care to remember I have never thought about living there, but perhaps the thought was understandable because one of my detractors was writing letters to the Immigration Department suggesting I was looking to flee the island, the same Attorney who claimed he did not have a clue when Watson disappeared from his office and the island in the middle of the night.

This belief was confirmed when despite the charges being dismissed on August 13th 2015, my Application in June of 2016 was put on hold. When I attended the Embassy on June 23rd I was advised that my Application would have to undergo further administrative investigation before a decision was made. Three weeks later I received an email from the Fraud Division of the US Embassy stating that though the dismissal of the charges is acknowledged, I needed to obtain a letter from the Registrar of the Supreme Court indicating that I faced no further charges.

This made it clear to me that the reason advanced for the revocation of my visa, namely that it was feared I may abscond, was a crock and that it was all tied up with reporting requirements with respect to suspected financial crime thanks no doubt to Leacock based on his perceived need to provide statistics to bodies monitoring financial offences like the Financial Action Task Force even if it mean manufacturing charges.

Immediately on receipt of the email I wrote the Registrar asking for the letter for the Embassy as required. For over a year, despite further requests, I had not received as much as a reply far less the required letter, by which time I was fuming. My mood was not helped by a chance meeting with another Attorney in the summer of 2017 that revealed to me the names of Attorneys who had been charged with similar offences that I had been charged with, some of which were still pending, and yet none had their visas revoked.

In June of 2017 I filed an Application seeking an Order of Mandamus against the Registrar to issue the letter or show cause why it could not be issued. The Commissioner of Police and the Director of Public Prosecutions were joined as Respondents in the suit.

My Application was granted a certificate of urgency, so the matter came on quickly on June 28th before Justice Pamela

Beckles. It is somewhat of an understatement to say that I was taken aback when the Attorney General's office representing the Registrar and the other Respondents informed the Court that the office of the DPP, through the then Deputy DPP, now the DPP, had in August 2016 written the Registrar advising that it was the intention of that office to refile the charges against me.

It was at once evident to me that given the form of the request from the US Embassy, it would have been pointless to continue to seek the letter from the Registrar. I recall a red mist descending over my eyes, because the letter from the office of the DPP had been written just over a year after the dismissal of the charges and was now being revealed nearly a year later. As it had been written in reply to a letter from the Registrar asking for guidance so that she could respond to my request for a letter to take to the US Embassy, it was clear to me that it was deliberately done to prevent such a letter being issued.

Justice Beckles nevertheless ordered the DPP to respond to my Application within two weeks and adjourned the matter to September. Before the two weeks had expired the DPP was to die with the inevitable delay that followed. However, because of another statement in Court, I was able to make further investigation in the Registry and was to discover that the DPP had indeed filed in February of 2017 an Application for a Voluntary Bill of Indictment to be issued refiling the charges. Of course it had nothing to do with the fact that I had filed a civil suit, CV 47 of 2017, six weeks before the Application for the Bill, naming Gale, the Commissioner of Police and the DPP as Defendants.

It was clear to me that the DPP was continuing his campaign of harassment because if the Voluntary Bill was granted the charges against me would have been laid in the High Court without me having the opportunity of contesting whether they should have reached that far, the whole purpose of the hearings in the Magistrate's Court which he had not bothered to prosecute for twenty-two months.

As if dealing with my visa problems was not bad enough, I would run into problems with my Application for an Electronic Travel Authorization to travel to Canada. Having declared on my Application that I had been arrested in response to one of the questions I was asked to submit Police Certificates of Character from countries I had lived in for more than three months since I was an adult.

If I was asked under pain of death to list the number of trips I have made to Canada since the early 1990s I could not because of my involvement with the Canada-Barbados Business Association, yet because of these charges I now had to provide information on my fitness to travel.

After I received notification of what was required I immediately wrote the office of the Commissioner of Police saying that the delay in issuing me the letter to sort out my USA visa was having a knock-on effect as I held to the belief, which I still do, that the blacklisting by the US was having an effect on me.

The response was that they would examine my complaint about the delay, but I needed to apply to the department in Sugar Cane Mall for the Certificate, which I already knew. I must assume that the police are still investigating why there was a delay in response to my previous letters, but to date I have heard absolutely nothing from them.

On two occasions I went to the office responsible for issuing the certificates. On each occasion I was told there were no more applications available for the day and that I needed to come back. This seemed ridiculous, so I called the Sergeant in Charge and after not getting him, wrote a letter asking for an appointment for me to apply for the certificate. There was still no response, so

I followed up with a call which did not go well, because I was told that by seeking an appointment I was jumping the queue, that he could not change the system, and that the only person who could was the Commissioner.

I could not believe what I was hearing and said so in another letter to the Commissioner—total bureaucratic nonsense. How could I, calling on a Monday to make an appointment later in the week, be jumping a queue? Well, in the mind of the Sergeant one needed to arrive early enough (I was told people lined up as early as 5:00 am) to secure one of the forms. By this time I was steaming, as in my mind all this nonsense had been caused by the ridiculous charge brought against me and once again, I was receiving little practical help in solving the issues that flowed from it.

When I compared the attitude I experienced in Barbados to that in Jamaica when I sought the same certificate it was sadly lacking not only from the point of view of willingness to help, but of plain commonsense. On December 9th I travelled to Jamaica for a prearranged function, landing at 10:00 am. By 2:00 pm I had not only applied for and paid for a Certificate of Character, but had obtained it as well. I had been assisted by an Attorney of about five years call, a former mentee student of mine, who called the relevant office and requested a speedy turnaround.

The irony was not lost on me that I was a Barbados Attorney for over thirty years but could not get any help from my own. After my return I wrote another letter enclosing a copy of the said Jamaican Certificate, and again asked for an appointment for one rather than trying to take part in a hundred metre dash up two flights of stairs after waiting in line for three hours. Towards the end of the year I received a call asking me to present at Central to apply for the Certificate and finally received it on

January 10th 2017.

However, two months prior the Canadians had denied my request for an ETA, presumably on the basis that I had not submitted the relevant certificates. It did not affect my travel then for a few days to attend the funeral of my Aunt's husband. I had lived with them while a student at Norman Manley Law School because the application process was not mandatory until a few days after I returned. So should I need to travel to Canada I need to start all over again.

Interestingly, I read in the paper on February 16th 2017 that as of February 20th persons desirous of Certificates of Character would need to make an appointment for the issuance of same. If I played a small part in changing the nonsense, then it was for the greater good.

What next?

NOTHING SHOULD SURPRISE us nowadays, but I couldn't believe my ears when I heard that the reduction in MPs' salaries is to be reinstated. Isn't that a boldfaced insult to Barbadians – especially when, over the last few days we've been reminded at length of these MPs' dismal record ? In contrast to the lyrics of **Biggie Irie's** song, that definitely wouldn't be "money well spent." On the other hand the Opposition seems to be taking the honourable position and refusing the reinstatement at this time.

Added to all the woes the Opposition Leader outlined, is the ongoing deterioration of our justice system. This was brought home forcefully in the recently published book by Philip Nicholls, entitled: **More Binding than Marriage**. Having read it, I certainly think it should be compulsory reading for all Barbadians, particularly those in schools and the law faculty of the University of the West Indies. Maybe some bright young minds might be inspired to bring about change once and for all.

We see evidence almost every day of the poor performance of this system in spite of all the highly paid individuals overseeing it, but Nicholls' book is a real eye-opener. In addition to the inordinate delays (in this case 13 years) how can we have judgements and injunctions from the High Court seemingly totally ignored, and to make matters worse, those concerned allowed to leave the country? Shouldn't travel documents be withheld in such circumstances? The severe impact which all these inefficiencies and obstructions have had on the author's life is clearly detailed in the book. I usually read in bed at night, but had to change this routine as the contents of the book prevented me from sleeping.

It's scary to realise that any one of us could suffer that fate for one reason or another. How can we accept this state of affairs even after the Caribbean Court of Justice has criticised it? No wonder the Rt Excellent Errol Barrow is reported to have said that If you want justice, stay far from the law courts.

I seem to recall it being mentioned in the book that lawyers aren't good business people. This is supported by the seemingly poor financial management and office systems common to many law firms. No doubt this is why we frequently see lawyers accused of "withholding" clients' funds.

It would seem sensible to keep clients' funds completely separate from operational funds and have both the client and the attorney sign any cheques drawn from the client account. Actually the Rt

FOR WHAT IT'S WORTH

BY FRANCES CHANDLER

Excellent Errol Barrow also had his say on this in a speech to the graduating class of the Hugh Wooding Law School in 1986.

Another thing I gleaned from the book is that the so called "legal fraternity" is anything but a fraternity if the meaning of fraternity is taken as "brotherhood, fellowship or kinship". Where are we going in this country?

Bearing all this in mind, I would say that if ever there was a time when we Barbadians needed hope it is now. So I commend Ms Mottley for her "Covenant of Hope". While we may not support all the content, I'm sure none would deny that we must "return to the values that sustained and distinguished us as Barbadians" and that we are badly in need of "good transparent governance"; governance that involves talking to the people, and recognising that government is to serve the people and not the other way around.

Although she voted against the no-confidence motion, Dr Maria Agard made some excellent recommendations during the debate: introduce measures to weed out the bad politicians, introduce legislation to deal with electoral reform and campaign financing, establish an independent commission with powers to force political parties to have audited accounts open to public scrutiny, publish and expose big-name political donors to make known what privileges and contracts they enjoyed when the party of their choice was elected to government.

In short, we Barbadians want our Barbados back. The Barbados that produced people of character like the late Mrs Dorothy Hinkson. I knew Mrs. Hinkson from my childhood, since we lived nearby at Three Houses Factory. I certainly agree with those who described her as an angel to the people of St Philip, an icon, unsung hero, a Good Samaritan, a Florence Nightingale. May she rest in peace.

● *Dr Frances Chandler is a former independent senator. email: fchandler@caribsurf.com*

Growing spiritual debility

I WAS WATCHING the **CBC Evening News** at
7 o'clock when the headlines to the broadcast broke
the story that an attorney had been charged with
some malfeasance. What's new was my first response.
Then in the body of the news item it was stated that
the attorney indicted was Philip Nicholls. I could not
believe my ears. Not "Lumpy" Nicholls I mused,
anybody but Nicholls.

I had been Nicholls' sixth form teacher and had
always thought of him as a boy of impeccable character.
You didn't get to be headboy of Harrison College under
the leadership of Albert G. Williams unless you were
squeaky clean. But children do change as they grow up.
Many lawyers in Barbados were my sixth form history
pupils, at least one of whom has been recently convicted
and disbarred for criminally unprofessional misconduct.
In Philip's case I decided to reserve judgment and
to listen out for the facts pertaining to the case.

A few weeks ago I finally received my copy of
Philip V. Nicholls' book entitled **More Binding Than
Marriage** autographed and delivered to my home by no
less a person than Nicholls himself. Let me admit that
concerning the legal matters contained in the book,
I am very sympathetic to Nicholls. Having read the text
I have become even more so, as I am convinced that in
the words taken from Shakespeare's King Lear, Nicholls
is a man "more sinned against than sinning".

The greatest indictment that can be levelled against
Nicholls is a charge of puerile naivety. But Nicholls
has already pleaded guilty to that on Page 85 when
he states "Boy was I naive?' How long does it take to
recognise when one is surrounded by "bad spirits" and
to forthwith distance oneself from them? Maybe not

has already pleaded guilty to that on Page 85 when he states "Boy was I naive?" How long does it take to recognise when one is surrounded by "bad spirits" and to forthwith, distance oneself from them? Maybe not being a lawyer myself, I underestimate the complexity of such disengagement, maybe.

Nicholls' book is a must-read from many points of view. As a student of the law I would want to study its legal soundings as it realities to issues of partnerships and the current state of the judiciary in Barbados. As a student of society in general and of contemporary Barbadian society in particular, it is compulsory reading. As personal human story about what it means to be a son, a father, a husband and a friend it is a revealing study of the exigencies of life.

What I found most disturbing in Nicholls' text relates to the behaviour of certain people in Barbados, that reflects what I call in this piece a growing spiritual debility. By that is implied, a lack of moral compunction particularly when it comes to issues involving money. Barbadians have always narrowly equated sin, "wutlessness" with sexuality propensity.

The real threat to Barbados over the next 50 years is not the fiscal deficit, but an increasing moral deficit that is exponentially eroding trust. What is worrying is that it is showing up in very high places not just among the boys on the block who break into your house to steal a flat-screen TV or a DVD player, but among ostensibly respectable people who will break into your or the company's account and clean you out to satisfy their naked greed and insatiable material hunger.

Two other things should be of concern to right-thinking Barbadians. One is a growing reluctance of people to stand up for what is right. What is ultimately most worrying is the fact that the justice system may be falling into an irreparable state of decline.

This article was submitted as a letter to the Editor.

APPENDIX 5B

May 10, 2016

Mr. Philip Nicholls
P.O. Box 93 W
Christ Church, Barbados

Dear Mr. Nicholls,

Thank you for your April 29, 2016 letter to Ambassador Taglialatela regarding your visa case. The Ambassador asked me to respond on her behalf.

According to our records, a consular officer revoked your visa on November 1, 2013, due to concerns about your eligibility following your arrest. Our standard procedure in visa revocation cases is to inform the holder of the visa of the intent to revoke, if practicable. If, however, the consular officer believes that the subject's departure is imminent or that a notice of the intent to revoke would prompt the alien to attempt immediate travel, the officer may decide to revoke the visa without notifying the subject. It is not clear from the officer's notes what occurred in your case. I regret any inconvenience you experienced.

In order to obtain a new visa, you will have to reapply. Please refer to our website at barbados.usembassy.gov for directions on how to do so. On the day of your interview, I recommend that you bring any documentation regarding the dismissal of the charges against you.

Yours Truly,

William Bent
Consul General

Subject: Fw: Additional Documentation

From: ████████████████ (@gmail.com)

To: ████████████████

Date: Tuesday, July 12, 2016 10:15 AM

Please print

Dear Mr Nicholls,

Our office acknowledge receipt of the letter from Magistrates Courts dated January 29, 2016, however, we are requesting a letter from the Registrar of Courts indicating that there are no pending charges in any of the Courts in Barbados.

Please provide this letter at your earliest convenience, so that we can continue the administrative processing of your case.

Sincerely,

Fraud Prevention Unit

U.S. Embassy Barbados & the Eastern Caribbean

63

APPENDIX 5C

Filed by:
PHILIP NICHOLLS & ASSOCIATES
Attorneys-at-Law
No. 8 Pine Gardens off Pine
   Plantation Road, St. Michael, Barbados
Tel. (246) 826-0054
Email: info.nichollslaw@gmail.com

BARBADOS

FIXED DATE CLAIM FORM
Form 2
(Rules 8.1(5), 27.2 and 59.4(2))

SUPREME COURT OF BARBADOS
IN THE HIGH COURT OF JUSTICE

CLAIM NO.   CV0893 of 2017

IN THE MATTER OF THE ADMINISTRATIVE JUSTICE ACT CAP. 109B OF THE LAWS OF BARBADOS

AND

IN THE MATTER OF A BREACH OF SECTION 4 OF THE SAID ACT AND IN THE MATTER OF AN ORDER FOR MANADAMUS AGAINST THE REGISTRAR OF THE SUPREME COURT, THE COMMISSIONER OF POLICE AND THE DIRECTOR OF PUBLIC PROSECUTIONS.

BETWEEN:

PHILIP VERNON NICHOLLS   **CLAIMANT**

AND

REGISTRAR OF THE SUPREME COURT   **FIRST DEFENDANT**
COMMISSIONER OF POLICE   **SECOND DEFENDANT**
DIRECTOR OF PUBLIC PROSECUTIONS   **THIRD DEFENDANT**

The Claimant, **PHILIP VERNON NICHOLLS** of No. 8 Pine Gardens, off Pine Plantation Road in the parish of Saint Michael in this Island claims against the Defendants The **REGISTRAR OF THE SUPREME COURT,** First Defendant of The Supreme Court of Barbados, Supreme Court Complex, Whitepark Road in the parish of Saint Michael in this Island, **THE COMMISSIONER OF POLICE,** the Second Defendant of Police Headquarters Royal Barbados Police, Lower Roebuck Street in the City of Bridgetown in this Island, and **THE DIRECTOR OF PUBLIC PROSECUTIONS**, the Third Defendant of Frank Walcott Building, Culloden Road in the parish of Saint Michael in this Island.

 I. An order that the First Second and Third Defendants or any of them provide the Claimant, a citizen of Barbados, with letters to the US Embassy and the Canadian Immigration stating that the charges brought against the Claimant by the Commissioner of Police were dismissed by the Magistrate of District A on August 13th, 2015 for want of prosecution after the Police failed to offer any evidence in support of the charges levelled against him on October 29th 2013 as a result of which the US Embassy cancelled his Visa on November 1st 2013 in order for the Claimant to be issued with a US Visa from the US Embassy and an Electronic Travel Authorization from Immigration in Canada.

 II. Any such other Orders that this Court may deem fit.

 III. Costs to be agreed or assessed.

The grounds for this Claim are as follows:

1. The Claimant was charged with Theft and Money Laundering on October 29th, 2013 by the Second and Third Defendants, which charges were dismissed for want of prosecution by the Magistrate of District A on August 13th, 2015.

2. The Claimant's US Visa was revoked by the US Embassy as a result of the said charges and the Claimant made an application for reissuance of the said US Visa

as instructed by the US Embassy but has been advised that he needs a letter stating that he has been cleared of all charges for his application to be processed.

3. The Claimant has been denied an Electronic Travel Authorization (ETA) from the Canadian Immigration which would allow him entry into Canada on the basis that there is no formal notification that the charges against him have been dismissed.

4. The Claimant has made several requests of the First and Second Defendant for the requisite letters to be issued but to no avail and no justification for the non-issuance of same has been given.

CERTIFICATE OF TRUTH

I certify that all facts set out in this Claim Form are true to the best of my knowledge, information and belief.

Dated the 19th day of June , 2017.

_____
Claimant's Signature

STATEMENT OF CLAIM

1. The Claimant is a citizen of Barbados having been born in this island on the 6th day of October 1960 and as such acquired citizenship when the Island gained Independence from the United Kingdom on the 30th November 1966. The Claimant is presently an Attorney-at-Law having been admitted to practice in 1986.

2. The First Defendant is responsible for the running of the Government Department known as the Registration Office of this Island which is the department responsible for keeping the records of all Civil and Criminal Cases in this island.

3. The Second Defendant is the head of the Police Force in the island responsible for investigating any Criminal Offences in the island and in his name institutes any criminal charges brought against individuals with the advice of the Third Defendant.

4. The Third Defendant is charged under the Constitution with the responsibility of instituting or discontinuing any criminal prosecutions in this island.

5. The Claimant was arrested on the 29th October 2013 and charged by the third Defendant with theft and money laundering on said day. He was bailed by the Magistrate of District A on the 30th October 2013.

6. The charges against the Claimant were dismissed by the Magistrate of District A on the 13th August 2015 for want of prosecution by the Third and Fourth Defendants.

7. The Embassy of the United States of America in Barbados revoked the Visitor's Visa of the Claimant that he has held since about 1966 on the 1st November 2013 which revocation only came to the attention of the Claimant on December 14th 2014. The Embassy advised the Claimant subsequently that the revocation was as a result of his arrest.

8. The Claimant on June 23rd 2016, as advised by the US Embassy, applied for and was interviewed for the issuance of a Visa to travel to the United States of America.

9. The said US Embassy advised the Claimant by email dated July 12th 2016 that it was necessary for him to provide a Letter from the First Defendant indicating that he faced no further charges before his application could be processed.

10. The Claimant wrote a letter to the First Defendant on the 12th July 2016 requesting said letter and has written five further letters on the subject. The Claimant has never received an acknowledgment of said letters, far less the letter required by the US Embassy.

11. The Claimant wrote a letter with respect to the request of the US Embassy to the Second Defendant on October 17, 2016 and had an acknowledgment of same on October 24, 2016.

12. The Claimant's application for an Electronic Travel Authorization (ETC) from the Government of Canada in September of 2016 has been denied as a result of his declaring as required his arrest on the 29th October 2013. The Claimant has been advised that as a result of his arrest he needs to provide certificates of character before the ETC can be issued.

13. The Claimant, because of the failure of the First, Second and Third Defendants has been unable to travel to the United States since November of 2013 and to Canada since November of 2016. As a result the Claimant continues to suffer hardship and loss by being unable to attempt to rebuild his practice in the Offshore Finance Sector which has disintegrated as a result of his arrest which was highly publicized by the Third Defendant.

14. The continued denial to produce the letter requested by the US Embassy by the First Defendant compounds the damage done to the personal and professional reputation of the Claimant as a result of the unsubstantiated charges for which the Claimant was arrested.

15. The Claimant seeks the following:

I.   An order that the First Second and Third Defendants or any of them provide the Claimant, a citizen of Barbados, with letters to the US.

II.   Embassy and the Canadian Immigration stating that the charges brought against the Claimant by the Commissioner of Police were dismissed by the Magistrate of District A on August 13th, 2015 for want of prosecution after the Police failed to offer any evidence in support of the charges in order for the Claimant to be issued with a US Visa from the US Embassy and an Electronic Travel Authorization from Canadian Immigration.

III.   Any such other Orders that this Court may deem fit.

IV.   Costs to be agreed and assessed.

Dated this 19th day of June , 2017.

PHILIP NICHOLLS & ASSOCIATES
Attorneys-at-Law for the Claimant

CHAPTER 6

My Brother's Keeper

ONE OF the abiding themes running through this whole saga has been the relationship that existed between the central characters, most of whom were or presently are members of the legal profession. From young when I was taken by my father to various cricketing events I came into contact with many of the true giants of the profession who not only inspired me to become an Attorney, but who after I qualified and indeed throughout my career provided me with a form of mentorship that today is sadly lacking in the profession. In this regard they were exemplifying the whole concept of being your 'Brother's Keeper'.

Men like Vere Carrington, Oliver Browne, Sir Clifford Husbands, not to mention the two senior Partners of the Firm when I joined—Joseph Armstrong and Frederick St. Clair Hutchinson, were not only either just a phone call away when I needed advice, but the Partners at Cottle had an open door policy in their office and were willing and readily gave me advice on anything troubling me.

Uncle Clifford Husbands went further, for after he found out about the perilous state of affairs at Cottle Catford he would several times summon me to Government House, for as he put it 'a little chat' that went on for hours. I was not alone in receiving this type of help from him. And of course there was my father who through it all has been a tower of strength support that continues to this day.

Having been the recipient of this mentorship at the start and during the course of my career, I made a conscious decision that whenever I could and as long as I was asked I would try to pass on the benefit of my experience to the next generation. Telling my story has been one way of doing that and I have lost count of the number of young Attorneys who have been among the many people who have spoken to me about what has occurred which has made them watch carefully the actions of some of these characters. In this respect I was simply trying to be my Brother's Keeper.

Sadly, the events that I have faced have illustrated that this feeling to one's fellow professional is disappearing as the profession becomes more and more akin to a barrel of crabs with each person scrambling for the top, leaving the devil to take the hindmost because those at the top of the ladder refuse to stop to think of assisting those trying to get on the ladder. It may suggest a lack of confidence in one's ability because of a fear that the new kid on the block will not eventually but straight away take your place.

If life's lessons are learned from other endeavors, be it sport or otherwise, you will see how the precocious talent of youth when nurtured and developed by a senior statesman who sees it as his duty to do so to allow for the passing of the baton that is inevitable is not met by a rejection of the senior but by an appreciation for his or her wisdom. Time does not stand still for any man and if one recognizes that, then one does not fear competition and eventually replacement from a younger person who will never forget the assistance you have given them in their rise to the top. If they don't their ascent to the top, while it may occur, will not earn them the respect of their peers.

I must thank Dean Jeffrey Gibson for buttressing my biblical knowledge so it was not too evident that it was deficient when he gave me a tutorial to unlock my early memories of the story of Cain and Abel in the Bible. My early remembrances from Divinity studies at school often made me draw parallels with the behaviour of some members of the legal profession over the last few years.

My reference to the Cain and Abel story is primarily one of symbolism, as the phrase associated with that story was "are you your brother's keeper?" a question asked that is often answered in the affirmative by your actions in your life. Your duty as a brother is that you look out for him, and not do as Cain did—murder him out of jealousy.

While no one has at this time physically killed me, it is clear to me that the so-called brotherhood of the legal profession is more of a romanticized view of the past than a present-day reality. In any profession one will have disagreements, which is expected, but deliberate falsehoods and use of your position to inflict misery on others is not only unethical but downright hypocritical. It also says something—that when you see a man struggling, instead of offering a hand of friendship to help him up you decide it is best to ensure that he no longer becomes a competitor of yours by any means fair or foul.

In modern times, the reference to 'your brother's keeper' must be given a wider meaning—that of a protector to suggestions that one has a duty to mankind to help persons in trouble. Of course the help may be limited to what an individual is able to do. To determine this, comparison with how the question of tortious liability is measured by reference to how a reasonable man would react is appropriate. The reasonable man has been described as the behavior of the average man on the Clapham omnibus (Bayfield bus or Pine minibus) or with respect to the legal profession, what is expected of the average well thinking Attorney. As the canons of the profession suggest, you should treat your fellow Attorney with respect and in a manner that you would wish to be treated. Sadly, a few clearly failed this test by whatever means you measure it.

I make no apologies for saying this and while many have not breached this standard, I have been saddened by the attitude of some in the profession who could have, if not prevented the events that occurred, certainly corrected them by simply pulling the rug from under those of their colleagues who chose to do me harm by their unethical actions. The result is that though no one has killed me literally, metaphorically I have suffered a death because of the actions of some who should know better.

Before protestations are made about my statements, let me make it clear that I am not speaking about all or even most of the members of the profession for that matter. Bearing in mind my statement that your ability to have acted in any circumstance would depend on your circumstances, I would be the last to expect that help could be forthcoming from most of my acquaintances in the profession.

While I have greatly appreciated the kindness and good wishes and offers to help with many mundane things of practice by many young Attorneys as they have neither the wherewithal nor contacts to make a difference to my problems, their actions contrast with those of many older practitioners who simply give the impression while expressing sympathy that 'I am glad it is you and not me'. I am left to wonder what the future holds for those now entering the profession, but remain hopeful that perhaps the bright-eyed wonder of youth will not be overcome by the cynicism that has overcome me once they recognise the pitfalls that befell me.

But just in case some do not remember let me remind what the Legal Profession provides—the Canons of the Profession—those dictates that may be compared to the moral stricture found in the Lord's admonition to Cain to be his Brother's Keeper. Thus, Attorneys must respect and pay deference to:

- the Court;
- their fellow Attorneys;
- the litigant on the other side.

The Law Society in England, the body charged with monitoring and ruling on disciplinary infractions of Solicitors, put it this way when talking about Ethics: '*A solicitor's commitment to behaving ethically is the heart of what it means to be a solicitor.*' The Law Society supports solicitors in recognizing and handling professional situations and making choices which can be substantiated by reference to the SRA code of Conduct.

- 'Ethics involves making a commitment to acting with integrity and in accordance with widely recognized moral principles.
- Ethics will guide a professional towards an appropriate way to behave in relation to moral dilemmas that arise in practice.
- Ethics is based on the principles of serving the interests of consumers of legal services and of acting in the interests of the administration of justice, in which, in the event of a conflict, acting in the interests of the administration of justice prevails.'

Simply put, your ethics should be towards ensuring that the administration of justice takes precedence. This is the governing consideration. It should not be seen as old-time law that has no relevance in today's world; it should be the basis on which your practice is founded.

For a seasoned Attorney, these should be known as a matter of course, let alone for a Queen's Counsel. After all, you only become a Q.C. after years of practice and even more years of life.

Queen's Counsels ('King' if the sovereign is male) were traditionally Barristers (advocates before the Courts of the land) who were elevated to silk in recognition of their outstanding advocacy. Admittance to the Inner Bar was not only an honour, it also allowed the Attorney to charge higher fees.

Several traditions surrounded the office, one of which was that the Silk never attended Court unaccompanied. He was always accompanied by a junior, who among other things was charged with holding his robes and papers for the matter at hand. Though a junior, he/she was expected to be as knowledgeable of the matter at hand as the senior. It is for this reason that the attitude in the UK is that if your senior is suddenly indisposed you should continue the matter without the need for an adjournment as is prevalent locally where the Q.C is unavailable.

With the fusion of the profession in Barbados circa 1971, there was no longer a distinction between Barristers and Solicitors and this eventually led to the admittance of those whose practice was that of Solicitors rather than Barristers to the rank of Queen's Counsel. Today most of those elevated are what traditionally was referred to as Solicitors Tradition, which had it that all heads of the major Law Firms in the island were accorded the designation as well as persons who were appointed Attorney-General or other senior positions with the State, such as the Solicitor General and the Director of Public Prosecutions.

At present, any person with more than ten years' call can apply to be appointed a silk. The Application is made to a Committee chaired by the Chief Justice and must be supported by two current silks. The Committee makes recommendations to the

Prime Minister who has the final say on who is appointed. It goes without saying that it helps to be supportive of whichever party is in power when the appointments are made approximately every five years.

I have never applied and have no intention of ever applying for appointment as silk. That is not to say that I would automatically have been successful, but my reason for saying so is simple. I am of the firm belief that elevation to the office should be because of judgment by your peers that your work has been of a quality to be admitted to the Inner Bar. It is my belief that several of the current Queen's Counsels have prior to their appointments not shown the necessary legal brilliance to warrant elevation. Many have benefitted from political patronage that has counted for more in counterbalancing their obvious shortfalls in legal knowledge.

My interaction with a few that carry the title has left me with the feeling by their conduct that they not only are a discredit to the office, but frankly should be removed from same. As such it is not a club that I aspire to enter, whether or not others may think I am qualified to.

While it is not my intention to cast a blanket of suspicion over all the members of what should be an esteemed club if the scoundrels were ejected, if you as a member fail to speak out against what other members within it are doing that tarnishes the reputation of all, then your silence may be viewed either as one of condoning or as indifference. Whichever one it is, it may be construed as a failure to uphold the canons of the profession.

In my previous book I devoted a chapter to Vernon Smith. I did so not out of any respect I have for him as a lawyer far less as a human being, but to draw attention to him and signify the absolute contempt in which I hold him. This would be like water off a duck's back for him. While his actions since then deserve my further comment, the actions of others are equally deserving of condemnation, especially as their actions not only belie the status of Queens Counsel but are an example of total hypocrisy.

While Smith may still be the cheerleader (a comparison which in itself is an insult to cheerleaders worldwide), it is evident that he is the figurative leader of a choir filled with hypocrites, men who by and large seek to exude an air of being self-righteous members of the profession and society, but are nothing but wolves in sheep's clothing.

The saga of the Watsons and Cottle in general is well illustrated in my previous book. It has been nearly twenty years since the Watsons have walked out on the use of nearly one point five million dollars that did not belong to them. In effect it is an unauthorized loan that they have determined has no requirement to be paid back or for interest to be paid during its period of loan.

Vernon Smith has been in the vanguard of attempts unethical in the main to prevent this recovery and I for one believe that his actions could, should there have been a DPP with the necessary balls, seen him charged as an accessory after the fact, namely the theft from Cottle. These antics by him illustrate some of his worst traits highlighted by the censure he received from the CCJ in the System Sales case. All he has done is to seek to delay the inevitable by raising any ridiculous point as a point of law and then arguing it as if it has some merit.

Smith's DNA would no doubt be comparable to that of Trump, an equally reviled person holding even higher office than he does, because of the similar traits, namely to never admit that he is wrong, never admit that the other side has an argument, and to do all in his power by any means—legal or illegal, ethical or unethical—to prevent an opponent recovering what is due to them.

This time I have his own words for impartial, fair-minded people to judge him against in the form of a transcript of proceedings before Justice Richards on April 24th 2014 when he tried to answer the question of how the money used by Delvina Watson was repaid by paying 32% of Judgment in favour of Cottle to me and then because the other 68% was paid to her husband and Joyce Griffith out of money borrowed by her husband this settles the claim.

On this basis alone Smith's actions would warrant an ethics investigation. However, worse was to follow, as in an attempt to justify his argument that the debt had been settled by the payment of the amounts due to the three Partners as he alleged was done, he had to concoct a reason for the payment of the Judgment to Watson and Griffith, as he alleged was done. I was stunned when he made his assertion in Court that the clients' account belongs to the Partners and as a result any moneys due the clients' account would be considered as repaid if paid to them in the proportion of their entitlement under the Partnership where the 32%/68% split arises.

It was an astounding assertion, and though made in 2014 it should have been highly relevant to any investigation surrounding the circumstances leading up to the murder of Marcelle Smith. Smith and Smith is a Partnership like Cottle Catford was, so when it collected rent to the tune of $100,000 from property owned jointly by her and her husband, it automatically became his private kitty according to his logic—a kitty that he has refused to repay up to today despite repeated requests from his sister-in-law prior to her death, the representatives of his brother and now to the legally appointed Administrators of their Estates.

That $100,000, and more patently how to recover same from Vernon Smith, was the subject of the last conversation I had with Marcelle Smith on the night of her disappearance;

a conversation which phone records suggest might have been her last. In the words that have become immortalized from the Watergate scandal and appear so relevant to the Mueller probe in the USA, just follow the money; something that apparently neither the Police nor the now deceased DPP cared to do.

Any right-thinking person, far less a legally trained one, would realize that the premise put forward by Smith as to the ownership of client's accounts is probably the view of one descending into senility. His wild legal views have been rebutted by many Courts and are in keeping with his theory that when the facts are against you, you argue the Law, and when the Law is against you, you argue the facts. However, when both facts and law are against you what do you do? You concoct a story. In this case it is fit for another Perry Mason episode entitled *The Case of The Disappearing Cheque* as to how this 68% was repaid by Mrs. Watson to her husband and Joyce Griffith in settlement of the default Judgment, but no trace of the payment can be made.

It may appear to some that this chapter could be named *Vernon Smith II*. Sadly, he is not the only one who has placed personal interest over doing what is right. I meet it daily in the tactics employed by others who should know better and who were not and are not man enough to look me in the eye or face me *mano et mano*, but send Juniors to do their bidding in Court while hiding behind the scenes in attempts to get others do their unethical biddings. Clandestine messages to the DPP with spurious and untruthful allegations at a time when you were President of the Bar are also suggestive of the hypocritical liar that persons of this trait have exhibited.

We all have sinned, but some of us have a conscience; sadly, several of my colleagues do not. It is thus of concern, as I have watched the profession develop over the years from one where new entrants were encouraged and freely offered advice to one where some seniors would look to exploit their inexperience to gain an advantage. I must say I am glad I am getting out of it, for certainly the profession is no longer representative of one's brother's keeper.

The hypocrisy makes me sick, but as will soon be evident, Attorneys do not have a monopoly on hypocrisy.

CHAPTER 7

God Does Not Like Ugly

OVER THE five years since my arrest I have often been told the phrase "God don't like ugly." It often follows or prefaces another, that "God is not sleeping." These statements have either been said to me in person or sent via the various versions of social media available today as a means of exhorting me to keep the faith and that better days are coming. Many others have uttered them while sympathizing with my plight, to remind me that God is seeing what you are going through and has a plan for you because He will not let you bear more than you can. I will confess to not being overtly religious, and I am sure I am not the first person who, while facing struggles, has questioned why I am being tested. What I can say is that it has become clear to me from the everyday happenings around me that He must indeed have a plan for me.

Many a night as I reflect while alone, I ponder what was the terrible crime that I did to deserve this torture. My first and only thought when it became clear that the practice at Cottle Catford was going under unless urgent measures were taken that my two Partners after years of talk were clearly unwilling to do, was how to preserve the Firm as a going concern. It was my hope that if this happened not only would the clients have recovered their money but the staff themselves would have continued in their employment.

To be fair I underestimated the magnitude of the problem. It was only after the end of the Partnership when I was able to examine the books in detail on my own and to perform a virtual audit that the extent of the total problem fully became clear. What I had not catered for in all of this was the unethical actions of others.

On Sunday July 9th 2017 I was at home looking forward to spending the day just watching cricket being played in the UK and the West Indies. A day of relaxation. Unexpectedly, my office phone rang. I sucked my teeth and let it ring. Sunday morning—must be a wrong number. It rang again, and I said to myself "gosh I can't get no rest." It rang a third time, so I got up from my chair and muttering to myself, went to check to see who was disturbing my homage in front the TV or, as that late great scribe Gladstone Holder penned once about a request from his wife to come to the phone, to tell the person he was at Lords and thus could not be disturbed.

I checked the caller display and recognised the call was from a cell phone of an Attorney that I knew. I said to myself "Why the hell did he not call my cell?" I returned the call to Tariq, about to upbraid him that I know he is not a cricket man but why on earth are you disturbing my peace this early?

He said, "Philip I have some bad news. Charles Leacock has died." I said to myself "He must be joking," because, as cruel as it may sound, given that he was aware of my travails with Leacock, I did not see how he could equate the two. I said to him "You looking to f… me up this Sunday morning? To start me up?" He said no and denied five times, like Peter denying the Lord, that the information was not a hoax and that it would soon break.

By this time I had started to think realistically. I said, "Well I will have to express my sympathy to his wife who was a former classmate at Harrison College, but time will see as to what happens." As is natural, I cast my mind back to the last time I had seen him which was in March in the President's Box at Kensington Oval during the One-Day International between West Indies and England. Our paths did not cross.

As I had been warned, my cellphone soon started ringing with calls or messages from persons, both Attorneys and other friends, some of whom were at the time overseas. Most wanted to know how I felt. My response was my feelings were not relevant currently. I was not a close friend and as is well known and documented, I took personal exception to some of his actions. It would be hypocritical of me to suggest that I was shedding a tear. However, given that it was unexpected and at a relatively young age, it must be devastating for his family, who I kept in my thoughts. The universal comment that I heard was that "God Doesn't Like Ugly."

For me there was an urgent practical problem. Just over a week prior to his death Justice Beckles had ordered him to file an Affidavit in response to my Application for an Order of Mandamus against the Registrar of the Supreme Court as First Respondent; I had named the Commissioner of Police and the Director of Public Prosecutions as the Second and Third Respondents.

While I am fully conscious of the maxim that one does not speak ill of the dead, I am also reminded of the maxim that "the evil that men do lives after them but the good is often interred with their bones." In my view the other often sited maxim that "the good die young" was being severely tested and I would simply refer to what the Constitution provides and compare it to his actions re my matter.

Section 18(1) of the Constitution provides as follows:

"If any person is charged with a criminal offence then, unless the charge is withdrawn, the case shall be afforded a fair hearing within a reasonable time by an independent and impartial court established by law."

How despite this and especially because of his failure to deal with the matter in the Magistrate's Court the filing by him of a Voluntary Bill of Indictment was in my view a clear abuse of powers.

Shortly after his death I was to get news of another death to which my feelings were not ambivalent. On the morning of Thursday, July 28th 2017 I learnt that Auntie Angela Nicholls, the widow of Daddy's eldest brother Courtney, had died in Trinidad after a brief illness. News of her passing made me reflect, as I had constantly done over the last fifteen years, about the predicament that I was still facing from the Cottle Catford & Co. saga. Through this predicament Auntie Angela had been a constant source of support and encouragement.

My mother's illness that was daily robbing her of more and more of her memory, plus the murder of Auntie Marcelle, had previously removed from within my immediate orbit that maternal support that all of us even if only subconsciously, rely on. Through it all Auntie Angela was often there not only at the end of a phone call but often coming up to visit. The Grim Reaper, whom we all try to cheat in our desire to continue our existence, had once again played his card and dealt me another personal loss.

Auntie Angela had attended my calling to the Bar in January of 1986, had played a supportive role at my wedding in September of 1990, had been ever present, often being the driving force behind the several family celebrations over the years to recognize various milestones—be it to celebrate Daddy's knighthood or to welcome the birth of my three daughters into the family, or to simply recognize those milestones passed as the journey of life continued.

She had always been in the thick of things, often offering a helping hand without having to be asked. After she along with Uncle Courtney returned to Trinidad after his stint as headmaster of Lodge had come to an end, she was always just a phone call away. Many mornings or sometimes in the early evening she would just call me with the words "My mind ran across you and the children and I was just calling to see how you all are doing."

Our conversations would always end with exhortations from her to me to keep strong. She would stress that above all I must keep in mind that my children were my prime responsibility, as stressful as other events may be. It was advice first given to me by Stephen Alleyne way back around 2005 and it was advice that as this ordeal went on I clung to even more and more.

Over the years as the children became older and more aware of things I had seen how my worries had impacted on them and how they in their own way would try to solve or resolve problems for themselves so as not to be a burden to me. It often left me feeling guilty when I found out as I felt that I had failed them, for after all one's childhood should be free of worry, and whilst some may still argue that their upbringing was more privileged than most, it still haunted me the effect that this lifelong debacle had on them and caused me not for the first time to inwardly curse the usual suspects.

Often a call from Auntie Angela would be to say that she and Uncle Courtney were coming up for a few days, and wanted to spend some time with the children. She continued visiting after his death even though all her life in Barbados was centered around him. She would arrive with all kinds of children's books that she would give to the children to read and ensure they had at least a head start by reading to them at bedtime. For us older ones, clippings from the Trinidadian newspapers that she thought may have been of interest to my parents or me.

She loved her cricket, was very knowledgeable about it and would talk about it for hours, even out-lasting me. She never forgot my friends from University and Law School days who would pick me up from their house when I went down for a few days. I was to learn after her death that two of my closest contemporaries from those days who had gone on to be Judges in Trinidad remained in contact with her, she often calling to give her opinion after reading about a trial that was reported in the paper and seeing that they were the Judge.

The last time that I had seen her was in December 2016 when I spent a couple of days in Trinidad on an exploratory trip to the Registry of the Caribbean Court of Justice. One of my nights there was reserved for dinner with her and we chatted on a variety of subjects, but always with an emphasis on her insistence on what was troubling me. She never complained about any personal problems, although in her last few years, having lost Uncle Courtney, I could sense a pervading loneliness. I thought I knew a lot of people, but our meal was constantly interrupted by someone she knew to whom she would give my life story, introducing me as her nephew.

In fact, while we were eating I was waiting for someone to collect some books I had taken down for my former Secretary Thea Corbin, then at Law School. The person collecting them turned out to be Thea's landlord, and when he arrived he found me because he knew her. Our dinner was delayed as they chatted like long-lost friends.

Her last visit to Barbados was on the evening of my book

launch in February of 2016. She was her usual effervescent self and the children as usual gravitated to her, lapping up her several stories of life today and in years bygone. It struck me how, while waiting for the function to begin at the Cricket Legends of Barbados, that she had taken the time to have a tour of the exhibit going back in history with the items on display from our cricketing greats of a bygone era. She was of course relating some anecdote from when she had met one of them and managed to do what I could not do: get the girls to view the exhibits which they routinely classified as boring, no doubt to antagonize me.

Both she and Uncle Courtney were at one in making it a point to attend important occasions, and I remember well how both had insisted on being in the island in October 1999 to attend what has come to be regarded as one of, if not the biggest meeting of the Barbados Cricket Association (BCA) to elect a Board of Management. I was elected Secretary of the Board that was led by Sir Conrad Hunte who sadly died a few weeks after taking office. Stephen Alleyne who succeeded Sir Conrad and I, could always count on their support in future elections and she would make a point in letting all and sundry know that her nephew was Secretary of the BCA whenever speaking on cricket matters.

There was thus no question in my mind that I would be attending her funeral, and so I began to put plans in place to be in Trinidad on Friday August 4th, 2017. Much to their sadness, the children would have been unable to attend as they had left the island on July 31st 2017 for five weeks in England, the land of their birth, with their mother.

It was thus with a very heavy heart that on the day before I was due to travel, I had to cancel my plans because of what was now becoming a recurring decimal for me—lack of finance. I was angry, and I called down the wrath of the Lord on all who had for these fifteen years been making my life a living hell. I then remembered her counsel and was comforted by the fact that she would fully understand what I was facing. July 2017 was thus a difficult month as I was reminded that many persons who had influences on my life had left the stage.

I must in closing this chapter celebrate one who is still here and recently celebrated her one-hundredth birthday. Avisene Carrington, known to many of us her former students as Auntie Avis and who has now been elevated to a Dame, has had a long connection with my family from the time my father and uncle attended St. Giles Boys School where she taught. It thus was not surprising that we three boys were sent to her primary school on Pine Road, officially known as Merrivale Preparatory School or Mrs. Carrington School, a schooling that has shaped not only our lives for the better, but many others who have gone on to play a prominent role in society.

Her late husband Vere was a former Registrar of the Supreme Court and after retiring joined Cottle as a Consultant. He retired from the Firm just before I joined, but would always call with a word of encouragement, something that I remembered fondly when I saw Auntie Avis at the launch of my book. An outstanding life and a lie to the maxim that the good die young.

CHAPTER 8

When Will the Hypocrisy End?

AS THE nightmare of the last two decades continued, I would marvel at the hypocrisy that I continued to face in my attempts simply to find a way out of the morass I was in. Whether the hypocrisy was being exhibited as a result of the actions of some who seemed hell bent on ensuring my destruction, or the indifference that I was encountering day to day as I tried to climb out of it, made little difference. The stark fact was that my financial predicament would have been unimaginable at the start of practice, far less than when the Partnership ended. That scenario was based on an assumption that everyone would play by the same rules, which did not occur, and when coupled with the downturn in the general economy, a perfect storm was created for my demise.

One sleepless night, again caused by my worrying over needs to source finance for another pressing claim, I decided to check the Oxford Dictionary as well as various search engines on the Internet for an accurate definition of the term 'Hypocrisy'. Some of the definitions I discovered were:

- 'the contrivance of a false appearance of virtue or goodness, while concealing real character or inclinations, especially with respect to religious and moral beliefs, hence in a general sense, hypocrisy may involve dissimulation, pretense, or a sham';

- 'the behaviour of people who do things that they tell other people not to do';
- 'a pretense of having some desirable or publicly approved attitude';
- 'is defined as saying or feeling one thing and doing another';
- 'pretending to be what one is not or to feel what one does not feel (e.g. empathy)';
- 'the practice of professing, beliefs, or virtues that one does not hold or possess; falseness';
- 'the practice of engaging in the same behavior or activity for which one criticizes another; moral self-contradiction whereby the behavior of one or more people belies their own claimed or implied possession of certain beliefs, standards or virtues';
- 'the claim or pretense of holding beliefs, feelings, standards, qualities, opinions, behaviours, virtues, motivations or other characteristics that one does not in actual fact hold'.

To these definitions I have not simply muttered to myself, but whether the time was appropriate or inappropriate I would shout from the rooftops that to this list I could simply add three words: the names of VERNON SMITH, MICHAEL SPRINGER and BARRY GALE. None of them deserve in my opinion the designation after their name of Q.C because none have displayed the type of behavior expected of such an exalted status. Instead they should simply be referred to as 'Hypocrite' and I challenge any of the three to dispute that they have lied, mischaracterized, and spread untold falsehoods about the situation at Cottle and my attempts to rectify the wrongs done by my former Partners. Virtually every day I uncover another form of deceit by one of them the latest being further evidence of the role that Gale played in engineering the charges that were brought against me.

While mulling over the title for this book the word hypocrisy often floated in and out of my thoughts, but in the end I determined that to use it as a theme running through the book may illustrate better the effect that this type of insidious behavior had not only on me but all who are subjected to it.

While at home on Saturday, July 29th 2017 I received a call asking if I was aware that there is an Appeal involving Cottle Catford & Co. in the Court of Appeal on Monday. I stated that I was unaware. After consulting with a few friends and colleagues, the consensus was that I should attend if only to see what it was about. I therefore asked Charmain Delice-Hunte to accompany me to Court. I muttered under my breath and wished all manner of purgatory on Smith as he was the only person in my view who could be bringing a motion on behalf of anyone with any kind of interest in the legal affairs of Cottle Catford.

Charmain had appeared for me with Elliott Mottley Q.C and Edmund Hinkson when the appeal brought by Griffith re the Cottle litigation had been dismissed on October 4th 2013, nearly four years prior and eight years since I had won the Judgment. Fourteen years and seven months had elapsed since the Partnership had ended and during that time I had recovered just over $100,000 with more than two million outstanding.

As I had not appeared in a formal Court session since January of 2014, I had to arrange with Eddie to borrow his bib, as I had no idea where mine was. More evidence if any were needed of the effect that this debacle had had on me as I no longer had a separate office where such things could be easily retrieved. To be frank, I was of the view that if I never saw the inside of a Court again it would be too soon. I was not the only person who was of the view that our Judicial system was a colossal waste of time.

I made enquiry of the Court Marshall on arrival and he indicated that there was an appeal involving Cottle Catford & Co. and a Delvina Watson. I simply sucked my teeth and took my seat. Typical Smith. The woman and her husband raped the clients' account of Cottle Catford to the tune of over two million dollars, only a $100,000 had been repaid and yet he was grandstanding in a Court in the belief that she had suffered a wrong. *A blasted unethical hypocritical criminal* were my polite thoughts. *When will it all end?*

Surely, I thought to myself, *he could not be so senile to be appealing the Order of Justice Richards of June 20th 2017 when she again confirmed that she had recused herself from further hearing of 151/152 of 2004 because of the scurrilous accusations made against her by Delvina Watson in a letter in October 2014 which was clearly drafted by Smith and or Springer but signed by her.*

This letter was written just before Justice Richards handed down her verbal decision on November 21st 2014, and at the time she had indicated that she was recusing herself from further hearings in the matter. She could not be faulted for so doing.

It is important to quote a very small snippet of the eleven-page letter that was signed by Delvina Watson dated October 28th 2014.

"Is it fair to me that the debt has been paid to the Plaintiff and I must still attend Court on Applications filed by the same Plaintiff before the same Judge without Notice to my Attorneys or to me seven years after payment of the debt? When will it end and who will pay my costs?

In the premises I must respectively, but regrettably,

state that such failure on the part of the trial Judge is clearly a gross dereliction of duty and constitutes such serious judicial misconduct as to warrant her removal from office.

Accordingly, I humbly ask that action be taken to protect and vindicate my constitutional rights in this matter without further delay."

Of course, whether the money had been paid was the bone of contention. There has been no evidence that it ever has been paid at least not to Cottle, from whose clients' account the money had been taken. But I need not be believed—the transcript of Smith and Watson perjuring themselves under oath on the subject is reproduced for all and sundry to determine for themselves.

When the matter was called, Smith entered an appearance on behalf of himself, Michael Springer and Springer's daughter, a young Attorney, on behalf of the Appellant Delvina Watson.

The President of the Court, Justice of Appeal Sandra Mason (sitting with Justices of Appeal Goodridge and Burgess) asked if anyone for the Defendant was there. I rose and indicated that I did not know whether to make an appearance as I had not been served with Notice of the Application and had no idea what it was about. Justice Mason stated that under the rules 62.2 the Application for Leave to Appeal could be made without notice, *in which case*, I thought to myself *why ask for someone for the Defendant*. In the circumstances I made no formal appearance.

Vernon Smith proceeded to factually mislead the Court in setting out his Application for leave to appeal as to what the matter was about. He proceeded to attack the Judgment obtained in 2004, more than thirteen years prior, arguing that I had no basis for obtaining same. *I mean to say his client's husband while Senior Partner of a Firm, writes cheques on its clients' account payable to his wife despite the Firm holding no money on her behalf and you going to argue that there is no basis for a Judgment for the money so paid fourteen years later.* And worse still is that three big people had nothing better to do than listen to him.

Whatever is the case, his arguments in the Court of Appeal were clearly unethical, irrational and a clear divergence from the facts which should have resulted in the Court of Appeal giving short shrift to the nonsense. Having not done so a year ago, I now have to apply for the leave he was granted to appeal to be set aside for want of prosecution. It seems clear that the other maxim that justice is blind was all too evident, for anyone else could have seen that his sole attempt as it has been over the years was to delay and delay my attempts at recovering the money due.

Smith continued his submissions by turning his attack to Justice Richards' decision to recuse herself. I have set out a small part of the letter from Delvina Watson asking for same, she having recused herself in 2014 and then again in 2017 when Watson applied for an Injunction to be lifted preventing her selling property, yet he is now appealing.

Justice of Appeal Burgess interrupted Smith's twenty-minute rambling to inform him that the Application for Leave was defective with respect to the names of the Intended Appellant, and not just the Appellant was required, after which the President stated that subject to that amendment, they were granting Leave to Appeal.

With what has transpired over the last decade with respect to my matters nothing surprises me anymore. I said nothing at the time, as my children were travelling that night to the UK to see their mother's family and I clearly did not want to upset them by the news that I had been arrested for contempt of Court because the only thing that I could have said was that the three of them were a bunch of lunatics. I will say, and frankly no longer care who it offends, as being nice and polite has got me nowhere.

Listening to Smith was bad enough, but allowing what he asked for was an example of a spineless performance of one's duties. It is not that I am biased, but good god, a blind man could see what Smith has been doing and for you not just to condone it but to be party to it is scandalous. The Marshall should have been ordered to chase him out of Court with a bull pistle with an Order for wasted costs affixed to his backside.

It would surprise no one that as we go into the final quarter of 2018, the Appeal still has not been prosecuted by Smith. Of course not, he simply wishes to continue the obstruction that he has been about for the last 15 years. But my problems have not only been of Smith's making. I get tired of writing, as my letters show, complaining that he has been and continues to be allowed to abuse the system.

It was not only Smith, but Springer is complicit in the crime of being an accomplice after the fact in the theft of money from Cottle. To file spurious motions after motions that are legally flawed to support a madman in his lunacy makes you as complicit as others. As for Gale, I will not comment further on him only because the law suit I have against him is still pending.

Their hypocrisy makes me sick.

APPENDIX 8A

Barry Gale

From: Barry Gale ████████████████████ on behalf of 'barry gale' ████████
Sent: Friday, July 22 2011 4:36 PM
To: ████████████████████
Cc: 'Barry Gale'
Subject: Re: Philip Nicholls

Dear Charles

I tried to reach you by telephone today without success to follow up on my previous letters to you and telephone conversations concerning the failure by the Police to prosecute Mr. Philip Nicholls for absconding with over $800,000.00 of monies belonging to my clients, Mr. & Mrs. Connor. I believe Inspector White was the officer at the Fraud Department in charge of this matter. I am very concerned that nothing is being done and in particular that the word on the street is that it is because of whose son he is that no action is being taken against him by the relevant authorities. This situation of course is a stark contrast of how other Attorneys are being treated in similar circumstances, for example, ████████ or yesterday, ████████

I am therefore again requesting that you use your good office so as to ensure that there is equality before the law and that the rule of the law is upheld otherwise the whole system will breakdown and naturally the public will lose confidence in all of us who are concerned in the upholding of the rule of the law.

If you wish to discuss this matter, please feel free to call me on my cell **230-3115**.

Kind regards

Barry L. V. Gale Q.C. LLB (HON.)
Barrister & Attorney-at-Law
%Trident Financial Centre
  Cnr. St. Matthias & Highway 7
  Christ Church BB 15150
  Barbados, West Indies
☎ Tel No: 1 (246) 427-9054
📠 Fax No: 1 (246) 429-8056
✉ E-mail: bgale@hastings-attorneys.com

B.L.V. GALE, Q.C. LL? (Hons.)
Barrister & Attorney-at-Law
TELEPHONE (246) 427-9264
FAX NO. (246) 429-8056
E-MAIL bgale@hastings-attorneys.com
VAT REG # 5402220155

TRIDENT FINANCIAL CENTRE
?. ST. MATTHIAS GAP & HIGHWAY 7
HASTINGS
CHRIST CHURCH BB 15156

18 September 2009

ATTENTION MR CHARLES LEACOCK, Q.C.

Director of Public Prosecutions
Frank Walcott Building
Culloden Road
ST MICHAEL

Dear Sir,

Re: Mrs. Kathleen Inniss

I act on behalf of Mrs. Kathleen Inniss of 23 Mount Standfast Plantation in the parish of Saint James and refer to our teleconference (Gale/Leacock) on 11th September 2009.

On or about 16th October 2008, my client made a report and provided a statement to the Criminal Investigation Department at the District "A" Police Station wherein it was reported that Philip Nicholls, Attorney-at-Law had fraudulently retained and used for his personal purposes the net proceeds of the sale of certain property amounting to **$861,672.00** from the vendors of that property for whom my client was Power of Attorney. She provided as part of her statement, letters of admission with promise to repay from Mr. Nicholls. (To date Mr. Nicholls has repaid $110,000.00). Follow up checks with the above-mentioned Criminal Investigation Department have only yielded that investigations will be carried out.

My client has recently instructed that based on information coming to her attention she is now very anxious that Mr. Nicholls may be in the process of closing his practice and may attempt to leave the jurisdiction without satisfying the debt owed.

I enclose herewith the following documents which set out in detail all relevant information in respect of this matter:

1. Copy of statement of Kathleen Inniss given to the CID Office at the District "A" Police Station;
2. Copy of Writ of Summons in High Court Action No. 640 of 2008 shortly entitled Hazel Sheila Connor and John Patrick Connor v Philip V. Nicholls along with – Copy of Default Judgment dated 6th June 2008; copy of Registration of Judgment; copy of Judgment Summons and approved draft Order made by the Master of the Supreme Court on 29th July 2009;
3. Copy of Complaint of Kathleen Inniss to the Disciplinary Committee of the Barbados Bar Association; (this complaint is yet to be heard).

Director of Public Prosecutions
Frank Walcott Building
Culloden Road
ST MICHAEL

Re: Mrs. Kathleen Inniss

The kind assistance of your office would be highly appreciated in ensuring that criminal charges are laid and prosecuted particularly given the fact that Mr. Nicholls has admitted his wrongdoing and that steps are taken to ensure Mr. Nicholls does not leave the jurisdiction until the criminal proceedings are completed and the debt fully satisfied.

Yours truly,

B.L.V. GALE, Q.C.

Encs.

Pc   Ms. Kathleen Inniss

BLVG/sg

APPENDIX 8B

Filed by:

PHILIP NICHOLLS & ASSOCIATES

Attorney's-at-Law

No. 8 Pine Gardens, Off Pine Plantation Road

St. Michael, Barbados

T: (246) 826-0054

E: info.nichollslaw@gmail.com

BARBADOS

SUPREME COURT OF BARBADOS

IN THE HIGH COURT OF JUSTICE

CIVIL DIVISION

No. 151/152 of 2004

BETWEEN:

COTTLE CATFORD & CO. (a Firm)　　　　**CLAIMANT**

AND

DELVINA WATSON　　　　**DEFENDANT**

ORDER

BEFORE Dr. the Honorable Madam Sonia Richards Judge of the High Court

On the 20th day of June 2017

Entered on the 19th day of July 2017

UPON the Defendant's Application dated the 22nd day of March 2017 and filed on the 5th day of April 2017 coming on for hearing.

UPON HEARING Mr. Vernon Smith. Q.C in association with Mr. Michael Springer, Q.C and Ms. K Springer for the Defendant who was not present.

99

AND UPON HEARING Mrs Charmain Delice-Hunte on behalf of the Plaintiff/Claimant who was present in the person of Mr. Philip Nicholls.

IT IS THE ORDER OF THE COURT THAT the Judge recuses herself from this matter consequent upon the Defendant's letter to the Chief Justice dated 29th October 2014 and the Judge's consideration of defamation proceedings against the Defendant.

_____
Dep. Registrar

Barbados $10

CERTIFIED A TRUE COPY

100

Philip Vernon Nicholls

LL.B (Hons) UWI, LL.M (Manch)
Attorney-at-Law

May 30, 2018

The Registrar
Supreme Court of Barbados
Supreme Court Complex
Whitepark Road
ST. MICHAEL

Dear Madam,

Re: Outstanding Court Matters flowing from the dissolution of Cottle Catford & Co. SCS 151 /152 of 2004 and 1612/1613 of 2005 and CV 290 of 2017 and 893 of 2017.

I refer to previous correspondence on the captioned subject (by my count numbering over fifty) and in particular my last letter to you of April 4, 2018. My letter of today's date is prompted by your letter of May 28, 2018 to the President of the Bar which was circulated to the general membership yesterday.

After examining the content of your letter, I sought the guidance of some of my colleagues and indeed persons not members of the Bar that my interpretation of the letter was correct. This was that the guidelines that you communicated would suggest that my matters would not qualify to be included amongst the files to be transferred to Manor Lodge.

The overwhelming advice that I received was that I should continue to write to draw attention to these several outstanding matters at caption even if it the lack of response in writing or action to my several please would suggest that my writing is an exercise in futility.

In case it has been forgotten, may I remind, point out that the latter two matters at caption filed in July and September of 2017 under a Certificate of Urgency are still awaiting a date of hearing. I have noted the recent comments of the Chief Justice at the opening of the Whitsun conference of the Bar that contrary to popular belief the Court can move with alacrity when it is necessary. In light of the fact that for more than six months now I have been waiting for a date of hearing in CV 290, and that in 1612/1613 it is approaching four years for a decision to be handed down, I must be forgiven for qualifying those comments by the addition of the phrase "if it is so minded."

P. O. Box 93w   Tel: (246) 571-7215
Christ Church
Barbados   e-mail: cartwinn@gmail.com

101

I therefore can only conclude that the rights of Commonwealth citizens, some of whom have taken up residence in this island but qualified under the three year threshold, during which time some of my matters were pending, are deemed more important than my right to have my matters disposed of by the Courts of Law in this island in a timely manner. The irony is that as a Barbadian and a member of this profession (for over thirty years, something daily I am becoming more and more ashamed of) I have suffered and continue to suffer far more damage than any damage that would have occurred if their actions were not so speedily disposed of.

I must be forgiven for thinking that something perverse is in play, especially when daily I am inundated with the need to settle claim and suffer abuse as to my integrity, while those who the Courts found nearly nine years ago are responsible for the problems that I face are not called to account.

History no doubt will have to be the Judge of that, and it appears that my recourse is to ensure that there is a paper trail for them to follow from my constant writings.

Yours faithfully,

Philip Nicholls
Attorney-at-Law

Cc: President Bar Association

2

102

Philip Vernon Nicholls

LL.B (Hons) UWI, LL.M (Manch)
Attorney-at-Law

December 19, 2017

The Registrar
Supreme Court of Barbados
Supreme Court Complex
Whitepark Road
ST. MICHAEL

Dear Madam,

December 31st will mark the fifteenth anniversary of the closure of the High Street office of Cottle Catford & Co. To commemorate the situation, I have decided once again to put my frustrations on paper even though many people have said to me and others that my writing is an exercise in futility. While there is clear evidence to support that contention, given that I have only received about a dozen replies to the over one hundred letters that I have written, it at least creates a paper trail for posterity.

The sad reality is that my writing has made no difference. While some would say that I must surely be a shining example of the saying that to keep doing the same thing over and over in the expectation of a different result is a sign of madness, I myself see it not as that, but as a sign of Perseverance in the face of tremendous odds. In fact, it is one of the reasons why I have maintained my sanity over the years.

It will not surprise you therefore that again I must prevail on you once again for answers to the following:

1. **1612/1613 of 2005 Allan Watson.**
   Is there any word on when the decision reserved since October 2014, with respect to an application for a final charging order in favour of the undersigned, the provisional charging order having been granted by the Chief Justice in May of 2014, over the interest in property owned jointly by Allan Watson et ux would be handed down? The only communication from your office sometime in June of 2016 was that a decision would be forthcoming after September 2016. The reality is that even though I have been a judgment creditor in the matter since 2009, I have suffered and continue to suffer daily from the actions of Watson and his cohorts. It is a sad indictment on our system that while I have lost my house, while the house of my parents continues to be threatened by legal action, his wife

P. O. Box 93w   Tel: (246) 571-7218
Christ Church Barbados   e-mail: cartwinn@gmail.com

103

(now widow) the Lady Macbeth behind it all continues to live in hers (his) with impunity surrounded by her children and grand.

2. **1612/1613 of 2005 Joyce Griffith**
   I have been attempting to have the defendant examined for the last two years only to be met with her refusal to attend Court. Since January of this year the inability of the Court Marshalls, despite my providing the address where she is living, to serve a Summons with a warning to attend issued by the Court is somewhat perplexing and as I write I have no idea when the matter will be heard.

The upshot of the two situations is that I have been unable to enforce the Judgments I obtained in 2009. The impact this has had on my personal and professional life, I have already documented and will shortly update persons with the publication of my second book.

3. **151/152 of 2004 Delvina Watson.**
   The circumstances of this case could not be made up. Allan Watson then Senior Partner of Cottle Catford & Co. over a period of some eighteen months in 2000 and 2001 issued cheques from the Client's account to his wife or to payees for her and his benefit in the amount of approximately $265,000.00. A default judgment was obtained in March of 2004 on behalf of the Plaintiff Cottle Catford& Co. Amazingly over thirteen years later having only repaid one third of the judgment this matter is now before the Court of Appeal. These appeals are yet again part of Smith's grand plan to aid the Watsons attempts to evade repayment of the money they have used. Filing appeals, one in December of 2014 and the other in July of 2017 and then not prosecuting them is the most effective way of doing this and I would ask that the status of these appeals be reviewed as soon as possible.

What is worst is that the Court of Appeal gave leave to hear an appeal against the recusal of Justice Richards from further hearing in the suit having been defamed in a letter written to the Chief Justice in October of 2014 demanding her removal from the matter by the defendant. It boggles the mind that having written demanding her removal, her recusal following, an Attorney now seeks leave to appeal against the recusal.

You do not need the list of Attorneys to find out who the Attorney behind this charade is as one Vernon Smith has engaged in every type of unethical behavior imaginable including contempt of court, to assist the Watsons in their defraud of Cottle Catford & Co.

Surely this behavior would not only warrant a charge of aiding and abetting the theft of client funds from Cottle Catford & Co., the fact, but also one of Money Laundering. That as no such charge has ever been laid against any of these parties must lead one to question why someone charged under the Constitution of this Island to be the leading Prosecutor in this island would pick me to file such charges.

The ridiculous money laundering charge levelled against me (when compared to how a blind eye was turned to the actions of my former Partners with the unethical assistance of some Attorneys) was the catalyst for the most egregious wrong done to me, namely the revocation of my USA visa. That it was precipitated by a man sworn to uphold the law suggests an ulterior motive.

As you are aware I have filed two suits namely 843/17 and 290/17 both granted certificates of urgency in June and October of 2017 to overcome this action. The last hearing was held on November 20, 2017 saw the matter being transferred from Justice Richards to the Chief Justice, so my final request is that the matter be accorded as early as possible a date in the New Year, so I may attempt to reclaim some normalcy in my life.

It would be remiss of me despite this all not to wish you and your family Seasons' Greetings and all the best for 2018.

Yours faithfully,

Philip Nicholls
Attorney-at-Law

CHAPTER 9

The Hypocritical Treatment of Our Cricketers

THE LAST tour to Australia at the end of 2015/early 2016 by the West Indies ended like many tours of the recent past with the team soundly beaten. The team returned home with its tail between its legs after a series of performances that would have made any person with a passing knowledge of the history of West Indies cricket cringe.

The defeat was made the more painful because of the nature of it, which to be frank was suggestive not of an elite team but of a group of club cricketers. When this was compared to the level of sustained excellence that our cricketers had achieved in the not too distant past, it made the team the butt of jokes, especially in Australia where many of our finest hours had occurred.

Towards the end of the tour an incident occurred in a domestic game in the T-20 League that was later to become dubbed as 'Blushgate'. The incident involved the current day West Indies icon Chris Gayle, one of the most recognizable of cricketers around the world, whose description of himself as the 'Universe Boss' has gained as much attention as his power hitting on the field of play. The incident quickly grabbed headlines around the sporting world and wider afield.

Gayle's clumsy attempt to ask a female reporter who was interviewing him after his dismissal in a T-2O game out on a date was exacerbated by his response of "Don't blush, Baby, don't blush" when he realized that his advances on live National TV were causing her much embarrassment.

The incident was soon blown out of all proportion on every available social media platform. The West Indies team, which at the time was struggling badly in the Tests, was soon thrown into the spotlight to further demonize Gayle's actions as he was portrayed as a money-grabbing mercenary, a gun for hire who had turned his back on his struggling compatriots.

Gayle's presence in the league had brought much commercial value to it, and with the resultant attention that his comments attracted it was an advertiser's dream. After all, publicity is publicity. The comparison could not have been starker with the dwindling interest in the Test Series which by then was one-sided.

With the Test Team struggling badly, many journalists including some of the former players who had suffered on the field of play during the days of West Indian dominance, started to bemoan the absence of the T-20 stars. Gayle was cited as the prime example, from the Test Series.

The criticism, whether explicit or by snide remarks, was designed to push a narrative that the T-20 players were putting money before their country by playing in the league. 'They had no nationalistic pride' was the theme of the criticism. This was a bit rich, as the criticism only started after the Gayle *faux pas*. It was not mentioned when their signings to play in the Big Bash were seen as coups to enhance its popularity. Gayle unfortunately was not helping the matter by doubling down on what were clearly inappropriate and perhaps sexist statements to the reporter.

The media reaction to the comments was not limited to that of the sporting press. Anyone with media access felt emboldened to weigh in and Gayle was hammered. His clearly insensitive and out of place comments were not seen as a slip up in an unguarded moment when competing in a sporting game, but became a *cause célèbre* to highlight a societal problem, namely sexual harassment in the workplace. A serious problem it indeed was, but to try to cast what took place as comparable to sexual harassment in the workplace was incredulous, given the fact that at no time was there any direct working relationship between Gayle and the reporter in question.

Spurious accusations of sexual harassment were not the only barbs thrown at Gayle. A call was made by the former Australian Captain Ian Chappell that he should be banished not only from the Big Bash, but from cricket worldwide. Chappell had forged a successful career after his playing days as a critic of the sport, but his comment was not only ludicrous, but clearly insulting to the commonsense not only of the average West Indian supporter, but impartial individuals anywhere.

It was more than ironic and clearly hypocritical that such a call for drastic action was made with respect to this verbal offence by Gayle, especially when coming from a man who saw it fit while a player to drop his pants and readjust his cricketing equipment, thereby displaying his naked backside to all and sundry watching on TV. The lynching in the media of a black man for having the effrontery to approach a white female reporter on National TV to ask for a date was in full force.

Chappell's call for him to be immediately banned gained traction and even though he was allowed to finish the competition (no doubt legal considerations about breach of contract weighed in this regard), it has been no surprise that Gayle has been deemed *persona non grata* in Australia and not been invited to participate since. For that he only has himself to blame for failing to realize his initial *faux pas* and offering an unconditional apology.

The criticism went further, and even led to the publication of an article in the newspaper which virtually dubbed him a serial sexual offender hiding behind his status of cricketer. Gayle was to win substantial damages for defamation in a Sydney courtroom a couple of years later after a jury rejected the scurrilous allegations that had their genesis in the accusations that he had sexually harassed the reporter and in others in similar circumstances.

The treatment that he received in the Press in Australia as part of a campaign to have him declared *persona non grata* for future Big Bash competitions was bad enough, but it was somewhat disappointing that there were no comments about Gayle's subsequent 'ban' from the competition in the region. After all, he had not infringed any cricketing rules, and his defamation case showed the comments in the Press attacking his character arising from the incident were found to be over the top.

The comparison between his treatment and the treatment afforded two Australian cricketers who not only were found to have breached the rules and mores of the game, but were still serving a ban from playing in their homeland as a result of the ball tampering scandal in a Test Match in South Africa, when included in our comparable league, was to say the least astonishing.

We welcomed them with open arms. That we saw it fit to invite them to play in ours, and that there was no public outcry at their presence while our own was banned, spoke volumes. In this case the hypocrisy that was displayed was from within, but as other examples will show, that is how we sometimes act having been conditioned into believing that the views of others may be best.

The deliberate portrayal by the Australian media of the West Indian cricketer as a bad boy cricket mercenary contrasted sharply with how the Australian cricketer was being portrayed. Their every move was deified, and it was unthinkable that they could do anything to sully the game. To think now that one of these players, Steve Smith, the captain nonetheless, is now the villain of the piece is incredulous. The portents were there, but the attitude of the Press was clearly nowhere, as discerning as it was as condescending to West Indian players, and thus no ulterior motives of the Australian cricketer were explored.

Smith's approach to the young and inexperienced West Indies captain Jason Holder to connive a result in the badly rain-hit Test Match at Sydney at the dawn of 2016 was not only welcomed, but praised extensively by the same personalities in the media who were so condemnatory of Gayle. They fell over themselves backwards to find words to describe what they viewed as the cowardly option by the West Indies Captain not to accept Smith's offer.

There was never a thought that something was amiss; that the actions of Smith were the beginning of the win at all cost mentality that was later to run him into hot water. The only thought was that he was making a dead game come to life. That willingness to accept the genuineness of one of their own was also apparent years earlier when Hanse Cronje convinced the English captain Nasser Hussein to make declarations in another rain hit match to achieve a result. Cronje of course was later banned for life as a Match Fixer. Neither, however, received criticism at the time from the traditional press which, compared to what they dished out to Gayle, considering future events when both Cronje and Smith were banned from the game, would suggest that the attitude to Gayle was at the very least hypocritical and at worst the product of racist views.

Condescending comments were made about Holder's turning down of the offer. It was suggested that accepting the offer may teach this young side how to scrap and win, not to mention enliven proceedings, but probably and this was never mentioned, to save a lot of money on bets that it would have been a three to nil sweep. The offer to the West Indies was akin to being given a loaded gun to point to your head and pull the trigger in the hope that the one loaded barrel in the chamber did not have your name on it.

The region's doyen cricket writer and commentator for over fifty years, the late Tony Cozier, published an article in the Barbados *Sunday Sun* of January 10th 2016 which more than adequately demonstrated why Smith's offer was not only unacceptable to the current West Indies team, but would have denigrated what Test Cricket is by reducing it to the state of and I quote: "Above all, it would have transformed even such a disrupted match into a complete pappy show, a glorified equivalent of a holiday fete match at Dover, denigrating the image of Test Cricket rather than enhancing it as Smith believed it would."

Smith was quoted as saying that he and the coach had checked the rules prior to their approach to the West Indies Captain and that the coach had concluded that there was nothing wrong with their plan. The same media that so roundly condemned Gayle for what he said despite his explanation, now was willing to accept Smith's interpretation of the Law. He was given a pass without even a cursory check, a courtesy that was never afforded to Gayle. Hypocrisy at its highest.

An examination of the latest regulations governing Test Matches of the International Cricket Council left me at a loss to understand why Smith was not in the dock for attempted Match Fixing. The standard playing conditions for Test Matches, which became applicable as of July 5th 2015, prohibited the limiting of an innings either in terms of overs or time by agreement, which is what Smith had offered should be done.

The ICC Anti-Corruption Code which came into force for all participants on November 2014 states under section 2.1 Corruption as follows:

> "Fixing or contriving in any way or otherwise influencing improperly or being a party to any agreement or effort to fix or contrive in any way or otherwise influence improperly, the result, progress, conduct or any other aspect of any International Match, including (without limitation) by deliberately underperforming therein."

On the face of it this would appear to have been contravened by the scenario set out by Smith. Had Holder agreed to it, he would have been a party to the fix. But not only was there no condemnation in the media, the silence from the ICC was deafening. Other areas of the player code do leave the possibility of a defense being raised that the offer was for tactical reasons, but then again, a defense suggests a charge, and none was forthcoming. It was never ever considered and certainly appears never to have been commented on by the match referee Chris Broad.

The lack of zeal exhibited by the match referee in this case for an apparent breach of the rules of the game is striking when an examination of some his recent decisions are made which would suggest, in modern parlance, he was an enforcer of discipline. For some time now I have had to take a deep breath when reading his decisions or listening to his comments, especially when handing out penalties to West Indian players and those from the subcontinent teams like India, Pakistan, Sri Lanka and Bangladesh.

The sanctions that he imposed were markedly different in

many cases from those he imposed on players from Australia for similar offences. As an Englishman and with a son in the current English team, he is obviously barred from officiating in games involving England because of perceived bias. It is my belief, however, that his overall actions when examined would reveal that he is clearly motivated by bias, of what kind I am not prepared to speculate.

These were some of the penalties imposed by Broad on cricketers from West Indies and Asia.

In November 2008, Broad suspended the Indian opening batsman Gautum Gambhir for one Test for elbowing Shane Watson from Australia while he was running, and though Watson was deemed the instigator in the matter, he got off with a fine of 10% of his match fee.

In the First Test between Australia and the West Indies at Perth in December 2009, Broad banned Suleiman Benn for two one-day internationals stemming from an altercation with two Australian players Brad Haddin and Mitch Johnson. The two Australians received fines, but significantly not even the heaviest allowed by contrast even though all three were involved in the same incident. Tony Cozier, reporting at the time, indicated that the disparity in sentence for involvement in the same incident was troubling, and though he did not say so, it was evidence yet again of the hypocritical difference in treatment that Broad meted out to players from certain countries.

Anyone caring to watch the YouTube clip of the incident would conclude that Benn appears to have been singled out for harsher punishment because he shaped to throw the cricket ball at Haddin while he was standing in his crease pointing his bat towards Benn. Many expletive verbals were hurled by all the players, but I fail to understand what difference there can be leading to different penalties between a bowler shaping to throw a ball at the batsman and the same batsman pointing his bat towards the bowler as Haddin did, threatening violence.

Broad also banished Shahid Afridi, the Pakistani cricketer, for four One-Day Internationals for brandishing his bat at a spectator after being heckled, and Hershchelle Gibbs, the coloured South African player, was banned by him for two Tests for making abusive comments towards the crowd, again after comments were made to him.

In 2010 the Pakistani cricket team was incensed when Broad sought to speak to the young 18-year-old Mohammed Amir (who later became infamous for a Spot Fixing conviction) for celebrating in the face of the Australian Captain Ricky Ponting who he had just dismissed, but overlooked the elbowing of Amir by the departing Ponting.

West Indians will remember how, at the last Champions Trophy in England in July 2013, Dinesh Ramdin was suspended for two games and fined 100% of his match fee for wrongly claiming a catch. Match referee Broad stated at the time "This is regarded as a serious offence as it is the responsibility of all players to act in the spirit of the game."

Consistent with this theme, he no doubt found the Sri Lankan wicketkeeper Dickwalla in 2017 to have breached the spirit of the game and he was fined 30% of his match fee for seeking to affect a stumping by waiting too long for the batsman to overbalance so he could remove the bails. To quote John McEnroe: "You cannot be serious." If it was so long, why did the Umpire not call the ball dead? Again, Broad is at the forefront of upholding the morals of the game and I will go to my grave believing that he instigated the complaint and was judge and juror against poor Dickwalla, who like Shannon Gabriel, copped a plea to the lesser charge.

In 2017 in a Test at Sabina Park Broad docked Shannon

Gabriel, the West Indian player, with 50% of his match fee for brushing the Pakistani wicket keeper batsman Sarfraz Ahmed in his follow through, deeming it unacceptable physical contact with an opponent. Several of us have suffered similar brushes when in a crowded lift, so trivial was the connection.

David Fraser, in his excellent book *Cricket and the Law – the Man in White is Always Right* says this of Broad's infractions when he was a player.

> "Broad demonstrated his own lack of self-control. During the Bicentennial Test in Sydney, after spending seven hours at the crease and scoring 139, he petulantly smashed the stumps with his bat after playing on to Waugh. His action was the mark of a man who finds it difficult to accept dismissal whatever his score at the time."

For being a poor loser and bringing the game into disrepute, he was fined 500 pounds by his own team management. In Pakistan, after being given out caught at the wicket, he refused to leave the crease, staying for almost a minute and departing after his partner Graham Gooch persuaded him to do so. He was issued, much to the disappointment of Pakistani officials and English writers, only a stern reprimand.

A renowned English journalist Martin Johnson wrote this at the time: *England in Pakistan 1987-88*, Wisden (1989) at page 910. In the context of England – Pakistan cricket it is hardly shocking that no more serious disciplinary action was taken. The English interpretation in such cases is that the Pakistani Umpires are either cheats or incompetent. Broad was wrong in displaying his disagreement because that is simply not done. The fact that he was given out by a Pakistani Umpire did, however, serve as a strong mitigating factor in his sentence.

I am sure that I am not the only one who finds such statements hypocritical, but it is testimony to how persons from certain parts of the cricketing globe are viewed. Given all of this it is all the more damming on the ICC that Broad can virtually carry on a quasi-judicial function involving players from these countries when the evidence is clear as to his biases against them. While infractions of the rules by any player deserve punishment, the admonition that he gave to Ramdin about the need to uphold the spirit of the game must have been said tongue in cheek, given his history. Ramdin was not the first and will not be the last who applied the Chappell doctrine that the decision is up to the Umpire and sometimes you get lucky and sometimes you don't, so you take the rough with the smooth.

After all, is cricket not about building character? Well it appears that the rules apply differently for the Broads, because a few weeks after his admonition of Ramdin, his son Stuart was involved in an incident that clearly shows that the apple does not fall far from the tree.

Broad junior had edged a ball into the lap of first slip during the First Test between Australia and England in 2013. He remained at the crease waiting for the Umpire to give his decision. He was given not out, a decision that received justifiable widespread condemnation from all and sundry, including comments from the then Australian Prime Minister that it was the worst decision he can recall on a cricket field. Allem Dar, one of the leading Umpires in the world, made the unfortunate error. Broad knew that Australia had used up all their challenges and could not ask for the decision to be reviewed, so it was rightly claimed that he was breaching the spirit of the game, as he knew he was out, a fact he later admitted.

But it was not this that was so revealing as the reaction of Broad senior who, when asked about it, said he had sent a text to his son to ask him how he kept such a straight face. That alone illustrates his hypocrisy, because a few weeks prior he was condemning a West Indian player for breaching the spirit of the game, the same spirit that his son now was oblivious to. Clearly a different set of rules apply depending on where you come from.

Michael Holding, the former great West Indian player, now a renowned commentator, was among a chorus of famous cricketers arguing that if Ramdin was banned for not indicating that he had not taken the catch (the TV replays suggested that while he knew he didn't take it he did not actually appeal, but did nothing to stop the rest of the team appealing) then Broad should suffer the same punishment if one is serious about acting in the spirit of the game.

Stuart Broad has had an interesting past. He certainly has had more infractions that have gone unpunished giving the impression that he is untouchable. The great Indian opener and former Captain Sunil Gavaskar alleged in an article in 2009 that there is a nexus between Broad not being punished for what others are punished for because of who his father is. In addition, two former English Captains have described his behaviour early in his career as boorish, making it reasonable to believe that he played the system knowing full well that he was being held to a different standard.

I have counted at least five occasions when Broad was sanctioned by referees, the most recent of which was for telling an Umpire to get on with it when the Umpire spoke to him about damaging the pitch. Mind you, Shaid Afridi was banned for a test when he was found guilty of doing a pirouette on the pitch in an effort to break it up to aid the spinners. If the equivalent was said in a football game, he would have been dismissed from the playing field and would have automatically missed the next game.

In 2010 Broad was fined 50% of his match fee for throwing the ball at a Pakistani batsman. He actually threw it, unlike just shaping to throw it like Benn who was banned for shaping to throw by his father.

Broad Jr. is in the Press referred to as the English enforcer, a title that appears now to have been transferred to the all-rounder Ben Stokes, a person who plays the game hard and wears his England crest on his heart, thereby his passion sometimes overflows. However, the same press sees players like Benn as surly and intemperate, whose transgressions are viewed as exceeding the bounds of tolerable behavior and need to be reined in so as to be, in the words of match referee Broad, taught a valuable lesson. Clearly a difference of treatment which can only be viewed as hypocritical.

It was not surprising that the actions of Smith in the Sydney Test did not seem out of the norm through Broad's lens. It is the same Smith who also avoided sanction by Broad for actions in India in a later series. The Indian Captain Virat Kholi almost went apoplectic when Smith, on being given out LBW during the second Test of the 2017 series in India, appeared to be trying to receive information from the dressing room as to whether he should seek to review the decision. This was clearly a no-no. The Umpires stepped in and sent him on his way, not giving him the chance to review. A war of words between the two camps erupted with the Indians feeling that the spirit of the game was being abused and that the Australians had been doing it throughout the game. Nothing was done, but Broad was prepared to accept their assurance that nothing was amiss. The hypocrisy is rife, but that is life.

CHAPTER 10

Reverse Hypocrisy: The Andre Russell Ban

HAVING GROWN up around the Law, encountering rules and perhaps more importantly obeying them became second nature. By and large our society is a law abiding one where rules are not only obeyed, but respected. Without rules it is fair to assume that chaos would reign. Problems however arise when rules that are designed by persons who live in places other than where the rules are enforced fail at times to take account of local circumstances.

A glaring example can be found in the decision by the Jamaica Anti-Doping Committee (JADCO) 2017 in January to find the Jamaican and West Indian cricketer Andre Russell guilty of an offence under the World Anti-Doping Agency (WADA) Code, and as a result he was banned from participation in cricket for a year. Russell was charged and found guilty of a breach of what some may argue is one of the more contentious rules in the Code known simply as the 'Whereabouts Clause'.

Russell is one of the most sought after T-20 cricketers around the world. Over the last five years he has plied his trade primarily with franchise teams in the lucrative Twenty/Twenty cricket leagues that have sprung up in the cricketing landscape all over the world over the last ten years. The existence of these leagues has challenged the norms of traditional cricket, especially in the West Indies, whereby some of the better players like Russell shun the longer form of the game. It is estimated that his annual earnings from such contracts are between $500,000 and a million US dollars per year.

WADA was established in 1999 in response to a dramatic increase in the use of drugs in sport. The twin scourges of drugs in sport and illegal betting and match fixing are two of the most chronic problems facing the International Sporting Community today. Sport has long since ceased to be a leisure activity for gentlemen to pursue as a pastime. It is big business whereby even run-of-the-mill players in many sports can make a living that is far more lucrative than from being employed in one of the traditional jobs.

Since 2004 WADA has published a list of drugs that were banned from use by athletes unless they obtained special dispensation for medical reasons. Medical evidence has shown that these drugs could be used for performance enhancement. In the same year, the World Anti-Doping Code was established to create uniformity around the world with respect not only to testing for abuse of drugs banned under the code, but the imposition of sentencing for those found guilty. Guilt was often proven by adoption of a strict liability standard—if it was in your system you owned it even if there was no intent to cheat. The intent to cheat meant that the length of your ban may be at the higher end of the scale, as distinct from the middle range of the infraction if it was because of negligence.

The present Code was adopted in 2015, however it was

the inclusion in the 2009 code of an amendment to make unannounced out of competition testing easier that saw the birth of the 'Whereabouts Clause'. To combat drug cheating, athletes were now subjected to unannounced drug testing to catch the use of banned drugs by out of competition testing, as these drugs would often be weaned out of the system by the time of competition during which testing occurred.

To enable such testing, it was necessary to require athletes to submit information in blocks of 90 days to their local anti-doping committee four times a year about their whereabouts. Information about where the athlete would be for an hour every day at a time of his choosing (outside of 11:00 pm to 6:00 am) so that he would be available for testing if need be. Where the athlete is a member of a team, he is only responsible for submitting this information for periods when he is not with the team. The information can be changed, but it is in the interest of the athlete to update any changes. Any three missed tests being a combination of not being at the designated place at the designated time or the failure to provide the information of whereabouts over a twelve-month period is the equivalent of a positive drug test which could result in a ban for up to two years.

The vast numbers of sporting persons would make the requirement for all to submit information unmanageable. As such, a pool of individual athletes subject to the testing procedures was established, known as a Registered Testing Pool (RTP). Any person who is included on the list is required to submit their whereabouts information. This list is comprised of elite athletes from a variety of sports like athletics and tennis, and those from team sports like cricket or football.

Russell was placed on the RTP list by JADCO and therefore subject to filing whereabouts information. Ironically, at this time he was not playing much for the West Indies, and because of this would not have been subjected to testing by the Governing Body for cricket, the International Cricket Council (ICC). This was because players who were to be tested were the top four as ranked in their specific discipline—batting, bowling, or all-rounder—from teams that were ranked in the Top 8. On this basis Russell would not have qualified, as he was neither in the top four and the West Indies had fallen out of the top 8.

His appearance on the list was at the discretion of the local NADO and for these purposes Russell was placed on the list by JADCO who no doubt was following the policies of the International Athletics Federation (IAAF) to determine which top ranked athletes are included in the testing program. Though similar to the system of ranking that the ICC used with respect to performance, the IAAF in addition exercised its discretion to include athletes on the list based on factors such as sudden improvement in performance during the year, return from injury, doping intelligence and the lack of a national level Testing Program.

With the improvement of Russell's performance on the field, it was perhaps not surprising that Russell was added to the pool by JADCO which administered the local testing program for Jamaica. The reason for his inclusion was the source of some dispute at his hearing, with Russell believing it was because of the money he was earning. Whatever the reason, he was subject as a Jamaican citizen to be included, but having included him it is arguable that JADCO had a duty to him to ensure that he not only understood the program, but how to comply with it.

JADCO'S testing program had been the source of much concern from about 2012. The continued exceptional performance of its athletes led by the indomitable Usain Bolt and Shelley Ann Fraser-Price was at times a cause for wonder in the International community as the local NADCO had been embroiled in problems. In fact, a few years before the Russell case the country as a whole faced sanctions from WADA because its program was not up to the required standard. As a result, the entire Board of JADCO resigned, paving the way for a new leaf to be turned over with the appointment of a new Board.

In 2015 Russell played 42 officially sanctioned T-20 games in 10 different countries, playing at 27 venues. Four of the countries he visited more than once in a year. He represented no fewer than seven teams during this time. On January 31st 2017 he was found by JADCO to have committed a doping offence because within a one-year period for the year 2015 he had failed to provide whereabouts information for the 90-day period on two occasions. He was then subsequently charged with a third missed filing because of his failure to explain why he had not filed the information. As a result, he was found to have committed a doping offence and banned for a year, half of the maximum time allowed because the Committee was satisfied there was no intent to cheat on his part.

It is instructive that only on one occasion was reference made as to the whereabouts information being submitted by the West Indies Cricket Board, one of the seven teams that he represented during the period that he was required to file whereabouts information. Given that the period in question for which the information was required was 180 days and that on average he played one game a week over the year, it was impossible for Russell alone to be responsible for the provision of the information according to the WADA rules which place the responsibility for submission of this information where the player was participating in a team sport on the team.

As the punishments that are levied for breaches of the rule vary significantly depending on whether it is broken by an individual or a team (see for example where Manchester City football club were fined £25,000 for failing to provide the information similar to what Russell was required to), this was a serious failing on the part of the committee to consider that Russell was to be treated as an individual athlete with the sole responsibility for submission of the information.

As if this was not bad enough it was clear from the transcript of the proceedings that Russell indicated that he did not understand what he was required to do. It was a serious failing on the part of the committee to rule that this responsibility was entirely his when he was playing a team sport and his schedule for his availability for the hour period would not be in his control.

In its decision the tribunal indicated that Russell had been tested around the world on several occasions, but had never returned an adverse result. It further stated that it was clear from the evidence that he was not attempting to evade testing by his failure to submit the whereabouts information. With these findings to subsequently ascribe to him the need to provide information that he was not required to do suggests that there was a determination that an example had to be made of someone whatever the circumstances. My belief that this occurred is heightened by the fact that Russell was not permitted to utilize defenses that appeals tribunals like the Court of Arbitration of Sport had allowed. When coupled with the procedural flaws, the decision is subject to criticism.

The decision of the JADCO committee is also disappointing because it did not take account of local circumstances with respect to the whereabouts of athletes. I do not say this lightly, as I have been involved in several disciplinary hearings for several Sports that require at times to take note of special local circumstances. Very often in an international context rules that are being applied are enacted for situations that are not completely relevant to local circumstances. One must be aware of this and be willing to make allowances.

The whereabouts of individual athletes could be an issue where programs designed for specialized training often saw athletes disappear for long periods of time into hilly terrains, as a result of which they were not easily accessible. This was not the situation with Russell in Jamaica, where his whereabouts could probably be easily ascertained if wanted by asking any person who could speak the Jamaican dialect liming on any street corner. Thus the greatest difficulty in finding where he was would be when playing overseas and under the rules it was not his responsibility to provide same.

After reading the decision and being aware of the issues that JADCO had faced in the years prior, I did not get the impression that the Committee was willing to bend over backwards within the rules to assist Russell. Rather I felt that he was thrown on the altar of expediency so that any criticism of the functioning of JADCO might be met by pointing to what it has done. In other words Russell's interests appeared to be deemed not as important as removing suspicion from the Jamaica testing program.

The issue surrounding Russel reminded me of an incident that occurred in the days before Match Referees in cricket, where responsibility for the on and off field conduct of players during a Test Match fell to be dealt with by the local disciplinary committee of the Association in the country that was hosting the game.

During the 1990 tour of the Caribbean by England there was a complaint lodged against Gordon Greenidge, alleging that he had verbally and physically assaulted Gladstone Small in the pavilion after some words were passed on the field of play during the Barbados game against the tourists.

Both players gave evidence and basically it came down to a 'he said', or 'she said' situation. As a relatively young man at the time who found himself asked to be part of a panel to adjudicate on the matter, I found myself in the midst of a hearing involving cricketers who at that time still had somewhat of a mystical status to me. It was mildly intimidating, to say the least. That was until I heard one of my fellow panelists say words to the effect that "If Stewart [the English coach who represented Small] feel that I am going to help him win a Test by suspending Greenidge over foolishness, he got another thought coming. Let them go behind the pavilion and finish it."

While there was no dispute that the required whereabouts information for Russell was not filed in the requisite time, the Committee appears to have approached this breach as fatal because of the strict liability doctrine applied with respect to the use of drugs under the Code. Once the presence of drugs in an athlete's system was detected it resulted in a four-year ban (in many instances a career ending event), which while harsh, was felt to be necessary as a deterrent. To apply such a standard to failure to file information required in circumstances where the athlete has never failed a drugs test, and the evidence is that he was not attempting to avoid testing, is surely questionable.

The use of a strict liability standard by the Committee to establish guilt was bad enough in this case, but when it was coupled with a failure to properly interpret the rules with respect to the responsibility for provision of whereabouts information, it virtually guaranteed a guilty verdict.

Even if criticism of this approach is not accepted, the failure of the Committee to find Russell not in breach by not examining or allowing him to present exculpatory reasons for his noncompliance ran counter to what the highest Court for appeals in Sporting matters—the Court of Arbitration for Sports—had ruled should be allowed, was to say the least disappointing.

When the whereabouts provision in the Code was first established in 2003 there were storms of protests from leading athletes. As a result a more relaxed requirement for provision of the information was established in 2009. Many prominent athletes at the time, especially the tennis stars Andy Murray, Raphael Nadal, Serena and Venus Williams, had criticized the requirements because in their view it was a gross violation of their right to privacy. By contrast Roger Federer took a different view, holding to the belief that in the interests of a clean sport, elite athletes had to be prepared to put up with some inconvenience.

A group of 60 Belgian athletes instituted legal action before the European Courts contending that the requirements were in breach of European law, and for a while FIFA refused to accept that the WADA Code would be part of its rules because of concerns that it had about the whereabouts requirements. The European Courts have recently ruled that the requirement for submitting the information was not an infringement of the athlete's human rights even though it recognized that the requirements were onerous. The Court was of the view that in the interest of clean sport, elite athletes would have to put up with the inconvenience.

As at the same time the French Courts were granting employees the right to turn off their work-related mobiles outside of work hours as demands by employers that they be left on were deemed to be intrusive, it was clear that the greater need for efficient drug testing trumped the individual rights. Bearing this is mind, it is realized that the elite athlete in the RTP is not even excused from compliance of providing the necessary information even when on holiday. In these circumstances an insistence on a strict liability test is not acceptable.

Prior to these challenges and before the revision of the rule on what whereabouts information was required in 2009, the former British Olympian Athlete Christine Ohuruogu challenged her suspension at the Court of Arbitration of Sports (CAS). She was appealing a one-year sanction imposed on her by the United Kingdom authorities for failing to update her whereabouts information. In this case the failure was over an eighteen-month period. The CAS upheld the suspension in a 2006 decision, but said as follows:

> "The burden on an athlete to provide accurate and up to date whereabouts information is no doubt onerous. However, the anti-doping rules are necessarily strict in order to catch athletes that do cheat by using drugs and the rules therefore can sometimes produce outcomes that many may consider unfair. This case should serve as a warning to all athletes that the relevant authorities take the provision of whereabouts information extremely seriously as they are a vital part of the ongoing fight against drugs in sport."

Not surprisingly, Ohuruogu was unimpressed by the decision and stated:

> "You are sunning yourself on a beach and, yet you still have to remember to text or email the anti-doping authorities before you go on a boat-trip or a shopping expedition, just in case a drug-tester turns up. I can think of no other profession where a person would be subject to such restrictions. Not even prisoners on parole get treated like that... We are athletes, but we are also human, with human fallibilities. Sometimes things don't always go to plan, which is why I ended up missing tests."

The noted BBC journalist Tom Fordyce did not just imagine the difficulties, he signed up to live under the program of informing of his whereabouts and within a month reported as follows:

> "A month into my experiment of living under the UK Anti-Doping whereabouts system, I have learnt many things—that athletes need to install very loud doorbells, that trip to your Mum's for Sunday lunch can lead to missed tests..."

He was to cite the words of Karen Pickering, a former gold medalist at the Commonwealth and World Games for England, the body representing the interests of British athletes, who outlined grave concerns about what athletes were required to do. She said:

> "I have issues with the whereabouts system from the beginning because of so many athletes being caught out... You were finding that athletes were being caught by making a mistake with the system, rather than with cheating, and I think that is a flaw in the system. I just question how much of a deterrent it is for the athletes who are going to cheat... I am uncomfortable with the fact that so many athletes have got strikes against their names because they did not fill the forms in properly or were not where they thought they would be. I would hate to see an athlete see their career ruined for being unorganized."

It is clear from the hearing that Russell was having problems not only with what to file, but how to file it, and in light of the fact that he should have had this responsibility removed from him because he was a member of a team sport, it is unfortunate that the Committee appears not to have realized that by applying a strict liability requirement would not allow him to present exculpatory evidence.

The question of the delegation of filing the whereabouts information by an agent became an issue in the Russell hearing because as he pointed out he was frequently away from Jamaica. The Committee decided that while it was permissible to do so, failure by the agent to file as required would not excuse the athlete from so doing. This contrasted markedly with a decision three years prior when in 2014 two Korean badminton players were found to have breached the whereabouts rule and were sanctioned for a year by the World Badminton Association. Their appeal to the CAS was successful on the grounds that because they had delegated the responsibility to file the whereabouts information to their national association as their agent, it would be unfair to penalize them. When this decision is coupled with the fact that under the rules he was not responsible for providing the information, it would appear that he was given a raw deal.

At the hearing Russell had also tried to dispute one of the Notices for failing to file within the requisite period. At the time of the hearing it was clearly outside the time stipulated for an appeal against the issuing of the Notice of default. As such the Committee rejected his attempt to dispute it. For some reason the panel seemed to be unaware of the case involving the British cyclist Lizzie Armistead. She was facing a sanction after three whereabouts failures, which with the automatic suspension for a year would mean that she would have missed the 2016 Rio Olympics. She challenged at the CAS in 2016 the first missed test which she had not done at the time.

Her excuse was that her phone was on silent at her team hotel during the Women's World Cup in Sweden and she did not hear the call from the testers. She argued that the testers could easily have found her when they arrived at the location, but simply did not look. She explained the further filing failures as due to an administrative oversight and that the other was due to a change of plans because of an emergency due to a serious illness in her family. She was allowed to contest the Notices at the appeal outside the time for appealing and prevailed at the CAS which overturned the Guilty verdict, allowing her to competed in the Rio Olympics.

To mitigate the very draconian penalties that may arise because of a whereabouts violation that leads to sanction, CAS has accepted that athletes be allowed to give reasons for failing to comply. This would suggest that the strict liability approach for guilt when drugs are found in the athlete's system is not the best for these situations.

Recent decisions by the equivalent bodies in other countries to JADCO indicate that the strict liability re ingestion of drugs is also now being softened. After all, how else can one square an acceptance by the USA authorities of the reason for a positive test for drugs was that the drugs were ingested while kissing your girlfriend who had a cold and was using a cough syrup that contained the offending drug?

Russell would have every right to be annoyed and it was a mystery to me why he did not take the matter to the CAS. Perhaps the authorities at JADCO should have noted how the Indian cricket authorities used an argument that to force Tendulkar and other stars to submit to advanced filing of their whereabouts would be a security concern and so excused their noncompliance.

Their willingness to throw their own under the bus was clearly not only wrong, but hypocritical; but what is new?

CHAPTER 11

The Mind-Boggling Hypocrisy of Sagicor

BEFORE SETTLING down to do some work or of late to write in the early morning, I would often scour news sites for the latest piece of idiocy tweeted by the President of the United States. The hypocrisy endemic in everything surrounding the Trump Presidency and his Republican enablers in the US Congress is a lesson in how to avoid issues that you would prefer not to deal with. It continues to amaze me that a country which prides itself on being the leader of the free world could have elected a man who in most other societies would have struggled to be elected as a dog catcher. Not surprisingly, his Presidency can be summarized after nearly two years of "Do what I say but not what I do." Hypocrisy at its highest. I never dreamed as I watched the hypocrisy first associated with his campaign and then his administration that I would myself be facing head on a form of hypocrisy from as prominent a corporate entity as there is in this country, namely Sagicor.

While reading, an unsolicited ad popped up on my computer screen advertising the SAGICOR 175 Endowment Plan 11.

Receiving such ads is one of the perils of using the internet. In this case I was not so much as annoyed as disgusted by the ad because my recent experience with Sagicor suggested that the ad was hypocritical. *Clearly designed to mislead* I thought, as its target audience were the young and vulnerable professionals by suggesting that they had their financial future at heart in advocating the Plan being advertised. At that early hour I found myself sinning my soul by wishing all sorts of malevolence on the Company as my anger fumed.

As I read the ad it struck a chord within me because of what I had experienced with Sagicor surrounding the Cottle Catford Pension Plan. For over seven years I had battled Sagicor with respect to my rights under the Plan. I therefore viewed such attempts to entice people into buying protection for your future financial security by the purchase of something similar with a level of disgust.

In my view Sagicor had lost its moral compass where pensions were concerned, as it had become trapped between the need to do what was right for the Plan member and its bottom line. The Ad was the final straw for me as it galvanized me into writing about the contemptuous refusal to obey a Court Order by Sagicor.

"We are here to help" the ad said, much like the jingle associated with its name that rings out that Sagicor stands for wise financial planning for the future. The ad was urging the need for sound financial planning to forestall that rainy day. Nothing unreasonable about that, in fact it was totally laudable, but what if it was not true?

That I should see parallels between Sagicor's actions and Trump's brand of hypocrisy and deceit distressed me. Part of the reason was that it illustrated forcibly that in today's world most of the time individuals as well as corporations consider narrow self-interests over considerations of doing what is morally right. In my case Sagicor's actions were compounded by the fact that after a legal decision in my favour they were prepared to disregard it and acted as if the decision was never made because it ran counter to their self-interest.

Sagicor's name has only become a household one over the last twenty years. The legacy of the company is however much longer, as Sagicor is the name given to the merged insurance businesses of the Barbados Mutual Life Assurance Society (BMLAS), formed over one hundred and seventy-five years ago, and Life of Barbados Limited (LOB), an indigenous insurance company which though formed less than fifty years ago had so established itself in the market and become a threat to BMLAS that it was taken over by BMLAS after a long and bitter struggle with a Trinidad rival. As my late friend Stephen was the CEO of LOB at the time, I had witnessed firsthand how that battle had played out on him and even had been subject to criticism by some who felt that any views I expressed on the subject where just talking points passed on to me by him.

In my early years at Cottle the Firm worked for both BMLAS and LOB with respect to its mortgage portfolio. I never participated much in that aspect of their work, but did quite a bit of the corporate work necessary for both companies as a junior to Mr. Armstrong. I recall in particular working on what ironically in light of what transpired later, the rules associated with the Health Scheme that LOB was to launch. Another area of work was with respect to many issues that arose in the administration of the Pension Plans by LOB.

The Cottle Pension Plan was established for its employees in 1963 at a time when I had not seen my third birthday. The Plan was with the Mutual Life Assurance based in Canada. Its portfolio was in the late eighties acquired by LOB, a transaction that I also worked on. All premiums under the Plan were paid by the Partners so that a pension would be paid to an employee on their retirement. Employees could enhance their pension by making a voluntary contribution to the Plan from their own income.

When Joyce Griffith and I became Partners of the Firm in 1992 we transitioned from employees, but no special amendment or change in the Plan was ever done. When she left the Firm at the end of 2002, as now the recognized Administrator of the Plan by LOB, I agreed to her request that her calculated pension entitlement at that date could have been paid to her or to be used to establish another pension plan. I cannot recall what eventually happened with hers. Thereafter whenever employees left the Firm for whatever reason any voluntary contributions were returned to them for disposal at their discretion.

However, as the accrued Pension entitlement for those individuals had arisen from premiums that had been paid by the Partnership, the amount so accrued was credited to the account of the Plan. The result of this was that there was a significant cash credit in the Plan which was used to pay the monthly premiums—a significant relief to me after 2002 as I battled with the deficits in the Firm and also to provide pensions for Freddie Hutchinson and Rudolph Hinkson because the finances of the Firm did not allow.

Given this historical context, it was my belief and hope that when I closed Cottle on October 31st 2009 the benefit that I was entitled to under the Plan could be tapped, not for my personal use, but to assist with acquiring finance for the deficit in the Clients account which was still in deficit.

Several of my letters originally to LOB and then to Sagicor were all on the subject of my urgent need to borrow against my entitlement. Justice Reifer put it succinctly in her Judgment when she said: "This Court also makes the observation that with increasing intensity the Claimant's actions were motivated by the desperate need to have access to the funds in the Plan in order to use them as security for his intended borrowing." If my situation was dire in 2010 during the exchange of letters, then what about in 2014 when the Judgment was given and pray tell what is it now, the full Judgment having not been honored?

Imagine my horror then, when after the time for filing an appeal had passed six weeks later in January 2015, I was informed by my Attorneys Rudolph Greenidge, Errol Niles, Charmaine Delice-Hunte and Eleanor Clarke, that Sagicor was deducting 25 per cent from the amount awarded claiming it was because of withholding tax. There was no discussion, no reaching out to hear the views of the other side, no examination of the Judgment, simply a statement that withholding tax must be paid in their view. To me it seemed that every two steps forward that I was taking was met with three steps back.

An examination of this position by Sagicor would find it dubious at best while at worst a flagrant and contemptuous violation of the Court Judgment. The Plan had been ended in October 2009, so on what basis could withholding tax deduction, a penalty for early withdrawal from the Plan, be relevant?

As arguments raged between the two sides, reference was made to the statement by Justice Reifer that the award was subject to any tax. A totally normal statement which most would interpret as a reference to income tax which is not deducted at source and would have been complied with by Sagicor reporting to the BRA of the amount that was paid pursuant to the Judgment. By its stance Sagicor was maintaining that its arguments before the Court which they had lost were the relevant ones. Having not appealed the Judgment, this was a particularly callous and cowardly position.

From around February 2015 through to November 2016 approximately six hearings were held to determine if Sagicor was right to as they stated deduct the 25% and pay it to the Barbados Revenue Authority. To this date they have never informed me in writing of the payment. Finally, in November 2016 there was a verbal agreement in Court between my Attorneys and theirs, Pat Cheltenham Q.C., that the deduction should not have been done. Justice Reifer then requested that the agreement be reduced to writing in the form of an Order which she would sign. Nearly two years later, despite repeated requests from my Attorney to agree to a formal Order, this has not been done.

I believe that in light of what has transpired it is understandable my reaction of annoyance on October 6th 2017 and 2018 to the robo-call greeting I received on my birthday. A year later when I received another robo-call, this time from Biggie Irie, with the status quo remaining the same I chose to vent my annoyance by writing. In my mind the birthday wishes were hypocritical in light of what had transpired and I said so.

As I devote my attention to finishing this book, I have to put on hold the filing of a suit to recover the twenty-five percent wrongfully deducted. That will probably be a story for my third book, as will be the misery that it has caused me.

APPENDIX 11A

Philip Vernon Nicholls

LL.B (Hons) UWI, LL.M (Manch)
Attorney-at-Law

October 15, 2018

Sagicor Life Inc
Sagicor Corporate Centre
Wildey
ST. MICHAEL

Dear Sirs,

Re: Philip Nicholls date of Birth October 6th 1960.

On October 6th, 2017 I received a call from a number in the UK on my mobile. When I answered it was a Happy Birthday Greeting according to the voice, from your friends at Sagicor. I was annoyed but other that mutter a curse to myself did nothing. This year I received the same call with the same greeting but this time the caller identified himself as Mr. Biggie Irie. As I am acquainted with Mr. Irie, I said to myself that whenever next I saw him I would give him a piece of my mind. On reflection I realized this would be only shooting the messenger not the purveyor of the message so I decided to write as follows.

1. On October 30th 2009, I wrote Life of Barbados indicating that Cottle Catford & Co. was closing and asked that the Firm's Pension Plan be wound up and the remaining beneficiaries including the undersigned be advised of their entitlements.
2. It took approximately two years for the Beneficiaries to be advised of their entitlements. At no time was it doubted that the plan was at an end.
3. Over three years correspondence between LOB, then Sagicor, and the Undersigned with respect to how my benefit was to be paid, broke down.
4. On 16th day of July, 2012 I filed CV 1211 of 2012 against Sagicor for a determination of my benefits.
5. Early in 2014 Sagicor cancelled my Health Insurance and Life Insurance for failure to pay my premiums over three months. In other words, the amounts due were about $2,000.00 but at that time Sagicor owed me over $400,000.00. Despite repeated request Sagacor has refused to reinstate the cancelled policies.
6. On 26th day of November 2014 I was awarded $425,469.89 By the Courts.

P. O. Box 93w
Christ Church
Barbados

Tel: (246) 571-7215

email: cartwinn@gmail.com

138

7. There was no appeal, but in February 2015 Sagicor deducted 25% of the judgment on the basis that it was a withholding tax to be deducted from withdrawals from a plan that all had considered closed.

8. As the Judgment clearly said Sagcior well knew of the Urgent need since 2010 of my urgent need for finance, a need all the more acute in 2018. A need that is all the more acute in 2018 as my upcoming book will illustrate.

Because of these actions please note that I do not consider Sagicor any sort of friend of mine nor do I consider it an Honourable Institution that seeks to secure your financial future. In fact I believe the opposite to be true and that actions of Sagicor are purely driven by self-greed and the need to protect your clearly illegal actions with respect to similar payments surrounding pension Plans.

Please therefore ensure that no such foolish robo calls are made to my phone in the future.

Yours faithfully

Philip Nicholls
Attorney-at-Law

CC: Mr. Pat Cheltenham Q.C

Appendix

SIR NEVILLE NICHOLLS

"Andover" Farm Gap, Green Hill, St. Michael, Barbados

August 5th 2015

Mr. Patterson Cheltenham, Q.C.
Attorney-at-Law
Charlton House
Whitepark Road
ST. MICHAEL

Dear: Mr. Cheltenham,

Re: C V No. 1211 of 2012 – Philip Vernon Nicholls v Sagicor Life Inc

I am taking the opportunity to write to you after my son Philip Nicholls reported that his Judgment Summons Application against your client Sagicor, for the balance due to him on the Judgment he was awarded in November last year, was adjourned on Tuesday the 21st July to sometime in 2018. The least said about that aberration the better.

You will recall that shortly after my son made an emergency application for a determination of his rights under the Pension Plan in the middle of 2012, we had several conversations as I attempted to explore with you an avenue to have the matter settled. My son's filing followed on over two years of writing to your client in an attempt to persuade them to honour his request which was firstly, to use his entitlement under the plan to secure a loan or subsequently, to purchase Government bonds with said entitlement, which as you know if held for five years would be free from any imposition of Income Tax if they were then sold.

It is no secret why my son was seeking to do this. He has been left holding the sole financial burden for the financial meltdown of Cottle Catford & Co. while his two former partners have remained virtually unscathed. Despite him securing an arrest warrant for the apprehension of Mr. Watson in April of this year and providing the authorities with his whereabouts in the U.S.A there appears to be no haste in executing it. The Judgments obtained against both him and Joyce Griffith remain unsatisfied and all efforts by him to realise same have been stalled by appeals to the Court of Appeal.

As you may be aware, Philip has had to borrow more than two million dollars to deal with the deficit in the Client's account at Cottle Catford as a result of the financial meltdown at Cottle. Philip estimates that the interest that accrues on these borrowings amounts to $500 a day while the interest on the judgements that he was awarded amounts to less than $250 a day. His predicament is easy to see and as there are still funds due to Clients as a result of his failure to recover the money from his former Partners he is no longer in a position to borrow to attempt to settle these claims.

His only reward to date has been that he is now facing criminal charges for funds due to a client from Cottle and being on the verge of bankruptcy. His destitute status partly as a result of these charges which has seen his floundering practice virtually decimated, has resulted in him depending monthly on assistance from me as his practice is no more. Having seen him work so hard over the last three decades, it is painful for me to watch, but my pain is exacerbated by the actions of many of his colleagues who have by unethical means delayed and obstructed his ability to enforce his Judgments against his former Partners and have thereby made his plight worsen.

I have noted that one of the client's owed money by Cottle Catford & Co. is Sagicor, and it is more than ironic that after six years of doing nothing a suit was filed in 2014 and Judgment recently entered against him two days after his matter was adjourned to 2018. In their action against Philip acknowledgement was made by Sagicor that some of the funds were the direct responsibility of his two former Partners, but as far as I am aware no action has been taken against them. Action has however been taken against him for funds due from Cottle Catford & Co for an amount far less than which he judgement against his Partners and I must be forgiven for thinking there is some form of persecution against him.

Regrettably, I am forced to conclude that the actions by his colleagues to which I refer as causing him distress, must now include actions by you. During our conversations as I tried to arrive at a settlement I got the impression that you regarded the matter as a simple one that could easily have been resolved. I watched with growing consternation how the matter became delayed and eventually the Defendant appeared unwilling to settle a matter which you agreed with me should have never been in Court and was only there at the instance of Philip because of the refusal of your client to honour its obligations under the plan a contention that the Courts have upheld.

As a former Chairman of the Financial Services Commission, the body now responsible for the oversight of Pension Plans, it was clear to me that Sagicor was seeking to apply rules that did not cover the Cottle Catford Co. plan, a plan that not only came into existence prior to the establishment of the Commission but crucially had come to an end before the Commission came into being. In this regard you will recall that the Commission found it necessary to publish a notice in the local press pointing out that it had no Jurisdiction over such plans. The Cottle Catford & Co. Plan fell within this category.

It was with a decree of consternation that I learnt from Philip that Sagicor presumably on your advice had withheld 25% of the amount of the Judgment and gave as the reason for so doing that it was on account of withholding tax. Many legal experts with whom I have consulted have confirmed to me that they have never heard of such a situation where an amount was awarded as due to the Claimant by the Court and a form of tax was deducted at source. In fact one has opined that the actions of Sagicor in so acting were a gross contempt of Court.

I should state at this point that in the event that after nearly 60 years of involvement with the Law I have misconstrued the reasoning of the learned Judge in making her decision and that indeed a deduction was permissible then in my opinion, Sagicor would be still liable for the tax charged because they failed to follow his clear instructions stated as long ago as 2010 that would have allowed him to receive the amount held to be due in a manner that would have led to the imposition of no tax. I refuse to believe that as experienced a person as you in the Law would fail to understand this and as such I am of the view that there is more at play.

I am informed that when the parties had sought clarification from the Court as to whether it was the intention that tax be paid that Justice Reifer indicated that she had not addressed herself to this point in her judgement. She also indicated that Sagicor may well be liable to Philip in negligence if this were the case and tax deducted. What has remained clear is that an award was made and not appealed against on the basis that a Plan had come to an end and was being wound up not that a withdrawal was made from a plan currently in existence. I therefore must repeat myself when I say that I find that for such an experienced counsel not to appear to be able to distinguish between a plan being wound up and a withdrawal from a plan under the relevant section of the Income Tax Act that attracts tax, deeply troubling.

I am therefore requesting of you as a matter of urgency, a meeting with you and your client to discuss the continued mistreatment of my son. Please advise within fourteen days whether your client is willing to meet with me, otherwise I will have to take my concerns elsewhere. Such a meeting would help me understand why your client continues to insist on this right of withholding 25% when there is a clear distinction between a withdrawal when the 25% deduction would apply and payment of benefits when a plan comes to an end in this case with the closure of Cottle Catford.

One conclusion which can be drawn is that your client appears to be concerned about the financial implications of incorrectly holding funds from Pension Plan beneficiaries over the years especially in connection with Plans with much larger membership than that of Cottle Catford .

My son's professional life is all but ruined and not only does he have to live with the opprobrium of ongoing criminal charges which nearly two years on the Police have been unable to offer any evidence and which despite ten adjournments the presiding Magistrate appears reluctant to dismiss, he is also faced with members of his profession who seek to exploit his present position despite knowing full well the history of this matter. It is insulting in such circumstances that some would be laughing at his predicament while others place continued obstacles in his path as he seeks to alleviate the stress he is under. When the continued actions of your client in denying him what he is entitled to are added to this, is it no wonders that his health is deteriorating from the stress he is under!

I look forward to hearing from you soonest.

Yours faithfully,

_____

Sir Neville Nicholls

CC: Mr. Rudolph Greenidge

    Mr. Errol Niles

    Mrs. Charmain Delcie-Hunte

    Sir Steve Emptage

    Mr. Philip Nicholls

Philip Vernon Nicholls

LL.B (Hons) UWI, LL.M (Manch)
Attorney-at-Law

October 26, 2015

Mr. Leslie Haynes, Q.C.
Attorney-at-Law
Ellangowan Strathclyde
ST. MICHAEL

Dear Sir,

I have been asked by my father to respond to your letter of 15th October received by him on the 19th instance. Both my father and I believe that it is bordering on the ridiculous that a letter written by him on August 6th 2015 which outlined many areas of concern as to what has befallen me, would only receive a response from you two months later and impose a deadline of a week from receipt to respond.

In light of your claim that my father has maligned your client, a claim that he totally rejects, he is availing himself of counsel as naturally I am conflicted. This is despite the fact that he was called to the English Bar at the Middle Temple in 1957, the Bar in Barbados in 1960 and has refused on more than one occasion to accept the offer of silk. During his public Service he was Chief Parliamentary Counsel and as Chief Legal Draftsman spent considerable time acquiring the legal skills that he used in the next stage of his professional life, first as General Legal Counsel before becoming Vice President and finally the President of the Caribbean Development Bank for 13 years.

Despite his achievements he is prudent enough to seek the advice of counsel who will respond to you in due course. To enable counsel to adequately respond to your claim he is going through the developments that have arisen since he first contacted your client after Sagicor informed him that their refusal to comply with my instructions and requests in connection with the Cottle Catford & Co. Pension Plan was based on the advice of their legal adviser – your client.

Since then my father held discussions by telephone on a number of occasions with your client about the interpretation and application of the relevant provisions of the Pension Plan and of the Income Tax Act and Regulations. I am informed by my father that during these discussions he formed the clear impression that your client agreed with his interpretation (which was later supported by the Court's judgement) and regarded the matter as a simple one which could easily be settled. Yet, when my father contacted Sagicor to question about their continued refusal to comply with my requests and instructions he was informed that they were acting in accordance with the advice of their legal adviser- your client.

Other actions by your client which have caused me distress and to which my father was referring in his letter of August 06 2015 are as follows:

P. O. Box 93w
Christ Church
Barbados

Tel: (246) 571-7215

email: **cartwinn@gmail.com**

144

(1) After the persistent refusal by Sagicor over a two year period to comply with y requests and instructions I was forced to file by way of Notice of Application under a Certificate of Urgency on July 16th 2012 an action in the Supreme Court to determine my rights under the Pension Plan. In spite of the Certificate of Urgency, at the first hearing your client applied to the Court for an adjournment although he had been dealing for some time with the matter before the Courts. I can be supported by my colleague Charmain Delice Hunte that on that occasion before Justice Worrell your client indicated to the Court that the matter was one that could easily disposed of with a short adjournment. More than six months elapsed before your client advised the Court that there could be no settlement after which with time needed to file a defence and your client's attendance at other previously scheduled court matters plus my subsequent need for surgery meant that the matter did not come on for hearing until Eighteen months after the filing of my certificate of Urgency.

(2) In spite of the Courts Judgement in November of that year 2014 which it should be noted that your Client's client did not appeal , in my favour where the Court's Order was for the payment by Sagicor of $425,469.89 plus costs, Sagicor, according to Affidavits sworn on its behalf has indicated that your client has advised that it must withhold 25% of the amount of the Judgment by way of withholding tax although this formed no part of the Order made by the Court.

(3) Your client's attempt to calculate the quantum of the costs awarded by the Court on the amount of the Judgment less 25% which again is not in the Order of the Court.

The abovementioned actions on the part of your client are some of the actions which my father was referring to as causing me distress when the comparison was made with the actions of other of my colleagues.

For myself I will add that I have spoken to more than Fifty Attorneys both here and overseas with respect to the deduction made by your client and no one has expressed any agreement with this action. Further to date your client on behalf of his client has not informed me of when this 'deduction' was paid to the BRA and I have been unable to trace it as being credited to any tax paid on my account.

But for the fact that courtesy demands a response on behalf of my father I now do so because your claim of an alleged act of defamation is without merit and as such the sum of $20,000 which you suggest would be appropriate to soothe your client's hurt feelings must be seen as a figure plucked from somewhere in the stratosphere in an attempt to scare and intimidate rather than as a realistic figure for damages for a perceived loan.

I myself have been present with others when your client has alluded to and have also been told privately by your client that he is aware of the extremely straightened circumstances that I have been facing over the last decade. During these times he expressed a desire that he wished wherever possible to assist me and whilst I would never expect him to act contrary to the wishes of his client or their instructions I do not consider that the matters that were spoken of go anywhere to this duty. In these circumstances the comments made by my father not only are not

2

145

defamatory as you allege of your client but are fair and reasonable comment on the actions of your client in this matter. I reiterate that your claim is completely rejected but if you wish to file suit against him please feel free to join me as I endorse and am in agreement with everything he said. I have noted that your letter makes no reference to the scandalous circumstance where further proceedings in this matter have been adjourned to 2018 which should be an affront, to one as you state is one of her Majesties Senior Counsel who has a duty to ensure where possible that our system of justice under hammer from the CCJ of late is beyond criticism, but which in this case is apparently of no concern to him.

Given that my father's letter received no reply for over two months it is unreasonable having made the allegations that you do, to expect a full legal response was from someone who is not intimately involved in the matter in the time you stipulate. One shall be made in the course of time. In the meantime I continue to copy my correspondence including your letter to the persons named below who other than my father were the Attorneys on record in the matter that my father has commented on.

Yours faithfully
PHILIP NICHOLLS & ASSOCIATION

Per: _____
         Attorney-at-Law

Cc: Sir Neville Nicholls
     Mr. Rudolph Greenidge
     Mr. Errol Niles
     Mrs. Charmain Delice-Hunte.

Sir Neville Vernon Nicholls
"Andover", Farm Gap,
Green Hill
St. Michael

___

October 28, 2015

Mr. Leslie Haynes, Q.C.
Attorney-at-Law
Ellangowan Strathclyde
ST. MICHAEL

Dear Sir,

Re: Patterson K. H. Cheltenham GCM. Q.C.

Please refer to our telephone conversation on Tuesday, October 27, 2015 initiated by you in connection with your letter to me of October 15, 2015 and the response thereto on my behalf by my son, Philip.

I note and accept your clarification that the reference in your letter to me of October 15, 2015 to damages and costs was not intended as a threat or intimidation but rather as an indication of willingness to avoid going the litigation route.

In turn I took the opportunity to express surprise that the passages in my letter of August 06, 2015 about which your client complained could have been interpreted by him as an accusation by me of unethical conduct on his part.

I made no such accusation in my letter nor was any accusation of unethical conduct on the part of your client intended. What I referring to in the passages in my letter of August 06, 2015 complained about was a number of actions by your client which in my opinion, caused distress to my son. These actions were itemized in my son Philip's letter to you of October 26. 2015.

I regret therefore any misunderstanding which may have been caused by the referenced passages in my letter of August 06, 2015 and trust that this letter and our telephone discussion of yesterday's date (October27, 2015) can suffice to being this matter to a satisfactory closure.

In closing, may I request your help in securing your client's assistance and cooperation with Mr. Rudolph Greenidge in connection with the following matter?

1. An approach/application to the Chief Justice with respect to the adjournment of his Judgement Summons Application to 2018;
2. The finalization of the payment of Costs awarded by the High Court in HCS No. 1211 of 2012 – PVN v. Sagicor Life Inc;
3. My son's Health Insurance and Policies of Insurance for his children were cancelled during the period under review and he has been unable to have same reinstated. At the

time he did not have the finances to meet the Premiums and in light of the ruling in his favour this action of cancellation for nonpayment seems unfair.

Yours faithfully,

Sir Neville Nicholls

June 13, 2017

Mr. Rudolph Greenidge
Attorney-at-Law

Carrington & Sealy Complex

Belmont Road

ST. MICHAEL

Dear Cappy,

Re: Claim CV No. 1211 of 2012 – Philip Vernon Nicholls v Sagicor Life Inc

In line with what is happening in the Judicial system, the fact that the above matter though five years old is nearer the end than the begging should not normally be the source of complaint. I must stress that before you became involved in the matter it was filed as an Urgent Application. On the first hearing in July of 2012 counsel on the other side, Pat Cheltenham Q.C, had assured the first Judge, it was assigned to Randall Worrell, that the matter could be amicably and quickly settled. He also repeated these assurances to my father.

The history of the matter need not detain us now but needless to say it was not settled, went to trial and judgment was obtained in November of 2014 in my favour. As no appeal was filed within the statutory six week period, I was within my rights to assume that the matter was finally nearing an end in January of 2015. How wrong I was, because it is now June of 2017 and the matter is still before the Courts.

In another life I have been very critical of certain Attorneys as being profligate with the time of the Court all in the aim of delaying my recovery. The behavior of the Attorney in this matter with respect to the deliberate frustration of the Order of the Court, so frustrated my father that he wrote him directly expressing his disappointment in his actions. His response was to threaten to sue him, a threat that was soon seen as merely a bluff, but now having had the matter adjourned before the CJ in December of 2015 to be returned before the Trial judge and now having had the matter before said Judge adjourned in December 2016 for the parties to agree on an order for her to make a final adjudication on the actions of the Defendant, it looks like Christmas of 2017 before I get anywhere. As you are aware the area of dispute is the deduction of withholding tax by the Defendant from the amount awarded to me, the Claimant. Whatever spin is put on whether the Judge meant that withholding tax was to come out, this is a dishonest argument because a clear judgment was given for a specific amount where a Plan was found to have ended and thus it beggars belief that a person admitted to the office of Q.C could be so lacking in common sense that he seeks to uphold what was done as a legitimate concern by the Defendant who was once in my opinion one of our leading if not leading Insurance Companies. There is no question that tax is payable but it is Income Tax and unless Sagcior have become deputized by the Revenue Authority I am a loss as to why they feel obligated to deduct anything.

For the last Eight years during the course of my dispute with Sagicor I have made no bones of the urgency of this matter for me. I have out of desperation turned to use of my Pension Fund with Sagicor to partly settle the crippling debts I have been left from the Cottle mess. Instead of trying to assist one who has worked for years with my former Firm when it represented the two entities that metamorphosed into Sagicor, at every turn they have deliberately frustrated me added to my problems. While owing me in excess Of Four Hundred Thousand dollars they cancelled my health insurance knowing that with a preexisting condition this was like a death knell because I was unable to pay them the premiums totaling about $1200 over three months. They have refused to reinstate me to the plan and try as I might I have been unable to get the Courts to rule on the matter.

Having no health insurance is of great concern to me especially in months like this when my medical bills have approached $5000. I don't even have the money retained by them illegally to be used as a buffer to help me meet these costs. May I therefore plead with you to contact Mr. Cheltenham and plead with him to take off the hat of obstructionism that he has been wearing for his client and simply aid me to manage a plight that he has expressed sympathy for .His continued refusal to expedite this matter by settling what is to go to the Judge must lead me to believe as was expressed more than two years ago that his actions must be taken as they are and not what he says they are.

Yours faithfully,

_____

Philip V. Nicholls, Attorney-at-Law

CC: Mr. Errol Niles
   Mrs. Charmain Delice Hunte
   Sir Neville Nicholls

Philip Vernon Nicholls

LL.B (Hons) UWI, LL.M (Manch)
Attorney-at-Law

July 27, 2018

Clarke Gittens Farmer
Attorneys-at-Law
Parker House
Wildey Business Park
Wildey
ST. MICHAEL

Attention Mr. Stephen Farmer Q.C

Dear Stephen,

I refer to our exchange of messages yesterday about the wrongfully withheld 25% by Sagicor of the Judgment that was awarded to me in November of 2014.

After our exchange I found myself just sitting in a car park waiting for some normalcy to return firstly to my heartbeat and also for the cold sweats that were overtaking me to subside. It was a feeling that I had experienced once before, and that was in late 2001 when I had discovered the extent of the raiding of the coffers of Cottle Catford & Co. Mr. Allan Watson and to a lesser extent Ms. Joyce Griffith, as has been established, were severely indebted to the Firm, which debt has now transferred to me pursuant to my borrowing in excess of two million dollars to keep the Firm afloat.

For the last seventeen years I have played catch up with trying to recover these funds and having in 2009 had to say Good bye to Cottle Catford, your message would suggest that the time has come for me to fold and give up. The refusal by a Company like Sagicor who prides its self as a Wise Financial Thinker, who entices individuals to do what I did namely to invest in a pension plan to secure ones future , to pay the remainder that the Court ordered them to play is nothing short of a hypocritical action of a Corporate parasite. This is what I have faced along my journey something that is well known to Sagicor.

P. O. Box 93w   Tel: (246) 571-7215
Christ Church
Barbados

e-mail: **cartwinn@gmail.com**

151

1. The refusal of the said Watson and Griffith to honor the agreement they signed in December 2002 to repay the money that was due from them;

2. The abuse of the Court system by the said two aided and abetted by Senior Attorneys to delay proceedings to such an effect that it took until September 2009 to have judgement entered against them for failure to honor their agreement;

3. The failure of the Judicial system since then in disposing of the matter in that it took until October of 2013 for the appeal to the Court of Appeal to be dismissed;

4. The continued failure of the Judicial system in that a decision on an application for a final charging order to allow me to sell property of Watson is outstanding since October 2014;

5. The failure of the Judicial system to penalize Joyce Griffith for failing to attend Court since 2015 to be examined as a Judgment debtor as to how she will settle the Million dollars owed to me.

With their combined debt to me now cumulatively approaching three million dollars still outstanding and with no financial institution prepared to extend to me any form of credit facility since 2008 I have been between the proverbial rock and a hard place, several claims from clients are still outstanding as I can no longer borrow to settle same as the Institutions with some justification are concerned about my ability to recover amounts due to me.

To settle such claims I have only been able to do so either by personal funds from earnings or by liquidating what assets I had managed to save. The former has been destroyed by the charges brought against me in October 2013, charges that to date were dismissed because no evidence was led but the mere fact of the charge has decimated my earning ability which all evidence I have gathered suggests was the intention.

2

That has left me with only one source of finance after I liquidated all my savings which I did by 2011 or 2012. This was to utilize my pension entitlement from Sagicor. It should be for my Pension but at least they can sleep well (something that I have not enjoyed in months) that I will not live to need it. Sagicor despite being made aware in writing from 2010 as to the need for these funds has fought me from then until now despite a clear order of the Court in 2014 from the suit filed in 2012 that the funds be paid to me. This fight was despite Pat Cheltenham assuring my father at the time "oh this will be settled soon".

As the matter dragged on the toll took its effect on my health leading to Heart surgery and continues now with side effects because of the daily stress I am under. Lest I forget that this upstanding Corporate citizen was during this time in 2014 minded to cancel both my Health and Life Insurance while owing me over $400,000.00, because I was unable to pay the monthly premiums for three months. My inability to pay was because I was using those funds to ensure that utilities were paid and that I could feed and clothe my children. To date neither of these cancelled products have been reinstated another cost that I have had to bear.

As I have indicated substantial amounts continued to be due to clients in addition to amounts due to Banks loans on which I have reneged, and which have cost my house to be repossessed and attempts made to do similarly to my Parent's property. My ability during this period to finance anything was to say the least nonexistent.

When I was awarded the Judgement, I budgeted how I would settle some of these claims never thinking that 25% would be deducted. I am yet to find a legal scholar in Barbados or throughout the Caribbean and indeed wider afield who supports the contention by Pat Cheltenham and his Junior Natasha Green that the deduction was legitimate. Since 2015 I have contested this deduction and I say without fear of contradiction that in November of 2016 Pat conceded in Court that the deduction was in error. To think that in July 2018 this has not been paid after this is nothing short of scandalous.

As claim after claim was being made against me the only option left to me was to settle these claims from funds I was holding. In effect Peter was paying for Paul a game of Russian roulette.

3

153

The perfect storm which was brewing now hit when the present funds were required as I had no others holding against which to set off. Many might argue that playing Russian Roulette was a risk but I ask you what alternative was there. Does anyone know, far less understand, the constant pressure I have lived under this last decade with this millstone around my neck, while my other two Partners have just disappeared and utilized unethical actions by certain Attorneys and a dysfunctional legal system to help them avoid the day of reckoning while at the same time trying to meet expectations of those who are due funds.

The recovery of this 25% is crucial for the matter at hand but even if this happened today I am aware of other problems in the next week. I had forecasted this present problem since June last year, I started pleading with Pat to let me have my money and have been disappointed that every day it is a different reason for the delay. I must therefore conclude that the cold fact of day is that the deduction of the 25% by Sagicor was in keeping with what they have been doing illegally in the past with regard to Pension plans that have come to an end. I am now sorry to say they are virtually seeking to cover their own backside.

So, while they look to ensure their financial wellbeing I am being cast out to dry to suffer the indignities of being called all manner of names and subjected to all sort of innuendo. My only recourse will be to bring to light the perjury that officers of Sagicor carried out while attempting to justify why they deducted the 25% by alleging payment of same to BRA, evidence of which I have never seen either from Sagicor or BRA.

Finally Stephen, as they have invoked a judgment against me by them, please note, that the issue they are talking about started when Rosalind Smith Millar was at Cottle Catford & Co. and was acting for Sagicor. This was before the breakup of the Partnership. As you know she left to join your firm so this matter had its genesis 20 years ago. I have always found it curious that Sagicor has never ever attempted to recover any of the money due to them from Cottle Catford & Co. from either Watson or Griffith, which has confirmed my suspicion that the actions against me is a personal one. My view is supported by the fact that the Judgement they refer to was obtained after my suit and that in an action for me to satisfy same an Affidavit drawn and prepared by your office suggested that I was well able to settle same having in addition to my legal income, income now as an Author.

4

Hopefully that will be true when Book two comes out, if God spares my life but I will certainly make clear with correspondence what has gone on.

I was told early in my problems by an Attorney friend in Jamaica then when I get to the bottom of who is pulling the strings against me I will solve my problems. The people at the end of the string are becoming clearer and clearer with each passing event and while some of my decisions may be questioned I can hold my

head high and state that I have never used any of the money in question for personal purposes. That is why I have a suit for defamation against one of our colleagues who gave comfort to my former Partner while seeking to destroy me. Problem for me is that with our Court system maybe my grandchildren will benefit one day not me another reason why I have had to resort to other means of finance as I have got no help from the Courts.

In closing, as Sagicor have brought in this judgment which is completely unrelated in a classic Trumpian move, I see no other recourse but for you to discontinue your efforts, not because I believe it may influence you in your assistance, but it now puts you in an invidious position with your client. I will face the music on my own and this crisis like all for the last fifteen years will hopefully soon end as I have turned to others for urgent assistance.

Thanks for your help. It will not go unnoticed.

Yours faithfully,
PHILIP NICHOLLS & ASSOCIATES

Per: _____
Attorney-at-Law

Cc: Sir Marston Gibson Chief Justice
Mr. Rudolph Greenidge
Mr. Errol Niles
Ms. Charmaine Delice Hunte
Sir Neville Nicholls
Mrs. O'Garro

CHAPTER 12

A Bolt Right Out of the Blue

I HAD not put pen to paper for over six months when I determined that I needed to continue to record my story. To be truthful my state of mind had not been conducive to writing. Not only was I angry because of my perception of the wrongs that had been done to me, but I was frustrated by the fact that I appeared to be running into road block after road block every which way I turned.

One of the ways that I have been able to stay sane is to try to create a sense of laughter with everything that I do, trying wherever possible to see the funny side of things. In some respects that has been to my detriment, as some people are fooled into thinking that everything is okay. It was my only route, as I was unable and unwilling to forego the bitterness that I felt over these years in accordance with the Mandela doctrine, where he wrote that he consciously decided when he walked through those prison gates, unless he left the bitterness behind him, he would forever be bound by it.

In many respects I have done that, as I only feel a sense of pity for what Watson and Griffith had become—virtually exiles within their own existence unable to venture out to do whatever they want. It is a life I could not have lived and while now I feel pity for them my anger has been transferred to cretins like Vernon Smith and Barry Gale because they have pretended to be men of virtue, but are nothing short of charlatans in robes.

When I was thinking of the name for my new book I toyed with the idea of publishing a book with the simple words "See previous book and then Ditto," pages blank otherwise, similar to that bestseller *What Men Know About Women* where the pages are blank. As the inquiries increased about when the next book was coming it added to the anxiety that I was facing and eventually I just determined not to force it.

These many requests, well intentioned as they were, left me quite depressed, as every time I thought about writing the stark reality that my situation had far from improved became more apparent. It was unbelievable to contemplate that no positive movement on any aspect of the several matters had occurred that was worth being placed on history's pages. I tended to keep this sense of despair as much as possible to myself, as from conversations with my children, my troubles were having an impact on them and they were constantly worrying about my well-being both physical and mental.

Around this time Daddy's increasing physical challenges—his mobility was reduced because of a chronic knee complaint coupled with Mummy's continued losing battle with the ravages of Alzheimer's—engendered a sense of helplessness within me. This led to me, when often asked by close friends and relatives out of genuine concern as to how I was doing, to more and more internalize things and keep them bottled up.

As all would know there has to be an escape valve, and if my children are to be believed it would be my sudden explosions of annoyance at the most trivial infractions of domestic life. Like in many other spheres of life what can be seen is often not the worst of the problem.

One of the consequences of this long running mental turmoil has been the impact it has had on my ability to sleep properly. I cannot remember the last time that I have had a full night's sleep—I define a full night's sleep as one where I do not wake until after six hours. I have long grown accustomed to sleeping at most three to four hours and then waking. Often, I have trouble returning to sleep after I wake and many nights as dawn broke, I would find myself in front of the computer maybe dozing off for an hour before it was time to get the new day started by waking the children.

I often envied the children while watching them sleep without an apparent care in the world and thought back to those long-lost days when I would go to sleep rather than fall asleep from exhaustion. Not for the first time in this saga as I watched the children apparently unconcerned while they slept or if they had a concern it was whether their streaks on snapchat were intact, I would often chuckle, for as soon as I could get them from their robotic state of sleep into some form of normalcy, there would appear as a pavlonian response to transferring to the land of the living, that appendage that we are now acquiring at an even earlier age: the cell phone.

I dreaded nightfall because it meant more tossing and turning while trying to sleep. At least during the day there would be something to do. The situation was a disaster waiting to happen.

On the night of June 20th I was in my favourite chair watching TV, catching up on the latest escapades of Trump when I drifted off to sleep. I was later to learn that I had been asleep for about an hour when I was jolted awake by what felt like an electric shock. For a few seconds I did not know where I was and was genuinely disoriented, but as the sleep left my eyes I figured out that the defibrillator implanted to monitor my heart had shocked me.

My first thought was of Dr. Greene, the Barbadian surgeon in the USA who had connected the device and who had told me that I would know when it went off. Previous read-outs from the device had shown it going off twice before in the middle of the night, but on those occasions I was unaware at the time. This time I was.

As I gathered my thoughts I called my father around midnight and asked him to ask Christopher to come and check me over. I got up from where I was to unlock the door so he could get in, and remember feeling that my legs were heavy, but otherwise nothing else was untoward. Christopher arrived within fifteen minutes and after checking my heart insisted on taking me to Sandy Crest for an EKG. I deferred to his medical propriety, but as expected the results came back normal.

Later that morning I called Dr. Massay's office and arranged for an appointment later that afternoon at 2:00 pm to have the defibrillator checked. Remembering his words from a couple of years back, there was no point in worrying—just marvel at technology that had once again prolonged my life, always remembering that it would have been the will of the Almighty that allowed it to function. *Easier said than done*, I thought again, but realistically as in other aspects of my life there was little that I could do to change it.

That afternoon I went to his office for the technicians to 'interrogate' the machine by placing a scan over where it is inserted to allow the download of its secrets. Ian revealed to me what had gone on. They noted that at midnight it had delivered a shock of 32 jules to my heart after monitoring that it had stopped for eleven seconds. They also discovered that it had sent another shock around 5:00 am. I did not recall that shock, but recalled waking up and finding the CPAP mask that I sleep with on the floor as I often had. This was because of my habit of pulling it off subconsciously while sleeping.

Discussions with the technicians and later with Dr. Massay pinpointed that not wearing the mask was the root of the problem, or simply put, the direct contributing factor, for as he noted every episode had occurred when I was asleep without the mask and presumably snoring. Once again, he suggested that I needed to find a way of not removing the mask when I slept at night. For assistance in this I turned to Natalie Edwards of Total Therapy in Dr. Roach's office, who was now providing me with my equipment in this regard, and given that I was still not able to travel to the US.

I was grateful that she was now a supplier locally. She suggested a couple of things—sleeping with socks on my hands so that my fingers would not have the dexterity to remove the mask. A second suggestion was to place the equivalent of a Du-rag on my head, something that created some amusement with the twins when they first saw me with it. Again the idea was to make it difficult for me to remove the mask during sleep. But of course, this headgear which they described as making me seem hip, naturally made them curious as to why, necessitating my explanation of what had happened. The fear in their young eyes at 16 was difficult not to notice.

Any time something so life-threatening happens one goes into a period of reflection. This period was not helped by my running into Craig Smith a few days later. Craig, the son of the late Sir Frederick Smith, is like most of the Smith family known to me. We have never been close friends, but he greeted me with the words that my name had come up over the weekend at Vernon's birthday party. It should have been his blasted wake.

I indicated to Craig that I know that Vernon is his relative, but warned him not to "start me on that animal at this time." I was not in the mood. Mention of his name brought back all the problems of Cottle which however you looked at it had to be a contributory cause for my present problems. And Vernon Smith will always remain *persona non grata*. He rivals Barry Gale for the loathing I have for two supposed brothers who, belying the acronym that they hold of Queen's Counsel, are nothing but vermin in my view, only fit for dining in the recent sewers of the South Coast.

It was while talking to him that I reflected on the odysseys of life. This piece of vermin was still stalking this earth while decent people who had so much to offer had passed on—friends like Barenda Brewster, Reuben Bailey and Stephen Alleyne, giving truth to the adage that the good die young. *Of course,* I thought, *there are exceptions to the rule,* but I will not name them like the barracker who on entering Empire cricket ground one afternoon and seeing another Smith—my close friend Allan standing—amongst three slips uttered this witticism: "they are three slips but two holes." *I not saying who I mean, but you can figure it out.*

Craig provoked me further by stating that he and the fellas know that I do not genuinely believe that Vernon had anything to do with Marcelle's death, no doubt recalling my well-publicized comment in the master's Court that Vernon "want locking up" over her death. I responded that while he may have been too feeble to do the actual killing, he certainly had motive as there is a $100,000 in rent collected from the property belonging to Auntie Marcelle and her husband Uncle Aurie, and just as he had done to me when casting suspicion on me for the problems at Cottle, I was returning the favour.

For some time now I had not given much thought to Vernon, having long ago relegated him to that of the lowest form of scum that infests the bar to whom the only parallel I could see was Gale. And as he Vernon is fond of saying, he knows where the Courts are, even if as I write they are presently itinerant like the Gypsy's of yore, that if either feel my characterization of them is not fair and accurate, they can visit.

I have often been warned that I am trespassing on dangerous ground re defamation, but my response is the same. I really do not care after what these two have done to me; let them file an action and give me license what I really want to.

I say further that there is no objective person who, once they have read a snippet of what has gone on with respect to Cottle, is left with any doubt about the animus of Smith with respect to his actions. It is an animus that has been referred to more than once by the CCJ with respect to his attitude towards other matters before the Law Courts and to some extent it is the parallel of what we are viewing on the International scene in the States. Never admit your actions are wrong despite the clear evidence to the contrary and be willing to do anything whether it be legal, illegal and or unethical to continue with your charade.

Yet despite this it has proven impossible for me to get the Courts in Barbados to rule definitively on any matter associated with his actions as he just files and files motion after motion, appeal after appeal, to keep alive matters that are clearly functus.

If only I can shock the system into life like happened to me things may look up.

CHAPTER 13

October Remember

ONCE YOU have been an Attorney for any length of time you have would have drafted a document along the lines of the following. I was born as I have often been told on October 6th 1960. On midnight of October 5th I entered my fifty-eighth year. I was up as usual around 5:00 am, not to unwrap the presents the girls had given me, but because of nature. I no longer sleep for periods of more than four hours due in part to the fact that I have not so much outgrown it, but no longer find the CPAP machine I have compatible and need to change it. That is a problem, as I still cannot travel to the United States. Try as I might, all efforts to source a more comfortable mask here in Barbados had drawn a blank.

Fast forward a year. As I enter my fifty-ninth year the differences are that the girls are not here at present as I have decided to treat myself to watching cricket, an activity which they have routinely determined as boring. In light of the shellacking that the West Indies got in India and Barbados in the Super 50 here at home, it would have done my soul better if I had followed their advice and not tuned in. One important difference was that I was able to source a new mask with the aid of Mrs. Edwards of Total

Therapy. However, my inability to sleep, a combination of many things, had had consequences.

In 2017 I was scheduled to attend Court later that day for the hearing of my Application under a Certificate of Urgency challenging the Application of the now deceased DPP for a Voluntary Bill of Indictment to be issued against me to answer in the High Court for the same charges that were thrown out on August 13th 2015.

Despite authorising charges on the basis of a Trumpian lie by Barry Gale, he had failed to support the allegations with any evidence for over twenty-two months, as a result of which the Magistrate dismissed them after giving the DPP more than one warning to proceed or it would be dismissed for want of prosecution in August 2015. Now in death he was still causing me misery because of his Application in February 2017 to reinstate charges by means of a Voluntary Bill of Indictment.

Lest it be thought that I am overtly litigious, for the record I detest Court. Nothing useful happens and it is a long, drawn-out process with adjournment after adjournment. As our former National Hero the Right Excellent Errol Barrow is reported to have said, "if you want justice keep out of the Courts." I am loathe to advise anyone to run into Court at the first opportunity, unlike some who get an orgasmic high at the thought. What I was seeking now was a decision that would allow my earlier approach to the Courts for assistance to obtain the letter from the Registrar requested by the US Embassy since July of 2016 to consider my Application for my visa to be reissued.

What I was in Court for was to challenge the actions of the now deceased DPP who was seeking to use the route of a without notice Application to the High Court, an Application that was usually heard by the Chief Justice, for a Voluntary Bill to be issued. This would have the effect that the charges which were filed against me on October 30th 2013, and dismissed for want of prosecution, would now be laid in the High Court on indictment. I alone was not of the view that his actions were questionable. Others throughout the Caribbean more familiar with criminal law felt that his actions were a clear abuse of his power.

My Application was to challenge the issuing of the Bill for abuse of powers by the DPP in violation of my rights under Section 18 of the Constitution for a speedy trial. It was due to be heard by Justice Richards, the duty Judge, on Friday October 6th. I awoke that morning and dared not hope that this would be the start of the end of this nightmare that at that time was nearly four years old. I was right to do so, and it is amazing that a further year on absolutely nothing has been done.

In Court that morning no one from the office of the DPP attended despite having been served, but they sought an adjournment on the grounds that they needed to file a response. I was not surprised, because the legacy of that office under Leacock is to pay scant regard to the rights of individuals. I mean to say who was I to complain when a man was on remand for murder for ten years before his charges were dropped in a matter of fact way and then annoyance expressed when he took legal action for his lengthy incarceration?

With the adjournment, I was able to focus solely on spending the rest of the day with the children. Birthdays are really for the young. The innocence of youth is still with them, but still they are aware of the events that have been troubling me with the consequential strain that the events have had on my health and my practice, and as a result on my finances. I have noticed how as they grow older and can appreciate what has been transpiring they have in their own way tried not to put further strain on me. Seeing how they have reacted has further fuelled my anger at what has transpired and especially towards those who have contributed to it, as it is grossly unfair that my children have the weight of this on their minds at this time in their young lives.

As I spent my birthday with them I noticed not for the first time how this younger generation lives. Their phones are an essential part of their bodies, an extension in effect, and it would be interesting to see the responses to a question "What would you prefer to give up, your phone or...?" They get all their information from it.

Newspapers are only read if there is a specific item that they want, or usually when told to do so by a teacher; otherwise news comes from some site on the phone. One of the perils of this is that the news that they receive is strictly limited to or from sites that they visit. Synonymous with the name 'smart phone', it tends to suggest items that fit into the pattern of sites they visit. Often days may pass and they are totally unaware of some major breaking news, and they are unaware of it because it does not fit into their profile.

October is the month of my father's birthday, he being born on the 11th. This month has over the last few years, in light of what has gone on, been one of introspection as I review what have been the changes over the year. Once again, this year it was depressingly apparent and frustrating that nothing has changed. The hearing that was adjourned from October 6th was eventually held on November 20th when the substantive matter of the Application was transferred to be heard by the Chief Justice.

The reasoning was that as the original Application by the former DPP in February 2017 was made before him, he would be the best person to deal with my challenge. It is unbelievable that considering all that has transpired that more than a year later the matter has still not been heard. I need say no more really.

October 11th was a date that had special significance for me other than the fact that it was Daddy's birthday. Sixteen years ago in 2002 I had finally said to Watson and Griffith that I had had enough. While that occasion had its sadness borne out of the fact that a way of life that I had known all my working life was coming to an end, October 11th 2017 was to be the end of the road for a close friend personally and professionally that my father had. We were to learn that day that Sir Clifford Husbands had passed away. As is well known, Sir Clifford was this country's longest serving Governor General, but through it all he was Uncle Clifford to me. Both Daddy and Uncle Clifford worked in what was the forerunner to the Attorney General's Chambers and at the time the families of the government legal officers lived in the Garrison Flats, which are now occupied by the Defence Force. It cannot have been a surprise that his eldest daughter Sandra Dawne and I entered the legal profession.

Uncle Clifford had a keen interest in several sports, one of which was my favourite—cricket. During my playing days at school and university he would often call me or later if he saw me in the Court precincts mention that he could not find my name in the newspaper which would have indicated that according to him I was wasting my father's hard-earned money with which he had purchased my cricket bats and other gear. He would in addition remind me of all the time my father spent bowling to me at the Garrison and suggest that it would appear to have been wasted energy.

Woe betide me if I mentioned that I had received a bad decision the weekend before which to him was no excuse for failure. The conversations were always jocular, and he would end by stating that he would continue examining the papers on Monday mornings to see if my name appeared. He was often disappointed. Often, he would comment on West Indies cricket and was as disappointed as many fans at the present state as we had slipped from our halcyon days. To many West Indians of his generation the pride that our team brought to them by their on-field performances when they were enduring the social harshness of living and studying in England had helped them through those hard times.

I recall how in 2005 or thereabouts I received a call from his private secretary Mrs. Layne saying that His Excellency needed to see me as a matter of urgency the next day. I was told to be at Government House at 10:00 am and that it took precedence over any other appointments. The next day I went up to Government House and was shown into his study. For most of the next three hours I was subjected to an interrogation. He got straight to the point.

"Philip," he said, "your father was here yesterday for a Privy Council meeting and after it ended we were talking as we often did. I was asking him about your daughters and shortly after informing of their well-being he started talking about Cottle Catford. I have never seen him so distressed in all my life, so I immediately asked Mrs. Layne to have you come and see me."

Over the next three hours I gave him the history up to then of my attempts at first to try and reach an amicable solution and the impossibility this had become because of the intervention of Vernon Smith and the delays he was orchestrating. The only thing I will report that he said about Vernon is that he repeated what he told my Dad: that Vernon can be a difficult man when he wants to be. I have said the same thing over and over in far more colourful language, and did so to him, whereupon he simply said "…it will not help you solve the problem."

During our talk he kept repeating that he did not know "this Watson fella…" could not recall setting eyes on him. He had seen

Griffith before, but did not know Watson. I then remembered that Watson had been awarded one of the Centennial Awards in 2000, and that I had seen a picture of the group at Government House. He had a copy brought to him and I had to point him out. Not for the first time a senior figure in the legal profession had expressed astonishment at what had transpired, and how these two simply had washed their hands of their responsibility. I understood because of his position there was absolutely no way that he could get personally involved in the matter, but his interest and advice I took to heart.

Every now and then he would ask me to come up for a chat about how things were going. It is my understanding that he also had these chats with people from all walks of life. In fact, one of these chats was with a young entrepreneur who had established a business known as Glass Creations which made all kinds of figurines from glass. Uncle Clifford had seen his work at some function and informed me that he had used his work as official Christmas presents. In conversation with him he indicated that he had formed a company, and that I was his lawyer and he immediately called me to ensure that everything was in order and that I must look out for him.

During the country's preparation for the staging of Cricket World Cup in 2007, Uncle Clifford more than once summoned the late Stephen Alleyne and I to Government House for a report on how things were going. Stephen would present the slides that he used all over the country to disseminate information about the plans for the tournament, after which we would have a robust discussion with him as to what he thought was feasible and what he thought was destined for trouble.

The meeting that was scheduled for an hour would often run for three hours. He was genuinely interested in ensuring that the tournament was staged successfully, as the reputation of the country was at stake, and offered wise counsel as to what he saw as potential pitfalls, often interjecting his statements with a humorous anecdote of some situation in the past to illustrate his point. Before we left he would enquire as to what else we young whipper-snappers were up to.

He would tease both of us that as we had only daughters we would have to develop interests in things that we would not have thought were important, such as ballet and modeling, to perform our roles as devoted fathers. The meeting would end with the instruction that he expected another report in a few weeks' time, and he would follow up by watching the roll out of information to the public on the implementation of his suggestions to disseminate our message.

After Stephen's funeral he called me to not only comment on my eulogy for which he was present, but to offer his thoughts on how I could use the friendship between Stephen and I in a positive manner to overcome the sudden and traumatic loss occasioned by his death. It helped me greatly.

However, for me personally it was his wise counsel after the traumatic events that I faced after my arrest in October of 2013 that I remember and appreciate the most. By this time he had retired, so it was down to his residence that I trekked for a talk. He listened for hours; in so doing he drained my anger at the world, at the legal system, at lawyers who had contributed to where I was as I got things off my chest.

He then spoke to me about understanding human behavior and about taking comfort in the fact that those who knew you best, who watched you grow (he would then interject even if it was wider than we had hoped) had your back and would assist you in ways you would not know and probably never know to help you through this ordeal.

In addition to personal visits we had several conversations on the phone during which he tried and succeeded in lifting me from the depression that I had sunk into. He was one of the few people to whom I felt comfortable bearing my soul and letting out the raw emotion within me over what I felt was an injustice being done by persons whose agenda was not altruistic. We spoke about the effect it was having on my parents, especially my father, and it was from him that I would learn of the pain that this whole event had caused him. He impressed on me that my father was my staunchest supporter. He was also able to turn what I viewed as a negative into a positive.

In our talks, when I advised him that I was writing a book, he encouraged me to do so and to be frank in all respects. This I have tried to do. It was always my intention to present him with a copy of my book, but before I could do so he advised me that a copy had been given to him and that he had enjoyed reading it. I was able to chuckle at some of his observations with his daughter Sandra Dawne with whom I grew up, observations which of course must, out of respect for him, remain private.

I am sure he is now reunited with his wife, Auntie Ruby, who preceded him to the next stage of our existence. I recall Auntie Ruby with equal fondness and recall how she took turns with my mother to be on duty when my brothers and I, her children and others from the neighbourhood would venture down behind the Drill Hall in the days before the Hilton as one of our summer holiday activities. May they both rest in peace, both having served this nation with distinction.

APPENDIX 13A

Filing Attorney:
PHILIP NICHOLLS & ASSOCIATES
Attorneys-at-Law
No 8 Pine Gardens off Pine Plantation
Road St. Michael
T: (246) 826-0054
Email: info.nichollslaw@gmail.com

BARBADOS

SUPREME COURT OF BARBADOS
IN THE HIGH COURT OF JUSTICE

CLAIM NO. | 290 of 2017

IN THE MATTER of an Application for a Voluntary Bill of Indictment against **Philip Vernon Nicholls**

AND IN THE MATTER of Section 4 of the Criminal Procedure Act Chapter 127

AND IN THE MATTER of a without notice Application by the Director of Public Prosecutions

AND IN THE MATTER of Section 18 (1) of the Constitution of Barbados

AND IN THE MATTER of Section 24 (1) of the Constitution of Barbados

AFFIDAVIT IN SUPPORT

I **PHILIP VERNON NICHOLLS** of No. 8 Pine Gardens, off Pine Plantation Road in the parish of Saint Michael in this Island, Attorney-at-Law **MAKE OATH AND SAY** as follows:

1. On October 29, 2013 I was arrested and charged with theft of funds from a client and money laundering with respect to the use of the said client funds for my personal use. I subsequently attended Court on the dates hereinafter mentioned before the matter was dismissed for want of prosecution on August 13, 2015. I have always fiercely denied these allegations as the client was never a personal client of mine but that of the former firm of

172

use.

2. As a result I instituted Claim No. CV 47 of 2017 on January 16, 2017 against Barry Gale for defamation as the instigator of the allegations that I misused the client funds, and against the Commissioner of Police and the Director of Public Prosecutions for wrongful arrest, false imprisonment and malicious prosecution (hereinafter referred to as "the COP" and "the DPP" respectively).

3. Due to the failure of the COP and/or DPP to lead any evidence against me in support of the charges laid against me on October 30, 2013 over a period of twenty months the charges were dismissed by the Magistrate of District A for want of prosecution on August 13, 2015.

4. The failure to lead any evidence against me prevented me from showing that the charges filed against me were as a result of allegations instigated by Barry Gale as a result of a civil suit and the denial of this the opportunity to clear my name in a Court of Law has hung over my head since then.

5. In addition to the besmirching of to my reputation both personally and professionally an additional loss that I have suffered is the cancellation of my U.S. Visa which I have held uninterrupted since about 1966 the reasons for which were confirmed by the US Embassy in a letter dated May 10, 2016.

6. Prior to the dismissal of the charges against me I attended Court on the following days:

   (i)   On February 19, 2014 I appeared before the Magistrate of District "A" to apply for the return of my passport which had been surrendered on my arrest. The confiscation of my passport had prevented me from travelling which had impacted negatively on my practice. The Passport was returned.

   (ii) On March 10 and June 6, 2014 the COP requested adjournments when my case was called on the basis that the file had not come down from the office of the DPP and as a result the COP was not in a position to proceed with the prosecution.

(iii)   On September 9, 2014 the COP indicated that it was not in a position to lead evidence pertaining to a matter that allegedly occurred in 2008 because investigations were still continuing.

(iv)   At my fourth court appearance on December 16, 2014 the matter was adjourned because the substantive Magistrate was on holiday

(v)   On January 12, 2015 at the fifth hearing of the matter, fifteen (15) months after the arrest of the Claimant, the COP intimated that the delay in its ability to proceed with the prosecution was because of the need to get orders for discovery of documents in the hands of commercial banks, from the High Court which the Banks were unwilling to produce. These same documents were among the documents mentioned in the search warrant executed on October 29, 2013 at the time of my arrest.

(vi)   At the sixth and seventh hearings of the charges on March 12, 2015 and May 22, 2015 the COP indicated that a request had been made for the office of the DPP to take over the prosecution because of its complexity due to the fact that it had recently learned of a judgment that I the deponent had obtained in 2009 against my former Partners and the decision of the Court of Appeal in 2013 affirming same. As a result the COP was waiting on Crown Counsel Watts, from the office of the DPP, to assist with the prosecution. The COP assured the presiding Magistrate that the promised discovery of documents supporting the charge would soon be handed over to me the deponent.

(vii)   Partial discovery was handed over to me the deponent on July 15, 2015 at the eighth hearing of the matter after Sergeant Howard, one of the arresting officers, was summoned to Court to do so. The COP indicated that it was still not in a position to proceed as the office of the DPP had not assigned anyone to take over the prosecution as Crown Counsel Watts was now on the bench.

(viii)   The matter was dismissed for want of prosecution on August 13, 2015 on the ninth occasion that the deponent attended Court when the COP failed to complete the previously ordered discovery by the Magistrate for District A and the COP indicated that it was still not in a position to start the prosecution and was awaiting the office of the DPP who had been advised of the situation.

7.   After the dismissal of the charges I sought to have the U.S. Visa which was cancelled on November 1, 2013 reissued and attended for an interview on June 23, 2016. I was subsequently advised by the U.S. Embassy in an email on July 12, 2016 that despite providing a letter from the Magistrate's Court that the charges were dismissed I would need to provide a letter from the Registrar of the Supreme Court stating that I faced no further charges and as such I wrote a letter the same day to the Registrar seeking such a letter.

8.   By letter of July 14, 2016 to the DPP the Registrar of the Supreme Court requested from the DPP confirmation in writing that no charges were pending against me.

9.   By letter dated August 3, 2016 from the Deputy DPP to the Registrar of the Supreme Court (some eleven (11) months after the charges were dismissed) the Registrar was advised by the DPP that a check with the Financial Investigation Unit and the Criminal Records Office disclosed no pending criminal charges against me the deponent but that the office of the **DPP had reviewed the matter and had reinstated these charges by a Voluntary Bill of Indictment but it had not been determined by the Courts.**

10. An Application for a Voluntary Bill of Indictment was filed on February 27, 2017 six months after the said letter. The Drawn and Prepared signature on same was Crown Counsel Watts while the person seeking the indictment was the DPP, now deceased. Neither the deponent nor his Attorneys on record had sight of same prior to September 15, 2017.

11. This was a particularly egregious action by the DPP given that the DPP was aware since July 14, 2016 that the deponent had requested information with

respect to pending charges and was awaiting confirmation so as to further process his Application for the reissuance of his Visa and that time was of the essence. His actions however were symptomatic of his repeated disregard for the rights of individuals affected by delays with respect to prosecutions under his charge.

12. It has been thirteen (13) months since the letter from the Deputy Director of Public Prosecutions to the Registrar of the Supreme Court, two (2) years since the dismissal of the charges against the deponent for want of prosecution and just short of four (4) years since my arrest on trumped up charges and yet the DPP still has no timeline for the start of prosecution of an alleged offence now nearly ten years old.

13. Such disdain for the rights of me the deponent is a clear and flagrant breach of the Constitutional rights of enshrined in Section 18(1) of the Constitution for the following reasons:

(1). The Application to seek Voluntary Bill of Indictment after the dismissal of the charges for want of prosecution is arbitrary ad by itself evidence of abuse of power by the DPP.

(2) The Bill discloses nothing that was not available to the DPP at the time the matter was dismissed for the inaction of the office of the DPP. As such the wrongfulness of the action exacerbates the delay already associated with the matter and must be seen evidently as a biased action against the Deponent for the following reasons:

   a) The institution of the of charges against the deponent, without either an examination or investigation of the facts and brought as a result of reliance solely on the defamatory allegations of Barry Gale in emails and letters sent to the DPP and other third parties (as displayed hereafter) from 2009 was negligent at best and a witch hunt at worst.

   b) At no time between the alleged occurrences of the events in 2008 that led to the charges which the DPP was aware of since the year 2009 was the deponent questioned about any of the allegations for which he was eventually charged. In fact, he was only questioned for about 90 minutes on the day of his arrest about a civil judgment after which criminal charges were filed including charges for money laundering.

c) The delay in prosecuting the charges over a twenty two (22) month period after the filing of charges was due in the main to the failure of Crown Counsel Watts and/or the office of the DPP to attend the Magistrate's Court and take over the prosecution from the COP as was requested on more than one occasion.

d) The filing of the Voluntary Bill of Indictment on February 27, 2017 contrary to the immanency of the filing suggested in the letter of August 6, 2016 that it was a retaliatory response to the filing of Claim No. CV 47 of 2017 and not as a result of a genuine belief that the interests of justice would be served by the deponent.

e) The filing of a Voluntary Bill is also designed to prevent the deponent having the opportunity of the Preliminary Inquiry were held to allege and illustrate that the charges were brought as a result of the actions of Barry Gale and not of any genuine complainant.

f) The continued refusal of the COP and/or the DPP either to file against the former Partners of the deponent who have been found by this Court to be liable for nearly three (3) times the amount that the deponent was charged with stealing or to seek the extradition of one of the said former Partners who had fled the island since January 2010 in compliance with an Arrest Warrant issued by this Court in April 2015 on the basis that said warrant arose as a result of Civil proceedings, shows the double standards that were applied when bringing charges against the deponent as the main basis of same as listed in the Indictment is a Default Civil Judgment.

14. In the circumstances this filing must be viewed as a continuation of a spiteful and vicious campaign engineered by Barry Gale against me the deponent in which he has enlisted and obtained the help of the office of the DPP. The same office that downgraded charges for trafficking of marijuana against his former wife so that she avoided the possibility of a jail sentence and the same office that discontinued charges for Money Laundering against two (2) foreign

nationals working in the financial services sector who are clients of the said Barry Gale with respect to matters involving millions of dollars which action is being challenged before these courts.

15. As such there is more than a reasonable presumption that the actions of the DPP in refiling these charges were as a result of a preconceived view of what transpired and as a result of extraneous pressure being exerted by someone with whom he was engaging in an improper relationship when it came to determining the application of the criminal law.

16. The behavior of the office of the DPP as outlined above is not that of an impartial prosecutor whose overriding consideration is the interests of justice but rather one that seeks to be carrying out the personal agenda of others with the result that the rights of the deponent have been trampled with and continue to be trampled with by the laying of a Voluntary Bill of Indictment with no effort at advancing the charges against the deponent which have been in existence if the Indictment has any effect for over four years without any effort at instituting a prosecution and is a clear abuse of the powers of the office of DPP.

In the circumstances I am making this Affidavit in support of my Application for the Application for a Voluntary Bill of Indictment against me to be set aside as an Abuse of Process.

SWORN TO by the deponent)
the said **PHILIP VERNON NICHOLLS**)
at the Registration Office, Whitepark)
Road, St. Michael on the 28ᵗʰ)
day of September 2017)

Before me:

Nadike Padmore
Legal Assistant

178

CHAPTER 14

The Tentacles of Money Laundering

I HAVE deliberately waited until most of this book is finished to deal with the subject of money laundering. The Money Laundering charge levelled against me has continued to impact on me, overshadowing all other events that I have faced over the years. To me the tentacles associated with being linked to money laundering were far reaching into all aspects of my life. So partly out of anger from my predicament and partly because the subject was a painful one for me, I delayed dealing with it for as long as possible.

My view in 2013, a view that has not changed five years later, was that the leveling of the money laundering charge brought against me by the now deceased DPP was an act borne out of pure petty vindictiveness rather than an objective review of any evidence of a crime. This view has been fortified over the five years by other facts that I have become privy to, which has affirmed my suspicions that this action was part and parcel of a wider conspiracy to cause me harm. For those who might feel these words are strong to use against someone now deceased, I remind that the evil that men do lives long after them. In my case his initial action was bad enough, but he has doubled down on it by later actions that have continued to this day to bedevil me.

One positive effect of the charge was that I made it my business to learn all I could about the intricacies of money laundering. I became obsessed with the subject and the more and more I read the angrier I got at the charge, because as I repeatedly said it was a stretch to accuse me of money laundering on the facts related to Cottle. Some of the things that Watson and his wife did with the assistance of Smith clearly amounted to it, but not surprisingly, given the relationship between Smith and Leacock, he was never charged far less arrested. Not for the want of my providing information as to where he had absconded to the authorities, but it was never acted on. There are other glaring examples of money laundering with persons with high ranking connections that appear to have had a blind eye turned to much to my astonishment.

One of the more recent books I purchased on the subject is authored by a young African woman named Maureen Mutua. The title is *Mastering Anti-Money Laundering*. It is an easy read and examines what money laundering is, how it occurs, and what are the efforts to combat it. As she traces the history, one cannot help but conclude that there is an element of self-protection in the efforts of some in the OECD and the EU with respect to attempts to curb the practice as rules after rules are promulgated for third world countries to follow, failing which they will be deemed havens. Hypocritically, the same rules are breached most often by countries that are members of the OECD or EU, but they seem to escape sanction.

During my hundreds of hours of research, I have failed to unearth a single case from jurisdictions all around the world where someone is charged far less convicted on the facts that surrounded my matter. What I did discover was that many of the cases have been brought after years of investigation, not brought prior to the conduct of investigation; worse still, when adjournment after adjournment is requested to allow time for the investigation which, if I am to believe a recent letter from the DPP, is still going on.

A charge of money laundering leaves a stigma on the person charged comparable in my view to the stigma that was associated with AIDS when it was rampaging uncontrollably around the world in the latter part of the 20th century. The difference is that whereas AIDS was a disease that affected many who through no fault of their own were stricken by it, thereby suffering unfairly, this stigma many times became less on realization that the disease was contracted through no fault of the sufferer. By contrast the stigma associated with a charge of money laundering, because of its criminal nature, continued whether the charge was proven or not.

The stigma in my case has virtually destroyed my practice and led to even the most mundane financial transactions that I must engage in being scrutinized. I no longer bother to make an issue of it, but find it ironic that I am subjected to such scrutiny because of an unproven allegation that I am associated with an activity that arises in the course of converting dirty money to clean money, when I have none at present. It boggles my mind.

The charge has directly impacted me in other ways. My offshore practice which consisted of several directorships on companies has been affected by the fact that since my arrest and charge I have not had a request to do any work in the sector or to sit on Boards of Companies as a Director. Quite the opposite is the case, for I have resigned from more than one given the nature of their business, which in my view could potentially have suffered from the apparent bad optics by my continued association with the company.

Having spent long hours of work in Barbados and abroad to build my practice in this sector, this has been particularly galling. The actions of companies in shunning me is entirely understandable given the global push to control money laundering. My charge was big news at the time of my arrest, but the same cannot be said of the dismissal.

During the call from the former Prime Minister Freundel Stuart that I received the night after returning home after my arrest, he indicated that upon learning of the news of my arrest that he had called the Chief Justice to enquire whether the long standing Cottle litigation had finished. He was told it had. I confirmed this, but added that as the Court of Appeal had only dismissed the appeal against the Judgments awarded in 2009 earlier that month in October 2013, there was no time for me to enforce same. Five years later I am still trying.

He was sympathetic to the situation I was now facing and indicated like many others who had called that his call was to indicate to me that he was aware of my struggles and that I should keep my head up and justice would eventually prevail. I took the opportunity to inform him that in my opinion, for whatever it was worth, the policy of the DPP to tack on a money laundering charge to any charge of financial crime will eventually come home to haunt us as a country.

His call was in October of 2013, and by March of 2017 the United States had named Barbados a money laundering haven. When this happened I did not feel vindicated, but saddened that through our own idiocy we had handed the possibility of doing this to them. That allegation, the country was to find out, was to have the same disastrous effect on a macro level as to what I had to face on a micro level. Like Caesar's wife, the reputation of the country as a beacon of a financial centre had to be above suspicion. The mere threat of scandal could cripple it and lead to persons shunning you with the result that much time and money in damage control had to be spent.

The baseless money laundering charges being thrown hither and thither by the DPP without an examination as to whether actual money laundering was occurring were now coming home to roost. Given the size of our population when the number of charges levelled were compared with those filed in larger jurisdictions, it was not surprising that the conclusion reached by some bureaucrat sitting at a desk thousands of miles away must have been that money laundering was endemic in our society. Already predisposed to consider the island a haven because of its low tax structures as part of a concerted effort to cripple offshore centers, it was not surprising.

At the time of the announcement in March 2017 that Barbados was one of twenty Caribbean countries considered a money laundering haven, a concerted movement had been under way for some time by the countries of the European Union (EU) in addition to the G7, later known as the G20 countries (some are members of both), to stymie what was seen as the existential threat to these countries posed by the increasing use of offshore financial centers by citizens of their own countries to mitigate their tax liability. The inherent vice associated with money laundering was a good basis to attack these centers.

There was nothing altruistic about these attempts to dismantle the centers, as it was all part of the movement to ensure that the money that had been transferred to these centers under schemes that were once deemed a legitimate form of tax avoidance, were now being deemed schemes financed by tax evasion and as such it was a form of money laundering. It was just coincidental that the evasion was from taxes in the developed countries. Unwittingly, by our policy of linking all crime involving finance to money laundering, we were playing into their hands by giving them a reason to condemn us.

It is impossible in the limited time and space left in this book to adequately deal with all the nuances of money laundering, so only a basic examination of its meaning and effect will be attempted. Anyone seeking further enlightenment I would refer to Ms. Mutua's book. A simple definition of money laundering is the taking of dirty money and making it clean. By that one means passing money obtained from illegal transactions and laundering it through the banking system, or by means of purchasing assets so that it appears as if it is from a legitimate business activity.

This activity is universally recognized as an illegal activity that has led to the setting up of specific rules and agencies to counteract the activity. Originally the target was the proceeds from organized crime and the negative impact that especially trafficking in illicit narcotics was having on people. It was determined that by following the money the ability to detect persons behind organized crime by their use of the financial system would be enhanced. The impetus behind initial money laundering legislation derived from a desire to compact narcotic related activities quickly spread to include terrorist financing and more recently to funds from any form of illegal activity.

This has culminated in the establishment of financial crime regulations to curtail tax evasion, which is illegal. Under this guise the attacks on offshore financial centers by countries within the G20 and the EU has intensified over the last two decades by the reclassification of activities that once were considered as tax avoidance, which was legal, into the realm of tax evasion, which is illegal, by means of arguments that the abuse of the financial system by money laundering was being facilitated by the centers. There was an obvious flaw in this argument as it related to Caribbean centers and Barbados in particular.

The amount of money that is laundered in one year is estimated to be between 2-5% of World Wide Gross Domestic Product or (GDP). To put a figure on it, this was between US $800 billion to $2 trillion.

Barbados' GDP for 2017 was 4.8 billion US dollars. It was, along with the following Caribbean countries: Jamaica 14.7 billion, Trinidad 8.6 billion, Guyana 3.7 billion, St. Lucia 1.7 billion, Antigua 1.5 billion, Grenada 1.1 billion, St. Kitts and Nevis 945.9 million and St. Vincent 789.6 million, named by the United States State Department as a money laundering haven in March of 2017. The nine countries had a combined total Gross Domestic Product of 40 billion.

The size of the economies of these countries, while not the only barometer to determine whether the country is a haven, would suggest that no serial money laundering would be carried on within the financial system for the simple reason that the size of the economies, even if this does not include activities in the sector, would suggest in light of the estimated amount of money laundered in a year that any activity of this nature cannot be significant by comparison.

The counter argument that is made is that it is the activities in the offshore sector through which the laundering occurs. In this regard it is only the Cayman Islands with its proliferation of banks that could fall under the microscope, but the sweeping generalization fails to recognize, in the case of Barbados for instance, that its highly regulated offshore banks, most of which are not in the business of accepting third party deposits, should not be subject to this criticism.

The overt emphasis on the banks operating in the offshore sector as a weak link with respect to money laundering is clearly misplaced. Where there is clear evidence of malfeasance, those institutions can be easily cut off from access to the global

SWIFT system controlled by the US. When the fact that over the last ten years banks in the USA have been fined a staggering 243 billion dollars for money laundering offences, with Bank of America alone fined 76 billion, one must wonder about the impartiality of those making the assessments. Even more so when it is considered that the USA has never been named as a haven. While one would not expect the USA to name itself, there can be no greater irony that while the USA is accusing others of being money launderers, its current President Donald Trump was the head of the Trump Organization which carried on practices that are viewed as the playbook for money laundering.

Dennis Cox, in his treatise on money laundering published in 2014, states as follows:

> "The growth industry which we refer to as money laundering has developed significantly over recent years. The industry really started with what might be considered a key public concern over organized crime and the negative impact that this was having on people. The governing authorities surmised that, by tracking the movement of cash, they would then be able to detect unusual patterns of behaviour. This led to a series of rules being put in place, originally locally but increasingly globally, to enable relevant authorities to identify organized crime through its use of the financial sector.
>
> The key element that underpins the regulation is that inappropriate funds were being moved within the banking system to disguise the original source of the funds, enabling organized crime, to make free use of the funds that may have originated from tainted sources, including drug trafficking. Essentially the plan was to use the movement of the gains to identify the criminal,

since the original criminal activity was so hard to detect. The impetus behind money laundering legislation in any country always comes from some form of issue which is considered to be of such magnitude that it actually gets on the political agenda. The legislation is generally developed in a hurry to meet these perceived and specific needs. We are seeing at present with the revised banking regulations, designed to try to prevent a financial crisis actually creating one of their own."

Money laundering, though primarily a secondary offence to other illegal activities, can be a predicate offence, for example when a person may offer services for a fee to clean tainted money. As the amount of money being laundered is usually significant, such a standalone operator is not easily in business, especially in the region, given the size of the economies within which it could be occurring. Any laundering tends be by the use of legitimate entities such as financial institutions to achieve their aim or by use of the real estate or the sale of luxury items, which again because of the size of the country would mitigate against it being of significance.

Money laundering is a three-part process. The first part of this process is called the Placement Process. The illegitimate funds may have been obtained from predicate activity like drug trafficking, bribery or another crime and then the illicit gains placed in the banking system to commence the money laundering process. This initial placement of cash is not the only way that the process can be started. Very often the illegally obtained cash can be used to buy high worth chattels like paintings or expensive cars or real estate which are subsequently sold before the cash is placed in a bank account. Though the secondary cash may not be suspicious because it was from a legitimate transaction, as the cash was realized by the sale of an asset that was purchased with the originally illicit money, a laundering process has started.

The second phase is called Layering. This phase is to disguise the source of the funds as stated above, but often can involve making investments into legitimate businesses or simply moving money from one account to another. This process is often done through the use of accounts in several different jurisdictions. For this reason, offshore centers are viewed with suspicion. However, for this to be possible these centers would have either to have bank secrecy laws or be not subject to oversight.

It is ironic that the country associated with some of the most extensive banking secrecy laws, Switzerland, with the infamous Swiss Bank account which is just a numbered account, has never been formally placed on such a list of havens, although in the recent past because of the insistence by the EU and G20 relaxation of some of the secrecy laws has occurred because of the intense pressure to get information on the beneficial ownership of these accounts. Another irony is that FIFA, headquartered in Switzerland, was thrown into chaos by money laundering charges against many of its main players because of use of the US banking system. The abuse of the system was in some cases ongoing, for as long as ten years, despite all the safeguards in place.

The third phase is Integration. This is where the funds are reintegrated into a legitimate financial system to be assimilated with other assets and the originally disguised money is deserted and used for the launderers' benefit.

This three-step process, though relatively simple, is often achieved by a complex roundabout method. Seldom do persons, having stolen money or earned it from drug trafficking or any other cash intensive business in this day and age, simply run and open an account and deposit same and expect that no questions will be asked. As anyone who has a bank account knows, any deposit over $10,000 requires a declaration which also applies if one takes cash or monetary instruments above that amount into another country.

It should be clear to anyone of an average IQ that this process requires some intent on behalf of the launderer, what the lawyers call *Mens rea*. The mere fact that one has illegal funds in their possession does not *ipso facto* mean that they are laundering same. There must be something further. The purchasing of real estate or a high value item that can disguise the source is one such example, but surely when a man steals money and goes into a fast food establishment to buy a snack box or for that matter goes into a retail store and buys a bed or stereo set, one cannot seriously allege that he is committing a money laundering offence.

The requirement of intent to launder highlights why the recent policy of the DPP to add on the charge on the basis that having committed one illegal act it must follow is a complete idiocy. I am firmly of the belief that the frequency of such charges has been the principal reason why the country has been classified by the United States as a haven. It is instructive to note that in a case decided in September 2018 a US District Court vacated a conviction to conceal illegal proceeds because of insufficient evidence of intent to do so.

The intent to launder, when combined with the ability to find places to launder, illustrates why countries like Barbados— which have neither the extensive financial sector or the high-end real estate as is prevalent in places like London a New York and Zurich to hide the proceeds—are preferred destinations by launderers. The high incidence of the purchase of property in London with Nigerian money was of such concern to the former Prime Minister David Cameron that one of the last things he did before leaving office was to host a conference to discuss the problem.

Though one may lack intent to launder, one could easily be an accessory after the fact, either by negligence or like a situation that I faced years ago as a result of blissful ignorance. In the middle of the 1990s before the alerts regarding money laundering had started the following situation occurred. At the time Cottle Catford was working for American Express. In addition to the corporate work re the Company's registration to do business in the island, at times I was required to collect money due from cardholders in default and then pay same over to Amex. A Swan Street merchant was in arrears to the tune of about $50,000 and promises to pay were not being met.

Out of the blue one afternoon after closing time I received a call from the default cardholder who advised that he had the money and wished to come and pay. I tried to get him to hold on until the next day, but he was insistent. I let him into the office and Mr. Hutchinson and I counted out the $50,000, issued him with a receipt, and placed the money in the vault. The next day the money was deposited into our Client's account.

I was clueless at the time that there was a possibility that money laundering was going on and it was only after I attended courses on the subject over the years that I realized that what was done was a classic case of how money laundering occurs. The money had become available from whatever source I do not want to speculate, and by being placed into our legal account, it now became clean. The merchant was then able to use his card and therefore had access to the money.

As the predicate offence for which I was charged was theft of funds from a client's account, the money laundering charge was secondary in that the allegation was that having stolen the funds I subsequently had laundered same. To date there has been no evidence presented against me that any of the three ingredients of laundering was ever present. This is not surprising, because I have never engaged in money laundering. In my view the charges were brought partly as a result of the defamatory badgering by Gale, but also because of Leacock's desire to curry favour with technocrats at agencies whose meetings he attended as a representative of Barbados on the question of fighting money laundering.

What made the charges even more egregious to my mind and roused my suspicions that something else was in play was that for more than three years prior to the charges, Leacock was well aware of the issues at Cottle Catford, having been informed of same by me at a social function we were attending at the house of Edmund Hinkson. In addition, by the time of the charge it was general knowledge within the legal community from the litigation between myself and former partners that I had borrowed in excess of two million dollars and paid the net proceeds of same into the said clients' account.

To then accuse me of stealing a sum of about a third of what I had paid into the said account and laundering the funds would appear to be disingenuous. When it is considered that some ten years after the events and five years after the charges the DPP has been unable to unearth any evidence to support either of the charges, then I am well within my rights to view that what was done was a deliberate act to cause me reputational harm by association with money laundering.

Not only was the question of theft from the account debatable, as the account in question was a part of the financial system and the money in the account was placed there from a legitimate transaction, what was the basis to establish a money laundering charge? There had been no placement, there was no attempt to layer, and it must follow that there could be no integration into the system. The charges as brought were clearly an attempt to condemn me by association as the factual matrix to tie the facts to money laundering was not present.

The tactic of the use of money laundering charges to achieve other purposes is a well-worn one. It is the modern-day equivalent of the charges that were proffered for tax evasion etc against known gangsters like Al Capone in the days of prohibition when such persons ran riot. The US authorities have not been shy to file them as secondary to other charges that the US system might have difficulty prosecuting because of the situs of the crime.

This tactic of levelling charges of money laundering for use of the US financial system to negotiate payments suspected of arising out of an illegal transaction is almost now par for the course when the Defendant is a person who is not a US Citizen or otherwise was living in the country. The charges are often concurrent with allegations of a breach of an Act called the Foreign Corrupt Practices Act, a 1977 Act which as the name suggests imposes liability criminally and civilly for offences committed extra territorially to the US.

Many notorious drug lords soon found themselves before US Courts facing money laundering charges along with the acts that resulted in the ill-gotten gains. In many cases legal wrangling arose about the jurisdiction to try the predicate offences, not to mention the practicality of proving crimes where the situs and witnesses may well be overseas. Many of the crimes committed were heinous—murders, rapes, kidnappings and drug trafficking such that no one would dispute that the crimes were illegal in any part of the world, and as such when money was earned from the committing of these crimes the depositing of same in the US financial system was clearly an Act of Money Laundering.

Recently a former Barbadian Government Minister, Donville

Inniss, was charged with money laundering in the United States. Much was made of the fact that he is also a permanent resident of the US. For the purposes of my discussion that fact is irrelevant, as there is nothing in the charges that arose because of this. The allegation against Inniss is that he deposited funds in the US Banking system from an illegal transaction, namely receiving a bribe contrary to the Corrupt Practices Act in Barbados, and by so doing committed an Act of Money Laundering. The sum alleged was $42,000 which in the scheme of amount laundered must be the equivalent of being accused of removing a grain of sand because it was attached to your slippers when leaving the beach. Clearly some other reason was in play.

Donville was very much a junior to me while at Harrison College. Our paths did not cross much then and have not crossed much since he has been in public life. As such I hold no brief for him. I have no knowledge of the predicate offence, taking a bribe, that he is charged with and make no comment on it. I take serious issue however with the manner of the charge in the US, because according to the indictment the money laundering occurred because it was the proceeds of a crime contrary to an Act in Barbados.

I find his charge disingenuous in the manner that the money laundering laws are being used in a manner to ensure a conviction. I am of the firm opinion that if he has committed an offence in Barbados he is to be tried and convicted in Barbados. If he is found guilty and thereafter the US wish to seek his extradition I fail to understand how an indictment for money laundering can be based on a supposed illegal action in Barbados that he has not been found guilty of, far less charged in the jurisdiction where it took place.

There is a clear distinction also with for instance the charges against the Mexican Drug Lord Joaquin Guzman, nicknamed

El Chapo, who is currently on trial for money laundering along with crimes of a heinous nature. No one can dispute the illegality of his actions, but in Inniss' case that cannot be presumed. What makes it more egregious in my view is that what he is charged with doing—accepting a bribe or using his influence to grant contracts contrary to a local act—has received the cloak of legality in the States under their lobbying statues. As such I hold to the view that the question of the legality of his actions should be determined in a Barbadian Court before it can be used as the basis to ground a charge in the US.

I am told, but can state conclusively that this is what happens, that the Department of Justice in the States will rely on evidence from our DPP Department either in the form of testimony at his trial or by way of Affidavit, that what he is alleged to have done in the indictment in the US as contrary to laws of Barbados, is illegal and on that basis the money laundering charge will be established.

If this procedure is correct, then I personally am left with a knot in my stomach, as Inniss will have no chance to challenge the alleged illegality of his actions before a Barbados Court. However great the US may be, I think we will all agree that it has no right to rule on Barbados law even though it may see itself as superior.

It is with regret that I must comment on the role of the DPP in the circumstances outlined. The rich history of that department would normally calm any fears one would have, but the recent direction leaves me uneasy. As I consider my matter I must note that if I was in the situation of using the US banking system and was charged with money laundering then I might well be convicted based on an Affidavit or testimony that what I did was illegal, yet in the situs of the alleged crime no evidence has been led against me after more than five years.

To my fellow Attorneys I would add another caution. It is evident that the net for financial crimes is widening even if it means use of unconventional means. Recent moves in the United Kingdom to target unregulated entities in the provision of money services are now extending to target lawyers and accountants with greater force because of their dealings with large sums of money. With the tightening of controls on banks, persons are turning to other avenues and it is only a matter of time before this aspect of Barbadian society comes under more scrutiny for regulation when the country goes under its biannual review from the FATF.

But the preparation of what to do and what to look for may have to be more imminent. A couple of years ago at a seminar put on at the Bar with the money laundering authority to educate the Bar about the need to be vigilant in preventing money laundering, I made the point that the traditional warnings that used to be circulated with a lot of Middle Eastern names are no longer relevant as an indicium of potential problems.

Few of them are likely to be seeking to utilize the services of an Attorney here. What is by far the greater existential threat to the local practice is the average American seeking to purchase property in the island, be it that villa in Sandy Lane or a West Coast condo, because of the change of emphasis in the United States between what is considered tax avoidance as compared to tax evasion.

I really see little choice than for Attorneys, accountants and real estate dealers to protect themselves by requesting that such clients produce a certificate from their US accountant that their taxes are in order. Failing this, you the innocent professional may well get caught up in an aiding and abetting charge by the US authorities who will be far more aggressive than the former DPP was with those who shamelessly aided and abetted the

Watsons, and in so doing aiding in the disposal of real estate to hide the trail of cash, committing a money laundering offence. That failure to charge when I was charged despite borrowing money to replace what they took suggests to me that others had a corrupt intent.

The ongoing scandal of the Danish Bank Danske is still being unraveled, but it involves by some estimates $200,000 billion. Now remember that Barbados' GDP was just over 4 billion last year and yet the United States named us as a haven. Do not expect such accusations to follow because of the laundering permitted by Danske and Deutsche Bank, the German Bank What was the phrase... 'Too big to fail'? In these cases, it may well be that too many big people are involved for it to be called out. It makes one wonder why our authorities are insisting that a 80 year old woman seeking to send a birthday gift of $200 to her granddaughter at University overseas must give proof of address, never mind proof of income.

Perhaps, as one of Clint Eastwood AKA Dirty Harry, Inspector Callaghan said, she should say she put on a dog and pony show for some customers. The Hypocrisy not so much of the West but of our own in blindly doing as they bid makes me seethe. The threats of delisting etc. are going to happen, so plan for it; be it a Caribbean clearing bank in a major financial centre or diving head first into the Crypto currency market. However, I probably would have departed by the time it gets a firm foothold.

CHAPTER 15

The Effect of the Bully Pulpit

THE ELECTION of Barack Obama in 2008 was the first US presidential election that I had paid rapt attention to. As a citizen of the world, one could not avoid knowing about the US elections because of the reach of the US news networks which inundated the world with any tidbit of news about the election. The twenty-four hour news cycle of the networks ensures the distribution of information not only of the current Elections/ Presidencies, but of one's past as well with the happenings of the past being dissected for evidence of trends relevant to the current elections. Thus for persons not of an adult age when the Watergate scandal occurred in the early 70s, it seems as if it happened yesterday as parallels are drawn with the Trump administration. Any viewer can easily suffer from news overload, but it is all part and parcel of the deliberate message that what transpires in the US is of utmost importance and thus for consumption worldwide.

The 2008 election, given the history of race relations in the US, was a monumental occasion, but still at the same time highlighted the good and the bad of US society. Having seen the election of a man who probably a decade before could not have been elected, it certainly gave credence to the view that the US was indeed the land of opportunities for all. To some observers the election of 2016 to some extent suggested that the experiment of 2008 was just an aberration, as it placed in charge a person holding similar views to many of his countrymen that what America wants was and is the only consideration. It was every man for himself and devil take the hindmost. The biggest bully in the class got whatever he wanted.

The stark difference arising out of a comparison of the worldwide coverage of the main power of a bygone era, namely the United Kingdom, with that of the not so much as the new but only superpower, was there for everyone to see. Whereas the election of a government in the UK was done and dusted in a couple of months at most when compared to the couple of years for an election in the US, this meant that the news cycle of events there dominated the airwaves for far longer. One result of this is that events in the country penetrated far and wide into the subconsciousness of people around the world, a classic example being our ready acceptance that the lexicon of Fake News is now to be associated with explaining what to all purposes is just outright lying and deceit.

I can still hear my friend David Comissiong's arguments during many a lunch time in that Sixth Form Arts class of Harrison College which we attended that this was what cultural penetration was about—the ability to ensure that your view of the world was what was disseminated and what became the norm against which all other events and views were measured. I myself had long recognized that this new form of colonization by the spoken word broadcast by TV and myriad other social platforms was just a new and more advanced way of ensuring that cultural penetration happened.

The concept of cultural penetration was nothing new. The

English did similarly when they ensured that their values were disseminated by the spreading not only of their system of Government around the Commonwealth, but of their recreational sports as can be seen for example by the spread of cricket to countries that were one-time part of the British Empire. For the former colonies defeat in this game today by the old colonial master was not simply a loss of game but at times cause for National anguish, as it opens old wounds.

That the baton of the new colonizer has long since passed can be seen by the embrace in many corners of the globe every year around the US Thanksgiving celebration of the concept of Black Friday shopping over the last five years. By comparison the UK version of blow out sales, the Boxing Day Bonanza, is still very much unknown outside those shores.

The ability to control the dissemination of news is thus of vital importance as history reveals, as radio and television stations are often the first target in any uprising.

It falls to reason that the leader of such a country can influence events around the world as much by word of mouth as by deed. When the US President uses his office to speak, especially when espousing criticism of opponents or events in other countries, the US media is quick to point out that the President is using the Bully Pulpit afforded by his office to give weight to his statements.

The maxim that to whom much is given much is expected would in the normal course of events be expected to be understood by any rational occupant of the office that the US Press readily dub as the leader of the free world. Unfortunately, as the world is finding out, the current occupant of the White House in many of his crass pronouncements makes it clear that his primary message is not one of embracing the moral responsibilities of lending leadership to the world that follow from being so regarded, but to simply state that others must 'follow my agenda voluntarily or you will be bullied into doing so.'

To be fair to Trump, in many respects he is not diverting from the traditional US policy, just expressing it in a more crass and insular manner. This policy, often when broken down, equates to 'do as I say and not as I do' with the effect that the devil take the hindmost to those not in its orbit.

Barbados has not been unique in suffering because of the use of the bully pulpit over the years in the manner described—to impose the views and or desires of a powerful nation onto a smaller nation. Other nations that have offshore centers have grown accustomed to the tactic of the US and indeed the collective countries of the EU using the medium of the Bully Pulpit in the case of the US, or the equivalent in the EU, of threats of blackmailing countries as being non-cooperative to get their way. By this method institutions like the United Nations or the OAS where numbers could often result in the policy being pressed by the colonizers being defeated, have been deliberately bypassed.

Trump's 'America First' policy should not be viewed as new or unique as it relates to a view of the financial sector of the world. Rather, it is a reset in albeit a more confrontational tone of the belief with respect to the world financial system that this should be controlled by the US.

For the last two decades the major financial economies of the world have engaged in a vicious hypocritical campaign to eradicate what they view as competition to their dominance of this sector. With numbers not on their side in bodies like the United Nations, the United States' shifted focus with respect to financial matters to organizations like the G7, now expanded to the G20, and its cousins the OECD and the FATF to advance their narrow interests.

At the same time the European Union joined this effort to wage war on the offshore domiciles of the World with the result that attacks were coming from all quarters. This war by the industrialized nations of the First World Order was fought by means of an attack on the taxation system of the centers which were based by and large in smaller countries. It was waged by use of the media to disseminate information and/or make attacks on the integrity of the centers on the basis that the centers did not conform with standards hypocritically drawn up by them to suit their own needs.

The attack on the offshore centers started under the Clinton administration 20 years ago with the designation of nations which operated the centers as Harmful Tax Domiciles. The harm being alleged was to the Nations that were members of the EU and the OECD, not the centers who generally were using their sectors to diversify their economies to provide a more prosperous living for their citizens.

The basis of the attack by the First World Order was that their legitimate expectation of tax revenue from their citizens, whether individual or corporate, was being compromised by its citizens utilizing structures in these centers to avoid paying tax in their countries of origin or residence. Of course, the fact that many of the centers were in previous colonies of the attackers who used to develop or under-develop their economies—depending on your perspective—was conveniently forgotten. Coupled with dwindling foreign aid or in the case of countries like Barbados who because of their success were graduated out of the countries entitled to concessionary development finance, the need to establish the sectors to diversify their economies was also conveniently overlooked.

Barbados, under the leadership of then Prime Minister Owen

Arthur, played a prominent role in defending the sector and prevailed at the time. But it was more a question of winning the battle and not the war. By using the basic argument that such investments from abroad to take advantage of robust tax planning to avoid paying the higher levels of taxation in industrialized nations was not what the generally accepted legal norm of tax avoidance, which was legal, the attacks mounted.

The goal posts were changed, a change that became clear during the Obama administration with the passage of FACTA legislation. FACTA legislation is a US domestic act which basically is a requirement that the rest of the world enforce US domestic tax laws on its citizens wherever they may be living. Failure to report to the Inland Revenue in the States of holdings by citizens in foreign countries would lead to the failing country being deemed non-compliant.

The forced enforcement of the country's domestic tax laws was by means of bullying threats that failure to cooperate would see the country sanctioned. That domestic law, being contrary to legal norms that no sovereign nation is required to enforce the domestic tax laws of another, was another clear example of application of the doctrine that might is right—do as I say not as I do.

As the world scurried to become FACTA compliant, a more insidious requirement was soon demanded of offshore centers by the OECD and EU backed up by threats of naming and shaming countries. The naming threat had significant consequences for the ability of countries to borrow on the world markets, and so the ploy was to use that old favourite of divide and rule of named countries in their attempts to be moved from firstly the list of the non-compliant to the list of the partially compliant, and finally fully compliant jurisdictions and thus break up the only effective counter that the jurisdictions had, which was to stand together.

These lists that counties were placed on depending on a review of their taxation system were determined by the OECD according to standards enunciated by them with respect to international taxation standards and matters pertaining thereto. Black listed countries were forced to change their taxation structure to comply with these rules before they were removed from the non-compliant list and transitioned to the fully compliant lists by agreeing to changes over a two year period after which sanctions would apply.

The latest and by far the most far reaching imposition is in the form of what is known as the Base Erosion and Profit-Sharing (BEPSS) standards. This enactment by the OECD set a level of taxation that the members of the OECD expected to be applied on profits by companies based in their jurisdictions.

To the extent that these levels were avoided by the shifting of profits under the guise of tax planning to offshore centers, this practice was deemed contrary to their interests, and as if by fiat they determined that all countries must fall in line with their dictates of what rules should apply. The result was that with one fell swoop one of the long-standing tenets of legal jurisprudence, namely the distinction between tax avoidance, considered legal, and tax evasion, considered illegal, as the BEPSS, had to be implemented. Barbados has recently had to virtually dismantle its International Business Sector for specialized companies built up over the last forty years under this pressure.

The basis of the attacks on the offshore centers was premised on the belief (hypocritical in the extreme) that the use of the centers was facilitating rather than preventing money laundering, and terrorist financing which was underpinning not only the world financial system but society. While such activity clearly does, this activity was not endemic in the centers as compared to the US and the countries of the EU, contrary to all the hype that was being spewed. Virtually every month another major banking scandal was coming to light with respect to money laundering in the United States and in members of the EU.

Typically, this clear empirical evidence was overlooked to give credence to the allegations that the centers were havens for money laundering, which was all the more surprising given that many researchers estimate that more than seventy percent of money laundered worldwide occurs in the United States and Europe.

The Antiguan Ambassador to the OAS, Sir Ronald Saunders, publishes on his website numerous articles looking at the stance that the US and the EU, both of which have vested interests in the OECD, have adopted in their battles to dismantle the offshore centers. His argument that their purpose is not as they state—to ensure that the financial centers are not misused—but is an attempt to have returned to their shores money deposited in the offshore centers of the Third World. His analysis that the United States is now one of the biggest if not the biggest tax haven in the world is a realistic assessment of the fact that as a result of the pressure against the activities of the centers, investors in those jurisdictions have been transferring money to the United States and utilizing similar structures in Denver, Colorado and South Dakota to those that exist in offshore centers.

The tactics of discrediting financial centers by means of accusing their tax regimes on the ground of encouraging abuse of the system for illegal purposes was not the only line of attack. Nations including Antigua, Dominica and St. Kitts that enacted programs of citizenship by investment were criticized as building same on the back of proceeds from money laundering to evade taxation or by persons who were seeking to acquire anonymity by the holding of a secondary passport and thereby make it easier to promote terrorism. This was a startling piece of hypocrisy, given that the United States and many other industrialized societies had not only adopted but still utilise such programs as they seek to attract persons to their countries.

By far, however, it was the sustained and untruthful allegation that the centers were engaged in facilitating money laundering that was pivotal to the sustained attack on the legitimacy of the centers. Whether or not there was any merit in the allegations was irrelevant, as the mere accusation had the desired effect of causing flight of investment. Similar to this is what is being done by the US with Iran, where it is using its control of the financial sector to get its way with respect to dealings with Iran even though to do so meant tearing up a legal binding treaty between several nations.

What the allegations did was to heap pressure on other players in the financial sectors to shun the named centers. Cognizant of the sizeable fines that were levied on institutions in the United States and indeed in other countries for breaching money laundering regulations, banks began withdrawing Correspondent Bank Relationships with banks in the Caribbean under the premise that any small profits made from such an association was not worth the risk given the possibility of a fine for being involved in money laundering.

The loss of such relationships has had serious practical considerations for the average person in the Caribbean. For instance, the ability to send and receive payments from the outside world would be compromised. Businesses such as those in the hotel industry that are often paid for in foreign markets would find it difficult to collect payments made to agents overseas for their services. The general cost of doing business would rise as the banks would have to utilize more expensive methods to continue to access the US financial markets now that the direct route through US correspondent banks was cut.

The rise in the cost of banking services was already a source of much disquiet in Barbados and the region. These rising costs, when added to the virtually zero payments that the banks were making in the form of interest on deposits placed in the bank, were the source of much anger. Every week it appeared as if there was an additional fee being charged for services that for years were part of the normal business offered to customers by banks. As many if not all the banks were making similar charges. The option of moving your account, already difficult with the increased requirements for opening a new account, became an option that was not readily available.

In fairness to the banks, part of the costs that they were incurring was as a result of additional costs associated with the increased level of compliance needed to satisfy the dictates of the requirements of the FATF passed on through the regional CFATF with respect to implementing measures to prevent money laundering. In many instances it meant the hiring of skilled individuals so that the banks themselves would not be found wanting in their compliance standards. Despite these levels of compliance, the attacks still continued.

The attitude of the corresponding banks in this regard did not consider the wider dislocation that their decisions would have on the society in the countries where delisting was occurring. It has resulted in the International Monetary Fund and indeed the US Government expressing their concern and urging that the generalized revocation of relationships be stopped and only done where there was a credible risk associated with continuing, which to some extent was going around in circles as it was the US that was screaming from the rooftops that the banks existed in societies in which money laundering was endemic.

The banks themselves to a certain extent were getting a dose of some of their own medicine in this regard. They had never been shy of utilizing the application of a blanket formula by which to judge all the customers doing business with them. As a result, there was a legitimate outcry when local gaming arcades found themselves prevented from utilizing the banking sector, as they were deemed risky businesses on the simple premises that they were a cash intensive business. Heaven help the entrepreneurs who one day soon will be able to deal in some places in medical marijuana.

Not for the first time I was of the view that our local regulatory agencies, in setting out parameters for assessing risks for money laundering, had not considered local conditions before implementing policies designed elsewhere. Local conditions demanded that these policies if not changed should be modified to fit local circumstances, rather than simply adopt a cut and paste method for accepting the measures handed down.

Gaming arcades are a prime example of this category. As a cash intensive operation, arcades are a magnet for money laundering schemes. So too are laundromats in the traditional sense, to pardon the pun. Gaming arcades in Barbados that operate primarily 25 cent machines should not be compared from a risk point of view with a traditional casino. If it is the activity that is being deemed not acceptable rather than the flow of cash, then why is there not a problem with taking money from horse racing betting where far more money is gambled on a good day than in a month in most arcades in Barbados. One must always be vigilant with a cash-intensive business and if suddenly deposits of large amounts of cash are being made then questions must be asked. To be suspicious simply because cash comes from a legitimate business is not being diligent, it is being ridiculous.

Of course, one has guidelines to follow and this is perhaps where our local regulatory authorities are failing in not insisting that the dictates handed down from overseas be tailored to comply with local requirements. Know your customer requirements. That persons must produce two pieces of identity to cash cheques is a case in point. For a significant portion of our population this requirement can be a challenge. The question that must be asked is whether in a small society where there is bound to be someone who can verify identities to the satisfaction of the bank, an insistence on the production of two pieces of ID is more being a slave to form than guarding against any form of deception.

In a similar vein is the requirement of a utility bill to prove your address. Many young people who wish to access the formal banking sector do not have such bills, especially if living at home, and I have always been at a loss as to how a utility bill can be a used as *bona fide* proof of your residence. I still receive utility bills addressed to a residence I left over five years ago, so I rest my case.

I understand that the rule makers overseas are not flexible and if you don't follow their rules a bad mark may result. However, dialogue to show that the problem you are seeking to overcome must take account of local conditions is important. When the organizing Committee of World Cup Barbados was dealing with the requirement for an exclusive zone of two miles from the Kensington Oval to be free of competing advertisements it was pointed out that to comply with the requirement would necessitate a zone of nearly two miles out to sea. The requirement was deemed redundant because of local conditions and not insisted on.

The Royal Bank, however, must take the cake with respect to unreasonable policies with respect to know your customer rules. For the last few years the Royal Bank has been making it increasingly more difficult to cash cheques drawn on their accounts if the payee is not a customer of the bank. I ran into the issue on more than one occasion and refused to leave, other than to file a suit on behalf of my client, who had issued the cheque which the bank was now refusing to cash because I was no longer a customer. This led to a furious argument with the supervisor, who had asked to come, especially when he told me that it was the bank's policy.

That was like a red rag to a bull, as I said that bank policy cannot override the Law of the land and the only reason you should disobey an order from your customer which the cheque is if there was either no money to comply with the order or you were unsure of my identity. Given that I had placed the funds on the Estate Account on behalf of the Estate, that was not the issue, and given that the teller had addressed me with the words that she could not cash the cheque as I no longer was a customer, it was clear that my identity was also not an issue.

It took about an hour, but the cheque was eventually cashed. Sadly, my letter of complaint to the Central Bank was met with the response that it was part of their due diligence re money laundering. If ever there was a bull---- response, that was it. Once the bank was satisfied that the money in its account was legitimate, it was irrelevant what I, the payee, was going to do with it. On the other hand, it highlighted for me the legacy that the allegation against me was causing, and the fact that those in charge seemed to have no idea on the subject.

CHAPTER 16

A Glimmer of Hope

HOPE SPRINGS Eternal; A Touch of Hope; West Indies Finally Find Hope were some of the headlines that were emblazoned across the world cricket press after the sensational run chase led by Shai Hope to guide the West Indies to a totally unexpected victory at Headingly on August 28th 2017 in the Second Test Match versus England. The victory was made all the more remarkable considering the trouncing that the team had received inside three days in the first Test at Edgbaston less than two weeks before.

Shai scored a century in each innings of the game, his first two Test centuries, an exceptional feat during a Test Match in itself, but made all the more amazing by the fact that it was the first time that the feat of two centuries in a first class match had been executed at the ground in over 100 years of cricket. That the ground was home to some of the most prolific of batsmen in the history of the game made the feat even more special. I watched both of his innings with a sense of pride as past President of Pickwick Cricket Club, of which Shai was a member and which club he had represented since he left his school, Queen's College.

I watched the last few hours of the game in the company of

my neighbor Cammie, a true friend through all my trials these last few years and a member of the tied Test Team in Australia of 1960. Cammie was ecstatic. He is not only a former player but was a long-time administrator of the game. I knew from many conversations with him that he felt the pain personally of the heavy defeats that the team had suffered over the years. His pain was of a kind that those of us who never donned that maroon cap would probably not understand.

After the game finished I sent Shai a congratulatory note and, typical of the outstanding and rounded young man he has become, he responded a few hours later thanking me for the continued support. It was a good feeling that I was able to send that type of message when just a week before I had been sending him one of commiseration and encouragement after the debacle at Edgbaston. I knew that whatever personal feelings I had of the achievements of a fellow Pickwick Club member would pale in comparison to the pride that his parents would feel. They had been ever present supporters of his through all the stages of his life doing what countless other parents do when supporting their offspring, no matter what their varied endeavours were.

Parental support through thick and thin is what sustains many persons. It comes unconditionally with parents often staying in the background during the good times, but is ever present and prominent during the low times when their support is strongest. I can relate well to this kind of support that all successful athletes receive, especially at those times when I was in the depth of despair. It was my closest friends and relatives and especially my father who carried me, if not literally then metaphorically.

I was not alone in my celebrations, and like thousands of West Indian fans I was hoping that perhaps the victory and more particularly the manner of it would be a forerunner to the birth of a new dawn. In that moment the despair felt at many of the recent results of the team seemed like a bad dream. As time has passed and pragmatism has set in, such hope might be more the result of what dreams are made of than grounded on any empirical evidence. So more than a year later, it is not so much like hope being misplaced, but the journey that is being undertaken is long and difficult with every step forward being overtaken by two back. Keeping hope alive is thus most important.

However, mindful of the modern jargon of the sports psychologists that one must find something positive from any game, the hope was that we were witnessing in Shai not so much the birth but the blossoming of the next great West Indies batsman. Hopefully over the next few years he would take over the mantle of our premier batsman and in so doing continue a trend started eons ago with Headley, continuing through the Three Ws, Kanhai, Nurse and Sobers, Lloyd, Richards, Greenidge, Haynes, Richardson, Lara, Chanderpaul and many others.

The euphoria that swept the region naturally gave people hope that the impossible was indeed possible under the right circumstances; that to climb Mount Everest one needed to take that first step, and that whatever the odds, whatever the obstacles, if you keep your head down and work hard eventually your reward will become evident.

I could not help myself but to pen a follow-up to my letter of September 15th 2014 in response to a Claim from an Insurance Company that the club was responsible for damage caused to the windscreen of one of their insured because of the negligence of Shai in hitting a ball out of the ground. Though not one to gloat, it seemed a good idea that by doing so I would not only be recognizing his achievement, but with tongue in cheek I would be thanking the company for its indirect assistance in being a part of his development as he practiced. Like my first letter, I have never received a response, which was not unexpected.

When I thought of the sacrifice that all young athletes go through away from the spotlight while perfecting their skill by the repetitive drills needed in practice, the lonely hours in a gym or on the road to build stamina for that far-off day when your breakthrough achievement will grab the headlines, it left me with hope that my situation would resolve. I was in no way trying to suggest that the trials and tribulations I was experiencing had compared with their athletic excellence. What struck me was the thought that if you fail to prepare you should prepare to fail, and if at first you do not succeed you must try and try again. That I thought was the story of my life and at present it was only hope that it might end that was keeping me going.

The victory nevertheless was a welcome distraction from the drudgery of the fight I was continuing to endure daily. For a few hours I was able to forget everything—all the antics of Smith (especially the underhand ones); all the failings of the judicial system. Many times I felt as if those in authority wished that I would just disappear or worse still that the stress of it all would finally take its toll. Every day I meet someone who says they do not know how I got through it. I myself wondered if it would ever end.

The ability to just forget the pressing problems and relax was something that I was not able to do frequently, hence my sleeping problems and my recent hospitalization. Only on Friday afternoons when I knew that for the next forty-eight hours the daily problems would take a back seat, but then come Sunday night there would be that tightening feeling of anxiety within my chest as I had to face another problem. As soon as one was solved, another one came a-calling or one that had been pushed aside would raise its ugly head. Even as I write this my mind recalls matters that have to be dealt with, any of which could spell my doom.

Over the last few years I have had to accept the advice that I needed to let go of some of the anxiety I was feeling because of not being able to solve the problem I was facing. It was really a self-help measure which no doubt has prolonged my life. Many persons tried to give me hope that it would end soon, but sadly, more than a year after the euphoria of that outstanding victory, my hopes have been dashed or perhaps it might be better to state that the hard reality of what I am facing has suggested that there is no hope. I have lost count of the number of letters I have written pleading for assistance. In fact, I once pondered about simply publishing all the letters with a commentary on them, but that would be defeatist.

This state of affairs has had an effect on me. I would definitely not be human if it did not, and at times I feel that any glimmer of hope has been extinguished. For more than two years I have toyed with the idea of taking the matter down to the CCJ, but the thought of trying to reduce 15 years of hell into an Affidavit short enough but succinct enough to allow for an Application to appeal the Court of Appeal decision of October 2012, in time to get the matter before the CCJ, is daunting enough.

I have now reached the stage where I have minimal interest in anything related to the profession. This has not helped my cause, and in fact I no longer approach anyone in the profession for help. What is the point? In fact, I despise the profession and recent reports of the largesse that has been granted to a few has not in any way improved my mood.

I no longer attend the annual admittance of new entrants to the profession. If memory serves me, the last time I did so was in 2010. Besides my disillusionment, there are a myriad other reasons for not doing so. As one gets older it is natural that one's knowledge of persons entering the profession would not be as great. In my case it is also a reminder that my connection with the younger generations that had been maintained during a nearly twenty-five year teaching association with the Faculty of Law has come to an end. This was a casualty of the events that had occurred. Now my acquaintance with the future is somewhat paradoxically through the past, as I am more acquainted with the parents of the newly qualified.

This year I was invited by a distant relative to attend the call, but politely declined for not wanting, as I said, to disrupt same by hurling invective at those who tend to like ceremony over substance and would be in attendance. That may sound petulant, but given what I have experienced with the failure of the judicial system, to sit and listen to the exhortation to all the new admissions from the Chief Justice about what it means to be an Attorney and how an Attorney should act would be just an exercise in moving one's lips to utter useless 'long talk'. Soon most will realize when they experience the real world that like much else, this would be just a lot of hot air.

So as not to dampen what should be a momentous day in their lives by my disenchantment, however justified as to its correctness, I have just opted out. At this time when the Court is virtually a nomadic entity, much needs to be done to restore faith in the system as a whole. Hopefully it will be in my lifetime, but I do not hold out hope.

I have long concluded that I will not get, nor do I want, any plaudits from my colleagues for trying to do what was right. There has been offered a lot of empathy and 'long talk' about the myriad of challenges that I faced, but as to practical help, there was little at all. In fact I have received more practical help from outside these shores. I have become quite cynical about it all, but my hope in humanity has been preserved by the actions of a number of people who, while not being able to influence the major issues that I am facing, have within their own sphere done what they could to ease my problems. Their efforts have and will be much appreciated. I think of persons like Mrs. Vaughn and Mrs. Burrowes who would tend to any request even if it is outside their department in the Registry, and several others whose names are not at the tip of my tongue as I write.

CHAPTER 17

Close of Play

FOR SOME time now at the end of a day's play in professional cricket matches there is a ritual that is followed. It involves a warm-down set of exercises (something that at first did not make sense to me), perhaps an ice bath, to be followed by a post mortem of the day's play and then to plan strategy for the next day's play. The team analyst, an addition to the back room staff for most teams over the last decade, would be prominent in the review of what had transpired, as his job is to supply the data to be used to review strengths and weaknesses of the team and perhaps more importantly to provide opposition research to plan the tactics for the next day.

Cynics, among which might include persons of an older generation, might scoff at these methods in the belief that this facet of the modern game is counterproductive because it prevents players from thinking for themselves. Certainly it is a departure from the era of a shower and discussions over a beer, whether with your team mates or the opposition, during which some of the functions of the modern-day analyst would take place. There is benefit in both approaches, but as the saying goes if you fail to prepare... prepare to fail, and it is clear that as the modern game like many other aspects of life is data-driven, resort to data is essential for planning.

For me the main problem with such an approach is not that

I did not have any data by which to go on, but that I had no control of what it was used for that is the Court system and as such I had no control of my destiny. In many respects a post mortem of my situation can, like a traditional *post mortem*, only be useful to see what could have been done differently. Two words would suffice—Forensic Audit—which no doubt would send shivers down the back of most practitioners.

As I review the current state of play 16 years after the Partnership was ended, I must face the stark reality that I have recovered less than One Hundred and Twenty-Five Thousand dollars of the One Million Three Hundred Thousand in Judgments awarded. That figure does not include any credit for interest or costs or for that matter any award for my time or that of other Attorneys expended over these years, not to mention me never bothering to claim for other amounts be it contribution to severance or payments that were to be shared during the transitional period because I just could not be bothered.

No one is more aware of the impact it has had on me. Let me correct that—now that I have read Anya's heartfelt letter. What I find depressing is that persons who by the letters after their names appear to have intelligence that is greater than most, have not appeared or simply do not care to make a connection between what has transpired and the effect it would have on me personally and persons related thereto. Maybe they have but as one of life's lessons is "it is not my problem." I may now be forgiven for adopting that attitude when asked about records of Cottle Catford. I am sorry if it offends but I am warned that constant worry is going to hasten my demise.

The animus that is clearly evident in the filing by the usual suspects with respect to the missing money from the Client's account seeking to absolve the Watsons of any responsibility so that Mrs. Watson who gave a first class impersonation of

Lady Macbeth in her scheming can now dispose of the ill-gotten gains so that she may continue living as she pleases, not to mention to pay their fees for not only their obstruction but unethical behaviour, would be dismissed as a sick joke except that I was served with the Application having just returned from the funeral of Aurie Smith. Not only has she been a party to the looting of the accounts at Cottle Catford with her now deceased husband, but she has been aided and abetted by others in avoiding repayment and worse still facilitated by the misuse of the system by several.

Like the condemned man who is allowed one last request, I granted myself one last letter of the over fifty to the Registrar. I care not who I offend, and if you wonder why, reread what my young daughter has said.

I have had three responses to all my letters. I never expected any because in many respects the questions raised are not in the purview of the office of the Registrar to answer. But given that the CCJ has ruled that Attorneys should not write Judges directly on any matter, however dissatisfied they are with what is transpiring and however provoked they may feel I have as always tried to follow the rules except when I bent them by paying by yearly fees of over $2000 primarily in coins. I got a rebuke then, but restrained myself from commenting because my father was present. Nevertheless that rebuke said it all.

I am often asked how I maintain my sanity. I always respond by saying that I try to look for something humorous in what is going on. Even though I am dealing with events that have had such a profound impact on my ability to meet everyday commitments, not to mention on my life itself, there is precious little else that I can do.

There has been a cost both monetarily and otherwise to what I face and continue to face as is evident by my chronic insomnia, despite the best efforts of the West Indies to keep me awake with their recent horror shows. I try to keep smiling. I will not say a positive attitude has perhaps been keeping me alive coupled no doubt with the plans of the Almighty.

One day it must come to an end, but at least I have had my say. At that point US WILL PART.

APPENDIX 17A

SUPREME COURT OF BARBADOS

Manor Lodge Complex, Lodge Hill, St. Michael
Tel. No. (246) 427-5537 PBX: 535-9700   Fax No. (246) 426-2405
E-MAIL: registrarsupremecourt@barbados.gov.bb

27th November, 2018

Mr. Philip Nicholls
Attorney-at-Law
P.O. Box 93w
Christ Church

Dear Sir

Your letter dated November 20, 2018 refers.

My apologies on the date in responding. As soon as I have been given instructions, I will contact you.

Yours faithfully

Barbara Cooke-Alleyne, Q.C.
Registrar of the Supreme Court

Philip Vernon Nicholls
LL.B (Hons) UWI, LL.M (March)
Attorney-at-Law

September 4, 2018

Deputy Director Public Prosecution
Sir Frank Walcott Building
Culloden Roads
ST. MICHAEL

Dear Sir,

**Re: Director of Public Prosecutions v. Philip Nicholls, Cottle Catford & Co.
and First Caribbean International Bank**

I am in receipt of your letter of August 29, 2018 on the captioned subject which left me Dying With Laughter.(DWL).

As I have just returned from a stay in the ICU I can testify that laughter is indeed a great healer for one's ailment.

You may wonder what has given rise to this mirth. I can assure you it has nothing to do with any lingering effects of the medication I was given, but your statement to wit: "The matter is being investigated expeditiously, and a response will be provided as soon as that process is completed."

It is with regret that I state that my interaction with the office of the DPP over this matter makes me of the view that I would have a better chance of having a response to my letter if I asked those with knowledge of such matters to arrange a séance with persons in your office and one departed.

Yours faithfully,

Philip Nicholls
Attorney-at-Law

P. O. Box 89u
Christ Church
Barbados

Tel.   (246) 273-7282

email   cartwien@gmail.com

222

Philip Vernon Nicholls

LL.B (Hons) UWI, LL.M (Manch)
Attorney-at-Law

October 1, 2018

The Registrar
Supreme Court of Barbados
Supreme Court Complex
Whitepark Road
ST. MICHAEL

Dear Madam,

Re: Claim No. 893/17 Philip Vernon Nicholls v The Registrar of the Supreme Court et al

I was recently advised that the above captioned matter has been given a date of hearing of January 7th, 2019.

You may recall that at the only substantive hearing of the matter, which from memory was June 30th 2017, counsel for the AG's Chambers disclosed that the Third Respondent, the office of the DPP, had advised that it was their intention to reinstate the charges that had been dismissed against me in August of 2015 by making an application for the issuance of a Voluntary Bill of Indictment.

It was later learnt that an application had been made on the 27th February 2017. As a result, when the matter was scheduled for hearing later in the same year it was adjourned, firstly, because Justice Beckles was on holiday and then because it was listed before you when you were acting as a Judge. Subsequently I requested that the matter be taken off the list as it was in my opinion a waste of, not only my time but the Courts as well to seek the issuance of the letter that the US Embassy was requesting from your Office. By filing for the Voluntary Bill, the late DPP, who well knew of the reason why the request was made for the letter, knew that this would nullify such a letter.

It was therefore necessary for me to make a challenge to the Application for the Voluntary Bill of Indictment and this I did in September of 2017. The basis of my application was that the actions of the now deceased DPP were capricious, unlawful and an abuse of power in that he was seeking to refile charges eighteen

P. O. Box 93w
Christ Church

Barbados

Tel: (246) 571-7215

email: **cartwinn@gmail.com**

months after they had been dismissed for his failure to prosecute same in a timely manner.

Justice Richards on the 20th November, 2017 transferred my Application to be heard by the Chief Justice on the ground that as the original application by the DPP was before him, he would be the best person to deal with it. Despite numerous letters I have failed to get a date of hearing since then, so despite my Application being under a Certificate of Urgency, more than a year later it still has not been heard.

It is now 5 years since I was charged, which the US Embassy stated was the reason for the revocation of my Visa. It is three years since the charges were dismissed and it should be clear to anyone with a basic understanding of English that my rights under Section 18 of the Constitution have been and continue to be flagrantly violated by the delays in resolving this matter, so that for five years now I can not travel for any purpose, including to seek Health care and have never had one shred of evidence ever laid against me to justify the ridiculous charges that were filed.

As hearing of and determination of this Application No. 290/17 is essential to allow for 893/17 to proceed, may I ask if it is too much to expect that a date for hearing this matter in a relatively short time.

Yours faithfully,

Philip Nicholls

Cc: Attorney General of Barbados
Ondene Kirton, Attorney- at- Law

224

APPENDIX 17B

151/152 of 2004

Filed in early 2004 for money used personally by the Watson clan from the Client's Account of Cottle between 2000 and 2001; just over $100,000 has been repaid to me. Of course, the fact that I had to fund the account out of borrowings to keep the Firm going was totally irrelevant to the three jackasses who spouted the argument that the repayment must be made to me as to 32% and the remaining 68% to Watson and Griffith. As the transcript shows there is real doubt as to whether that 68 % was ever paid or from what source. Was it from money that Griffith and Springer lent to Mrs. Watson or was it the same loan that Mrs. Watson suggested her husband borrowed? Whichever, it means that they both Griffith and Watson according to Smith the primary jackass borrowed to repay themselves.

1612/1613 of 2005

Judgment obtained in September 2009. Appealed. Appeal dismissed by Court of Appeal in October 2013. Enforcement proceedings against Watson; still awaiting a decision since October 2014 as to whether the Judgment obtained was flawed per Jackass 1 so that a charging Order over his property can be sold.

As against Griffith all attempts to summon her to attend Court from early 2017 failed. A new Court date was promised in early 2018, but I am unaware of same.

Result: the Judgements which with interest and costs

amount now to over two million dollars are not worth the paper they are written on.

211 of 2012 Nicholls Vs Sagicor Life

Despite the clear Judgment of the Court Sagicor deducted 25% of the amount awarded and paid it to the BRA. To this date they have never formally written me indicating the reason for so doing although they have responded to legal challenges on the ground that it was Withholding Tax. I am presently trying to finish my Xmas present to them in the form of a suit for the actions and the damages it has caused me.

893/17

Application for Madamus vs the Registrar to issue the letter that the US Embassy has requested since July 2016 to process my visa Application is now listed to be heard in January of 2019.

290/17

Application by now deceased DPP in February 2017 to refile the charges laid against me on October 30th, 2013 and dismissed for want of prosecution on August 13th, by means of Voluntary Bill of Indictment on November 20 2017 my application challenging this was transferred to the CJ as the VBI was made to him. To date neither has been heard.

APPENDIX 17C

List of Letters to Registrar and the Chief Justice

2013
February 11, 2013
February 19, 2013
April 5, 2013
March 18, 2013
June 19, 2013
June 28, 2013
September 18, 2013
December 12, 2013

2014
February 4, 2014
March 6, 2014
March 31, 2014
May 12, 2014
July 15, 2014
September 16, 2014
November 13, 2014

2015
January 15, 2015
April 2, 2015
April 13, 2015
November 4, 2015
September 22, 2015

2016

January 4, 2016
March 15, 2016
April 11, 2016
April 26, 2016
April 27, 2016
June 8, 2016
June 9, 2016
June 21, 2016
July 6, 2016
July 12, 2016
July 26, 2016
September 2, 2016
October 7, 2016
October 10, 2016
November 10, 2016
November 11, 2016
November 16, 2016
December 8, 2016

2017
March 6, 2017
March 7, 2017
April 12, 2017
June 8, 2017
July 19, 2017
October 3, 2017
November 6, 2017
December 19, 2017

2018
January 5, 2018
February 28, 2018

March 14, 2018
April 4, 2018
May 30, 2018
July 23, 2018
August 27, 2018
October 1, 2018
October 15, 2018
October 22, 2018
November 20, 2018

APPENDIX 17D

Director of Public Prosecutions
Chambers, 4th Floor, Frank Walcott Building,
Culloden Road, St Michael, BB14018

Our Ref: DPP 6

Tel. Nos: **(246) 535-0495**
         (246) 535-0496
Fax No. **(246) 271-2338**
E-mail:dppbarbados@caribsurf.com

29th August, 2018

Mr. Philip Nicholls
Attorney-at-Law
P.O. Box 93 W
Christ Church

Dear Mr. Nicholls

Re: Director of Public Prosecutions v. Philip Nicholls, Cottle Catford & Company and First Caribbean International Bank

The Office of the Director of Public Prosecutions acknowledges receipt of your letter dated 16th August, 2018 and received on 20th August, 2018 concerning the matter at caption.

2.   The matter is being investigated expeditiously, and a response will be provided as soon as that process is completed.

Yours faithfully,

Oliver Thomas
Crown Counsel
for Director of Public Prosecutions

230

Philip Vernon Nicholls

LL.B (Hons) UWI, LL.M (Merch)
Attorney-at-Law

November 2, 2018

Director of Public Prosecution
Sir Frank Walcott Building
Culloden Roads
ST. MICHAEL.

Attention: Mrs. Donna Babb- Agard Q.C.

Dear Madam,

I enclose a copy of two letters to your office dated August 16, 2018 and September 4, 2018, the latter a response to a letter signed by Mr. Oliver Thomas dated August 29, 2018 for your attention. I can only presume that Mr. Thomas knows absolutely nothing of the farce that has befallen because of the malevolent actions of the former DPP, Charles Leacock now deceased, given the manner of his response.

This month marks just over 5 years since my arrest and subsequent charge for two offences. As you should be aware the charges were dismissed for want of prosecution on August 13th, 2015 after my tenth appearance in Court after twenty-two months. The dismissal was prompted by the failure of the Commissioner of Police to complete discovery that the Magistrate on two prior occasions had ordered to be done, after empty promises to this effect had been made for a better part of a year while seeking further adjournments.

Another reason for this was the failure of anyone from your office to be present to assist with the prosecution after the prosecution, in making a case for an adjournment to be granted, had advised that he had requested and been assured that someone would be coming to take over the prosecution. If you doubt me you might want to check with Sergeant Watson who was the lead prosecutor in the Magistrate's Court but who is now with your chambers.

The farce that was taking place at the time beggars belief when section 18 of the Constitution stipulates that once charged a person should have a speedy trial. It is a section that the office of the DPP appears not to have any regard for especially in light of the fact that having failed over twenty two months to start a preliminary

P. O. Box 03w
Christ Church
Barbados

Tel   (246) 171-7119

email   carteinn@gmail.com

enquiry, it should now seek to have a second bite at the cherry by filing, fifteen months later in February 2017, an application to reinstate the charges against me by means of a voluntary bill of Indictment. I am sure that this decision had nothing to do with my filing, six weeks prior, a civil suit against the Department and others.

While I must acknowledge that during the nine years between the alleged offence and the refiling of the charges you were not the substantive DPP, you certainly knew of the actions by your former colleague. Given that several judicial and other legal luminaries throughout the region have advised me that this action was high handed, capricious and a clear abuse of office, the continued oversight of this process by you must now be your sole responsibility.

I have made it clear that I do not seek any favours from anyone. What I have asked and continue to ask is that my rights not only be respected but that they not be trampled with, which is clearly happening because although the charges have been dismissed, for over three years now, because of the ridiculous application it is preventing me from clearing my name with the US Embassy which was tarnished by the vindictive actions of your predecessor.

In closing I will state that the ludicrous money laundering charges filed against me for which there is and can be no evidence however long you dig continues to cause me much grief. My grief pales in comparison with that of my father however, who when you were a toddler was attached to the forerunner of the DPP's office. As one who is cognizant of what money laundering is as well as the standards for a prosecution he has been forced to watch silently and with incredulity how his legacy of service as a Public Officer culminating as Chief Parliamentary Counsel is bastardised by the actions of a few in an attempt to boost numbers to report to International agencies. One of the results is that the country has been deemed a Haven for money laundering, a ludicrous assertion given the level of money transactions here compared to other jurisdictions. For that designation the policy of your department, started under your predecessor in flinging money laundering charges at any accusation of a financial crime, is solely responsible.

2

232

I intend to make this letter known to the wider public. I will give you the opportunity of having a reply published at the same time if you manage to respond by November 16, 2018. Given the pace at which your department moves that may well be impossible but that is clearly beyond my control. The fall out I really do not care about, just as you have shown scant regard for what the actions of your department have done to me in the past and continue to do.

Yours faithfully,

Philip Nicholls
Attorney-at-Law

Cc: Mr. Dale Marshall Q.C., Attorney General

Philip Vernon Nicholls

LL.B (Hons) UWI, LL.M (Manch)
Attorney-at-Law

November 20, 2018

The Registrar
Supreme Court of Barbados
Manor Lodge Complex
Lodge Hill
ST. MICHAEL

Attention: Mrs. Barbara Cooke-Alleyne

Dear Madam,

Re: 290/17 and other matters involving Philip Nicholls

Today marks one year since the matter at Caption was transferred to be heard by the Chief Justice. As I have drawn to your attention several times in the past despite the application being Certified as Urgent and despite the common knowledge that until this is resolves my application for the reissuance of my Visa that was revoked because of the fiasco of my arrest, appears to be of little concern with respect to scheduling a date of hearing. In your letter to me of October 9, 2018 you had indicated that you had passed my request for a date to be set to the Chief Justice but as I have heard nothing further from you or from the office of the Chief Justice I must presume it has fallen on deaf ears.

My present letter is the latest of over 50 written since 2013 with respect to matters that are outstanding before the Courts and which continue to affect me, not only in my ability to practice but to live a normal life. It is clear from this inaction that there is absolutely no concern to the plight that I am daily facing which will only intensify after March 31st 2019 when, if I am unable to satisfy a judgment against me, I will be held in contempt of Court.

At least it gives me about four month to prepare and hopefully your office will arrange with the relevant authorities to have available the necessary medical equipment and treatment to allow me to continue breathing when that day arises and I am held in contempt because despite judgments amounting to in excess of two million dollars Which have been granted in my favour I have been unable to enforce same despite my trying several avenues to do so.

P. O. Box 93w
Christ Church

Barbados

Tel: (246) 571-7215

email: **cartwinn@gmail.com**

234

Enclosed is a list of the dates of the letters that I have written. I am not bothering to enclose copies of them because once you have received one you virtually have seen all. Hopefully my readers will be able to determine who has been trying and who has been drawing a salary (I am not referring to you) under false pretenses because when broken down a refusal to do, unless there is a just reason, what one is appointed to do must be considered a dereliction of duty.

At a time when the rank and file are being sent home in keeping with the austerity cuts of Government it may be of interest to those aggrieved especially ones who have been hard working that perhaps 5 or 6 of these could have been saved if the cuts had taken into account productivity at all levels.

Yours faithfully,

Philip Nicholls

Blessing at Book Launch at The Cricket Legends, March 24th 2016. Left to right: Dean Jeffrey Gibson, MC for the evening Roland Holder, and the author Philip Nicholls.

Invited guests at the Book Launch. Far right (third row) is Maxine Babb, the last surviving employee of Cottle Catford. In front of her is Auntie Angela Nicholls. To left of the picture is Dame Avis Carrington.

With Dennis Morrison, President of the Court of Appeal of Jamaica, the best lecturer I ever had and a valued friend together with Beverley Smith Hinkson, my book distributor, at my Book Launch in Jamaica on July 29th 2016.

Dinner with Dennis Morrison. Former students of Dennis Morrison at Norman Manley Law School held a dinner in his honour at Champers on November 12th 2015. Left to right in front row: Andrew Pilgrim, Marguerite Knight Williams, Dennis Morrison, Gillian Clarke, Marguerite Woodstock Riley. Back row: Lorna Duncan, Marlon Gordon, Philp Pilgrim, Philip Nicholls, Alicia Richards Hill, Junior Allsopp, Debbie Fraser, Toni Jones, Errol Niles.

Signing books after the launch for Sherlock Wall, a long-time associate at Cottle Catford. To his right is Henderson Holmes, the Executive Director of BIBA. Next to me is Roland Holder and in the background my hardworking publisher Carol Pitt.

Listening to Charmain Delice-Hunte, one of my colleagues, at the Book Launch.

Wonders will never cease. The girls decide to visit Pickwick Cricket Club at Foursquare St. Philip with me. Probably cost me lunch. While growing up they always grumbled that I spent too much time at that 'boring' place.

With my Goddaughter Erica Hinkson, tireless promoter of my book, at the Book Signing at Sky Mall.

With Harold Hoyte, Editor Emeritus of the *Nation*, at Book Signing at Sky Mall.

With Dr. Ricardo Coppin, an old Kolij schoolmate, at Book Signing at Sky Mall.

With my Godfather Sir George Alleyne and Member of Parliament Ralph Thorne Q.C at the Test Match vs Pakistan at Kensington Oval in May of 2017.

With the Hope Brothers, Kyle (to my immediate right) and Shai, at Pickwick Cricket Club just before they left for the tour of England in 2017.

With my long-suffering trainer Kim in the Gym. My smile indicates it was taken before my session with her.

With Cammie Smith, recipient of one of the awards to mark our 50th Anniversary of Independence. Cammie is one of the most jovial people I know, a former President of the BCA, and former West Indian cricketer.

Being presented with a Long Service Award by President of the Barbados Cricket Association Joel 'Big Bird' Garner, a West Indian Legend and good friend at the BCA Awards Ceremony in 2016.

TRANSCRIPT OF EVIDENCE

The following pages, almost 100 in number, are the Transcript of Evidence given by Vernon Smith and Delvina Watson on April 24th 2014, before Justice Richards re the repayment of $270,000 paid to Delvina Watson by Allan Watson out of the Client's Account at Cottle Catford.

Despite not defending the claim filed in 2004, it took three years before Smith paid 32% of the Judgment to me, claiming that this plus 68% received by Griffith and Watson satisfied the Judgement. Now Smith was not the Attorney for the Plaintiff, so just on what basis he could claim to be stating that the basis of settlement of the Claim is beyond me in the first place?

That apart, other than a cheque to me for the 32%, there is considerable doubt as to whether the rest of the money was actually repaid. And if it was, it meant that money was being repaid by Mrs. Watson to Griffith, and more amazingly to her husband, who paid it to herself from the Accounts of Cottle between 2000 and 2001 and at a time when he was no longer connected to Cottle.

Further was the claim that the source of the money was from loans made to either of the Watsons, which would mean in one case that he borrowed money from Griffith to repay her and himself, or she borrowed the money from Griffith et al to repay Griffith and her husband. And this scheme was not considered Money Laundering; hardly surprising as Smith was always in the office of the late DPP ensuring that his fur was clean, similar to how cats clean themselves. To get the transcripts prepared cost me $1,100.

1   that correct?

2   A.   It was not that the suit was not -- that the suit

3   was not defended. It was the defendant consented to

4   judgment, admitted the claim and consented to judgment.

5   Q.   So the claim was recorded as a judgment in

6   default; is that correct?

7   A.   It is not in default, it was a consent judgment.

8   Q.   As a consent judgment, was the judgment

9   subsequently settled by the defendant?

10   A.   Yes, the judgment was settled by the defendant:

11 The judgment was paid.

12   Q.   In what manner?

13   THE COURT: Just a minute counsel.

14   MR. NICHOLLS: Sorry.

15 BY MR. NICHOLLS:

16   Q.   In what manner?

17   A.   Just like how any debt is paid.

18   Q.   The defendant the plaintiff in the matter was

19 Cottle Catford and Company, was the amount of the judgment

20 approximately $270,000 paid to Cottle Catford and Company?

21   A.   Yes, it was paid. The whole debt was paid to

22 Cottle Catford and Company which was the company that was

23 dissolved on the 31 of December, 2002.

24   Q.   Do you have?

25   THE COURT: Just a minute.

NOS. 151 AND 152 OF 2004 COTTLE CATFORD & CO. (a Firm)v.
DELVINA WATSON

1   MR. NICHOLLS: Sorry.

2   THE COURT: Which was dissolved on, on what date

3 counsel? Which was dissolved on?

4   THE WITNESS: On the 31st of December, 2002.

5   THE COURT: Okay. Yes?

6 BY MR. NICHOLLS:

7   Q. Are you aware that Cottle Catford and Company

8 continued to practice or continued to act as

9 attorneys-at-law after 2002?

10   THE COURT: After 31st of December?

11   MR. NICHOLLS: 31st of December, 2002.

12   A. I.

13 BY MR. NICHOLLS:

14   Q. Are you aware that Cottle Catford and Company

15 continued to be in existence after 2002?

16   A. No, it did not. Not the one that --

17   THE COURT: No. That's not what he is asking you. He

18 is asking you if you are aware that Cottle Catford

19 continued.

20   MR. BASS: He can't answer that.

21   THE WITNESS: With respect, Madam, it did not continue.

22 It dissolved on the 31st of December, 2002. The Cottle

23 Catford that --

24 BY MR. NICHOLLS:

25   Q. Ma'am, Mr. Smith is being asked questions not

1   on the law. He said it dissolved in 2002?

2   A.   Yes.

3   Q.   Cottle Catford dissolved in 2002 or a partnership

4   dissolved in 2002 in your opinion?

5   A.   Cottle Catford is the registered business name of

6   the Firm of Cottle Catford, comprising at the time when it

7   was dissolved the three partners.

8   Q.   Right?

9   A.   Mr. Watson, Ms. Joyce Griffith and Mr. Phillip

10   Nicholls.

11   Q.   Right?

12   A.   That dissolved.

13   Q.   Okay?

14   A.   Ceased to exist.

15   Q.   Thank you. When the suit was filed in 2004 in the

16   name of Cottle Catford, did you make this objection to the

17   suit?

18   THE COURT: You mean an objection on the basis that the

19   plaintiff did not exist.

20   MR. NICHOLLS: Did not exist.

21   THE WITNESS: With respect, Madam.

22   THE COURT: Yes or no.

23   MR. NICHOLLS: Yes or no.

24   THE COURT: Yes or no Mr. Smith, this one is simple.

25   THE WITNESS: When Cottle Catford in 2004 sued the

248

NOS. 151 AND 152 OF 2004 COTTLE CATFORD & CO. (a Firm) v.
DELVINA WATSON

1   defendant in this matter, it was the Partnership of Cottle

2   Catford that existed before 2002 that sued Ms. Watson.

3   MR. NICHOLLS: Ma'am, I would like to remind,

4   Mr. Smith, he is under oath, because in his affidavit and in

5   the affidavit of Mrs. Watson they keep saying that

6   Mr. Watson and Mr. Griffith exited the Partnership in 2003.

7   How can a suit filed in 2004 be on that basis?

8   THE WITNESS: The law is, Madam, that on the

9   dissolution.

10   THE COURT: You are not here for expert evidence on the

11   law. You are just here to respond to the questions asked by

12   counsel.

13   THE WITNESS: And I am responding to it.

14   MR. NICHOLLS: Ma'am, with respect, Mr. Smith, has been

15   down this line, he has been thrown out by the Court of

16   Appeal on it. There was a plaintiff in the name of Cottle

17   Catford and Company who had --

18   THE COURT: And the question is still the same. Did

19   you take an objection to Cottle Catford bringing a suit for

20   debt against your client? Did you take an objection?

21   THE WITNESS: A firm on dissolution --

22   THE COURT: Did you take an objection, counsel?

23   THE WITNESS: Take objection to what, Madam?

24   MR. NICHOLLS: To the suit.

25   THE COURT: To the suit.

NOS. 151 AND 152 OF 2004 COTTLE CATFORD & CO. (a Firm)v.
DELVINA WATSON

1   MR. NICHOLLS: Yes or no.

2   THE WITNESS: To what ma'am?

3   THE COURT: To suit against your client on the basis

4   that there was no entity known as Cottle Catford.

5   THE WITNESS: I did not take objection because there

6   was no need to take an objection, because the Cottle Catford

7   and Company that sued Mrs. Watson was the Cottle Catford and

8   Company that existed before 2002. There was no need to take

9   an objection in the circumstances and that was the company

10 to which Mr. Watson owed the debt, that is the company or

11 the Partnership to which Mrs. Watson owed the debt.

12 BY MR. NICHOLLS:

13   Q. Mr. Smith, you have just stated before that there

14 was a consent order in 2004 and the name of the plaintiff

15 was Cottle Catford and Company a Firm is that correct?

16 THE COURT: Was the name of the plaintiff in the 2004

17 matter Cottle Catford and Company a Firm?

18 THE WITNESS: A Firm, yes, ma'am, and that was the Firm

19 comprising the three partners Watson, Griffith and Nicholls.

20 MR. NICHOLLS: But, Mr. Smith, you have just indicated

21 that Watson and Griffith left the Firm at the end of 2003.

22 THE COURT: Is that correct to your knowledge?

23 MR. NICHOLLS: End of 2002.

24 THE COURT: To your knowledge, did Watson and Griffith

25 leave the Firm at the end of 2003?

1   THE WITNESS: They continued the Firm.

2   THE COURT: Is it to your knowledge?

3   THE WITNESS: They continued the Firm for the purposes

4   —

5   THE COURT: The question is, the question is --

6   THE WITNESS: But I am answering it.

7   THE COURT: Is it to your knowledge that these two

8 persons left the Firm at the end of 2003?

9   THE WITNESS: Not the one that sued in 2004, because

10 after the dissolution of partnership, the Partnership

11 continues for the purposes of —

12   MR. BABB: Settling accounts.

13   THE WITNESS: -- of settling accounts.

14   THE COURT: No, you cannot be speaking him when he is

15 giving evidence.

16   THE WITNESS: No, no.

17   THE COURT: You cannot be doing that Mr. Babb.

18   MR. BABB: My apologies.

19   THE WITNESS: No, no, for the purposes of settling the

20 accounts —

21   THE COURT: Just a minute please.

22   THE WITNESS: -- and winding up the Partnership it

23 continues, the law clearly states it; the Act states it.

24 The Partnership states it that all the powers of the

25 Partnership of the partners continue for the purposes of

1   winding up the Partnership, that is, collecting the debts

2   and collecting the assets and sorting out the accounts.

3   BY MR. NICHOLLS:

4   Q.   So, Mr. Smith, on that basis all the three

5   partners are liable; is that correct?

6   A.   All three of the partners are?

7   Q.   Liable for debts and -- all three partners are

8   liable for the debts?

9   A.   All three partners are liable for the debts.

10   Q.   Now, were you aware the basis for the suit in

11   2004? Were you aware the basis for the suit in 2004?

12   A.   The basis for the?

13   Q.   For the suit in 2004?

14   A.   Yes.

15   Q.   Right. To recover money from debts due to losses?

16   A.   Yes.

17   Q.   Were you aware in 2000?

18   THE COURT: Just a minute counsel.

19   BY MR. NICHOLLS:

20   Q.   Sorry. Were you aware in 2004 that the money that

21   was being recovered was money paid from the Clients'

22   Accounts of Cuttle Catford?

23   A.   That the?

24   Q.   Yes or no, were you aware?

25   THE COURT: I don't think he heard you.

NOS. 151 AND 152 OF 2004 COTTLE CATFORD & CO. (a Firm)v.
DELVINA WATSON

1   BY MR. NICHOLLS:

2   Q.   Were you aware in 2004 that the claim that was

3   being made about €270,000 was for money that was paid from

4   Cottle Catford Clients' Account?

5   A.   Yes, yes, I am very aware.

6   Q.   Does?

7   THE COURT: Just a minute.

8   BY MR. NICHOLLS:

9   Q.   Does the Clients' Account belong to the partners?

10   A.   It belongs to the all the partners.

11   THE COURT: The Client Account. The Client Account is

12   what he is asking about.

13   THE WITNESS: All the accounts are Cottle Catford's

14   accounts.

15   THE COURT: He is asking specifically about the Client

16   Account. Your answer is: "The Client Account belongs to

17   the partners." That is your response?

18   THE WITNESS: Yes, all the accounts of Cottle Catford

19   belong to all the partners.

20   THE COURT: Including the Client Account?

21   MR. SMITH Q.C: Including the Clients' Accounts. All

22   the accounts are Cottle Catford's accounts.

23   BY MR. NICHOLLS:

24   Q.   Is there --

25   THE COURT: Just a minute counsel.

1   MR. NICHOLLS: Sorry, ma'am.

2   Mr. Smith?

3   THE COURT: So the Client Account is not a Trust

4 Account?

5   THE WITNESS: All accounts are Cottle Catford's

6 accounts.

7   THE COURT: So the Client Account is not a Trust

8 Account?

9   THE WITNESS: It's a credit account -- a Trust Account

10 held by Cottle Catford and Company. Cottle Catford and

11 Company are the signatories and the only signatories to that

12 account as they are to all the other accounts of Cottle

13 Catford.

14 BY MR. NICHOLLS:

15   Q. Mr. Smith, is there a difference between a

16 signatory to account and owner of the account?

17   A. All the accounts are owned by Cottle Catford,

18 whether they are office accounts, Clients' Accounts. All

19 accounts are Cottle Catford's accounts.

20   THE COURT: That's not the question. The question is,

21 if there is a difference between the owner of an account and

22 a signatory to the account.

23   THE WITNESS: The owners are the signatories to the

24 accounts.

25   THE COURT: In this.

NOS. 151 AND 152 OF 2004 COTTLE CATFORD & CO. (a Firm)v.
DELVINA WATSON

1   THE WITNESS: In all the Partnership's accounts.

2   BY MR. NICHOLLS:

3   Q.   Are you —

4   A.   The signatories are the people.   They are the only

5   people who can control the account or withdraw from the

6   accounts.

7   Q.   Are you aware Mr. Smith that several other

8   employees of Cottle Catford were signatories of the

9   accounts, even though they were not partners, including a

10   relative of yours, who is an attorney-at-law.

11   A.   They are not owners of the accounts.

12   THE COURT: So you are saying some of the signatories

13   to the Client Account were not owners of the account.   Is

14   that what you are saying?

15   THE WITNESS: But they would have to have the authority

16   of the partners.

17   THE COURT: That's not what I am asking.   Are you

18   saying that some of the signatories then to the Client

19   Account were not the owners of Client Account.   Is that what

20   you are saying?

21   THE WITNESS: Signatories would not be the owners of

22   the accounts necessary.

23   THE COURT: Would not necessary be the owners of the

24   Account.

25   THE WITNESS: Not necessary be the owner of the

255

1   Account.

2   BY MR. NICHOLLS:

3   Q.   So the fact that a partner was a signatory does

4   not make him an owner?

5   A.   Only the partners would be the owners of the

6   accounts. Only the partners.

7   Q.   So when you ceased being a partner, do you own the

8   Account still?

9   A.   When you ceased to be a partner, the accounts that

10 were held by the Partnership are still owned by the partners

11 for the purposes of the winding up.

12   Q.   Do you recall on or about the 16th of April, 2007,

13 issuing a cheque approximately $100,000 in the name, sorry,

14 30th of April, 2007, issuing a cheque for approximately

15 $100,000 in the name of Phillip Vernon Nicholls?

16   A.   Yes, I recall issuing a cheque to Phillip

17 Nicholls.

18   THE COURT: In what sum please?

19   MR. NICHOLLS: $100,000.

20   THE WITNESS: $100,000.

21   MR. NICHOLLS: 491.16.

22   THE COURT: Of approximately $100,000.

23 BY MR. NICHOLLS:

24   Q.   And do you recall sending that cheque to Phillip

25 Nicholls on the cover of a letter addressed to Messrs Cuttle

1 Catford and Co., at Alphonso House, Attention Mr. Phillip

2 Nicholls?

3   A.   Yes.   That's correct.

4   Q.   Now is this the same, so what you are saying is

5 this was sent to Cottle Catford and Co., who did not exist

6 at the time?

7   A.   That was not the Cottle Catford in respect of whom

8 the debt was paid to.

9   Q.   So who was the debt paid to, may I ask?

10   A.   It was paid to Phillip Nicholls as a partner of

11 the previous Cottle Catford which was dissolved.

12   Q.   How long have you been an attorney in Barbados?

13   THE COURT: Just a minute counsel.

14   MR. NICHOLLS: Sorry.

15   THE WITNESS: I beg your pardon?

16 BY MR. NICHOLLS:

17   Q.   How long have you been an attorney in Barbados

18 Mr. Smith?

19   A.   How long I have?

20   Q.   Have you been an attorney in Barbados?

21   A.   I have been an attorney since 1974.

22   Q.   Forty years.   In that time have you had many

23 transactions with Cottle Catford?

24   A.   Numerous transactions with Cottle Catford.

25   Q.   Have you ever written a cheque for one of the

1   partners?

2   THE COURT: I am writing.

3   MR. NICHOLLS: Sorry ma'am. In that time --

4   THE COURT: Had numerous transactions.

5   MR. NICHOLLS: -- with Cottle Catford.

6   BY MR. NICHOLLS:

7   Q. Have you ever written a cheque in one of the names

8   of the partners?

9   A. I can't recall. I can't recall.

10   Q. Do you usually write cheques in the names --

11   THE COURT: Please Mr. Nicholls.

12   MR. NICHOLLS: Sorry, sorry, ma'am.

13   THE COURT: It only happens like that on T V.

14   MR. NICHOLLS: Yes, sorry, ma'am. My apologies.

15   You don't recall.

16   THE COURT: You can't recall writing a cheque to --

17   MR. NICHOLLS: -- in the name of one of the partners.

18   THE COURT: Oh yes.

19 BY MR. NICHOLLS:

20   Q. Did you usually write cheques in the name of

21 Cottle Catford? Did you usually write cheques in the name

22 of Cottle Catford?

23   A. I would have written cheques to Cottle Catford and

24 Company.

25   Q. So you recognise the distinction between Cottle

1   name of one of the partners and not Cottle Catford?

2   A.   If you read the letter that I wrote to Phillip

3   Nicholls with the cheque of $100,000 it sets out the

4   reference and the circumstances under which it was paid.

5   Q.   It does. And I would quote, ma'am, it says?

6   A.   And it was written.

7   Q.   That it was in full satisfaction of my 32 percent

8   share in Cottle Catford.

9   A.   That's correct.

10   Q.   Inclusive of all interest accrued, together with

11 tax costs?

12   A.   That's correct, and it was your share of the debt

13 owed by Mrs. Watson to Cottle Catford and Company which

14 comprised three partners.

15   Q.   And who received the rest of the debt?

16   A.   Beg your pardon?

17   Q.   Who received the rest of the debt? Who received

18 the rest of the debt?

19   A.   They received their share of the debt: Mr. Watson

20 and Mr. Griffith.

21   Q.   Did you write them a cheque too?

22   A.   Yes, I think I did. Yes, I did.

23   Q.   Can you produce those cheques?

24   A.   No.

25   Q.   Why not?

NOS. 151 AND 152 OF 2004 CUTTLE CATFORD & CO. (a Firm)v.
DELVINA WATSON

1   A.   Those cheques are not.

2   Q.   Bank records are kept for seven years?

3   A.   I have a receipt. They issued me receipts of

4   having received --

5   Q.   Ma'am it seems --

6   THE COURT: Just a minute. I wrote them a cheque as

7   well. I do not have -- he said he doesn't have the?

8   THE WITNESS: I do not have those cheques.

9   MR. NICHOLLS: He has a receipt, I did not ask

10   Mr. Smith if he has the receipt. I asked Mr. Smith if he

11   wrote them a cheque, if he could produce the cheque, if not

12   the cheque, do you have a record in the Firm whether in your

13   ledger that --

14   THE COURT: One thing at a time.

15   MR. NICHOLLS: Sorry.

16   THE COURT: You'd spoken about the cheque. He cannot

17   produce the cheque. You are asking him now whether his Firm

18   can produce a ledger.

19   MR. NICHOLLS: A ledger, an entry or anything. A stub,

20   anything reflecting that he wrote cheques to Phillip

21   Nicholls, Allan Watson and Joyce Griffith.

22   THE WITNESS: A letter was sent to them as well.

23   THE COURT: He didn't ask you --

24   THE WITNESS: In the same vein.

25   THE COURT: He did not ask you about a letter. Look at

1   no counsel.

2   THE WITNESS: In actual fact.

3   THE COURT: Counsel, counsel, the question is read my

4   lips please, if you have difficulty hearing. Counsel, the

5   question is —

6   THE WITNESS: I am hearing.

7   THE COURT: -- does the Firm, does your firm have any

8   entry in a ledger? Not a letter, a ledger of the Firm where

9   the payment to the other two partners would be?

10   THE WITNESS: We would have that in our accounts.

11   THE COURT: Okay.

12   MR. SMITH Q.C: But those accounts are --

13   THE COURT: Your Firm would have that entry?

14   THE WITNESS: Those would have been in our accounts.

15 BY MR. NICHOLLS:

16   Q.   Can you produce them?

17   A.   No.

18   Q.   Why not?

19   A.   Because they are not available.

20   Q.   Madam, I'll like to make a --

21   THE COURT: Just a minute please.

22   Yes, Mr. Nicholls?

23   MR. NICHOLLS: Madam, as the core of this matter is the

24   receipt of this money and where I have acknowledged

25   receiving the money and depositing it into a bank account, I

NOS. 151 AND 152 OF 2004 CUTTLE CATFORD & CO. (a Firm)v.
DELVINA WATSON

1   am requesting that the records of Smith and Smith which is

2   Smith and Smith which were previously ordered I believe by

3   Justice Crane-Scott or certainly in another matter be

4   produced to substantiate that these cheques were written to

5   Allan Watson and Joyce Griffith.

6   THE COURT: So you want them to produce for an

7   acknowledgment?

8   MR. NICHOLLS: Not the acknowledgment, ma'am, I would

9   like them because, ma'am --

10   THE COURT: What do you want produced?

11   MR. NICHOLLS: I want either a ledger entry, a cheque

12 stub, a Client's Account showing deficit, nothing to do with

13 anything else. All relating to the payment of these funds.

14 Nothing. I don't want anything else from Mr. Smith, ma'am,

15 I am only interested in the cheques paid that he said were

16 paid to Allan Watson and Joyce Griffith.

17   THE WITNESS: In actual fact, Madam, I have -- there

18 are two receipts which were filed --

19   MR. NICHOLLS: Madam, Mr. Smith cannot lead evidence of

20 a receipt not signed by him. If he wants to lead evidence of

21 a receipt signed by Allan Watson or Joyce Griffith, bring

22 them here.

23   THE WITNESS: They are here.

24   MR. NICHOLLS: Not the receipts.

25   THE WITNESS: You can't get those. You can't get

1   those.

2   MR. NICHOLLS: Ma'am, Mr. Allan Watson.

3   THE COURT: The application as I understand it, is for

4   you to produce —

5   THE WITNESS: They are not available.

6   THE COURT: Something from your Firm.

7   THE WITNESS: They are not available.

8   THE COURT: Why are they not available.

9   THE WITNESS: They are not available.

10   THE COURT: Why?

11   THE WITNESS: Because we don't keep cheques that long.

12 We don't keep cheques that long.

13   MR. NICHOLLS: Ma'am, I am was told by the Inland

14 Revenue up to the other day that you cannot by law dispose

15 of anything under seven years.

16   MR. BABB: Hearsay.

17   MR. NICHOLLS: Still within seven years. The seven

18 years expired last week, so it's just convenient that he

19 destroyed them last week.

20   THE WITNESS: Don't have them.

21   THE COURT: But the ledger entry would have --

22   MR. NICHOLLS: Would still be there.

23   THE COURT: -- been destroyed as well?

24   MR. NICHOLLS: No.

25   THE COURT: The ledger entry would be nonexistent as

NOS. 151 AND 152 OF 2004 COTTLE CATFORD & CO. (a Firm) v.
DELVINA WATSON

1   wo117

2   THE WITNESS: The?

3   THE COURT: The ledger entry.

4   THE WITNESS: Those would be -- in actual fact those

5   are actually evident by the receipts --

6   MR. NICHOLLS: No.

7   THE WITNESS: -- issued --

8   THE COURT: That is not what counsel is asking you for.

9   THE WITNESS: I am saying that we don't, we wouldn't

10 have need for those.

11   THE COURT: You would have need?

12   THE WITNESS: We would have to keep those. We have the

13 receipts.

14   THE COURT: So they would be no ledger entry at Smith

15 and Smith?

16   THE WITNESS: No. No ledger entries. No ledger

17 entries.

18 BY MR. NICHOLLS:

19   Q. Mr. Smith?

20   THE COURT: Just a minute counsel.

21   THE WITNESS: In actual fact, if I am not mistaken,

22 Madam, these moneys were paid by cheques which were sent

23 to — which were paid to Smith and Smith for Mrs. Watson.

24   THE COURT: I beg your pardon?

25   THE WITNESS: Moneys which paid Mr. Watson and

1   Mr. Griffith were moneys that were borrowed by Mrs. Watson

2   to pay them.

3   BY MR. NICHOLLS:

4   Q.   May I ask from whom?

5   A.   Mr. Springer was one of people who paid them.

6   Q.   Mr. springer?

7   A.   Mr. Michael Springer.

8   THE COURT: Just a minute moneys paid to Mrs. Griffith

9   and Mr. Watson.

10   THE WITNESS: Were paid by cheques from Mr. Springer.

11   THE COURT: Were from moneys borrowed by them? Were

12   from moneys borrowed by Mr. Watson?

13   THE WITNESS: By Mrs. Watson.

14   BY MR. NICHOLLS:

15   Q.   And is that?

16   THE COURT: Just a minute.

17   MR. NICHOLLS: Sorry.

18   THE COURT: And the question was from whom did

19   Mrs. Watson borrowed this money?

20   THE WITNESS: Mr. Springer was one of the people she

21   borrowed the money from.

22   BY MR. NICHOLLS:

23   Q.   Who was the other?

24   A.   I can't remember.

25   Q.   Ma'am, you will see on the file, I can't remember

1   the date I'll get it. That there is a mortgage, alleged

2   mortgage granted by Mrs. Watson to Mr. Michel Springer who

3   is next door to Mr. Smith and Mrs. Joyce Griffith for the sum

4   of about $330,000. The date of the mortgage is the 20th of

5   April.

6   A.   And the payment of those moneys are verified by

7   receipts issued by both Mr.

8   THE COURT: He hasn't asked you that.

9   BY MR. NICHOLLS:

10   Q.   Mr. Smith, just for argument sake. Are you saying

11   that the money that was paid to Me, Mrs. Griffith and

12   Mr. Watson in our capacity as partners of Cottle Catford

13   came from the mortgage loan from Michael Springer?

14   A.   Was taken from -- the ones that paid you came from

15   Smith and Smith.

16   Q.   So you paid money to me?

17   A.   Yes.

18   Q.   On behalf of?

19   A.   That was out of my account.

20   Q.   On behalf of them? Where did the money come from?

21   A.   That was money that I had gotten from Mrs. Watson

22   to pay you.

23   Q.   To pay me?

24   A.   Yes.

25   Q.   And you got back your money?

1   A.   I got back my money.

2   Q.   And where did you get your money back from?

3   A.   I got my money from when the property that she

4   gave as security. So --

5   Q.   In 2012?

6   A.   Yes.

7   Q.   So you had no money between 2007?

8   A.   None, none before.

9   Q.   So in that period of time Mr. Smith there was also

10   money as you are saying by the receipts payable to

11   Mr. Watson and Mrs. Griffith; is that correct.

12   A.   Yes. Those were borrowed by Mrs. Watson from

13   Mr. Springer.

14   Q.   So Mrs. Watson borrowed money from Joyce Griffith

15   and Mr. Springer to pay Joyce Griffith?

16   A.   No, no.

17   Q.   But that's what you are telling me, sir.

18   A.   No, I did not say that.

19   Q.   But that's the logical answer.

20   A.   I did not say that.

21   THE COURT: What did he say that Mrs. Watson borrowed

22   money.

23   MR. NICHOLLS: From Michael Springer and Joyce

24   Griffith.

25   THE WITNESS: No, I did not say Joyce.

267

NOS. 151 AND 152 OF 2004 CUTTLE CATFORD & CO. (a Firm) v.
DELVINA WATSON

1   BY MR. NICHOLLS:

2   Q.   There is a mortgage from Michael Springer and

3   Joyce Griffith.

4   A.   I did not say Joyce Griffith. I did not say he

5   borrowed money, she borrowed money from Joyce Griffith.

6   THE COURT: Who did she borrow money from then --

7   BY MR. NICHOLLS:

8   Q.   Who did she borrow money from?

9   A.   I don't —

10   THE COURT: -- other than your Smith and Smith who did

11   she borrow money from?

12   THE WITNESS: I know that I lent her money.

13   THE COURT: You said she borrowed money from

14   Mr. Springer.

15   THE WITNESS: Mr. Springer lent her money to pay them.

16   MR. NICHOLLS: Right.

17   THE COURT: Mrs. Watson borrowed from

18   Mr. Springer.

19   BY MR. NICHOLLS:

20   Q.   So Mr. Griffith's name on the mortgage from

21   Mr. Springer is purely fortuitous?

22   A.   Sorry.

23   THE COURT: Fortuitous or fictitious, what's that?

24   MR. NICHOLLS: Fortuitous. Mr. Griffith's name on the

25   mortgage and Mr. Springer is purely fortuitous?

268

1   A.   I couldn't tell you.

2   Q.   So is that the same mortgage —

3   THE COURT: Counsel I can't tell you.

4   MR. NICHOLLS: You couldn't tell me.

5   THE COURT: If Ms. —

6   THE WITNESS: What I can say is.

7   THE COURT: Just a minute I am writing.

8   THE WITNESS: Let me.

9   THE COURT: Just a minute, please.

10   MR. NICHOLLS: Just a minute.

11   THE COURT: Yes, thank you.

12 BY MR. NICHOLLS:

13   Q.   The mortgage from Mr. Springer that Ms. Watson

14 gave Mr. Springer and Ms. Griffith for $330,000 was purely,

15 Ms. Griffith name there was just fortuitous?

16   THE COURT: He says no he can't tell.

17   THE WITNESS: If I am not mistaken --

18   THE COURT: He can't tell if Ms. Griffith's name —

19   THE WITNESS: If I am.

20   MR. NICHOLLS: He drew up -- prepare the document,

21 ma'am. He drew up, prepared the document, ma'am.

22   THE COURT: Well, maybe you need to ask him that for

23 the record.

24 BY MR. NICHOLLS:

25   Q.   Do you recall drawing and preparing a mortgage

1   deed between the --

2   A.   Yes, yes.

3   Q.   And what was the basis of that document? Why was

4   that document prepared?

5   A.   Because Mrs. Watson had borrowed the money to pay

6   you and Mr. Griffith and Mr. Watson.

7   Q.   But you just said that you paid. You advanced the

8   money that was paid?

9   A.   Yes.

10   Q.   So how did she then have to borrow to pay me?

11   A.   No, no. I am not saying she borrowed money to pay

12 you, because I paid, that was money advanced to the Firm.

13   Q.   She borrowed money -- She borrowed money to pay

14 Mr. Griffith and Mr. Watson?

15   A.   Yes.

16   Q.   From Mr. Griffith herself?

17   A.   I couldn't tell you.

18   Q.   No, no. You just said you did the mortgage

19 Mr. Smith?

20   A.   I did the mortgage.

21   Q.   And the mortgage said the money came from

22 Mr. Griffith and Mr. Springer?

23   A.   No, I did not say that.

24   Q.   That's the mortgage document.

25   A.   I did not say that.

1   Q. That's the mortgage document.

2   A. I did not say that the money came from

3 Mr. Griffith and Mr. —

4   THE COURT: Okay. So does the — Okay. Does the

5 mortgage document say the source of the money?

6   THE WITNESS: No, it does not.

7   MR. NICHOLLS: It says the loan is from —

8   THE WITNESS: It does not -- it does not say that.

9   MR. NICHOLLS: It says that Mr. Griffith and Michael

10 Springer lent Delvina Watson $330,000.

11   THE WITNESS: It does not say that.

12   THE COURT: Do you have the document there you can show

13 to it to him?

14   MR. NICHOLLS: The document is on record, ma'am.

15   THE COURT: I have three files here.

16   MR. NICHOLLS: Yes, I know.

17   THE WITNESS: Let me say this.

18   THE COURT: Just a minute, counsel. Just a minute.

19   THE WITNESS: Let me say this. I did not say the money

20 was borrowed from Mr. Griffith.

21   THE COURT: He has a copy of it there with —

22   MR. NICHOLLS: Oh he has a copy.

23   THE COURT: Yes.

24 BY MR. NICHOLLS:

25   Q. And Mr. Smith I am looking at the document dated

NOS. 151 AND 152 OF 2004 COTTLE CATFORD & CO. (a Firm)v. DELVINA WATSON

1   the 20th of April, 2007.

2   A.   Yes, yes.

3   Q.   Drawn and prepared by you?

4   A.   Yes, that's correct. I have it.

5   Q.   Right. And it's between Delvina Watson and

6   Michael Taylor and Joyce Griffith. For avoidance of doubt

7   is the Michael Springer, Michael Taylor Springer the

8   gentleman sitting down on your left?

9   A.   Yes.

10   Q.   Is the Joyce Janet Griffith the same Joyce Janet

11   Griffith who is a partner of Cottle Catford?

12   A.   Who was a partner, yes.

13   Q.   Was. Is she still partner? Is she still a

14   partner?

15   A.   I couldn't tell you.

16   Q.   Is there a notice that she ceased being a partner

17   that you are aware of?

18   A.   Yes, yes.

19   Q.   Right.

20   THE COURT: So she is no longer a partner of Cottle

21   Catford? Ms. Griffith is no longer a partner of Cottle

22   Catford?

23   THE WITNESS: She wasn't after the 31st of December,

24   2002, she was not a partner.

25

272

1   BY MR. NICHOLLS:

2   Q.   So why did you pay her money?

3   A.   What?

4   Q.   Why did you pay her money and --

5   A.   Because she continued as a partner for the

6   purposes of the winding up of the Company of the

7   Partnership.

8   Q.   If that is correct, sir --

9   THE COURT: Don't let's get sidetracked, we are dealing

10   with whether or not the source of the money, the source of

11   the mortgage.

12   BY MR. NICHOLLS:

13   Q.   Okay. The mortgage. The mortgage. This mortgage

14   though it was executed on the 20th of April, 2007, was not

15   recorded until September, 2009, Joyce Janet Griffith and

16   Michael Springer loaned I believe you said the amount is

17   $350,000.

18   THE COURT: Could you point him to where it says that,

19   what page are you at?

20   MR. NICHOLLS: On the second paragraph of the page,

21   ma'am.

22   THE COURT: On the first page. On the second paragraph

23   he has --

24   MR. NICHOLLS: He has —

25   THE WITNESS: The second paragraph reads follows:

NOS. 151 AND 152 OF 2004 CUTTLE CATFORD & CO. (a Firm)v.
DELVINA WATSON

1   "Witnesses that the mortgagor hereby mortgages all that land

2   and property described in the schedule to the mortgagee for

3   the principal sum of that."

4   BY MR. NICHOLLS:

5   Q.   It gives the amount?

6   A.   I can tell you. I drafted the mortgage.

7   Q.   I know. You drafted the release too?

8   A.   And it was drafted in the name of Mr. Springer and

9   Mr. Griffith as trustees.

10   Q.   Trustees now.

11   A.   They were trustees for the money that I paid you

12   as well.

13   Q.   With respect, ma'am, that is not on the face of

14   the document and Mr. Smith will have to produce —

15   A.   It doesn't have to be. You don't put trusteeship

16   on the face of a document.

17   Q.   I don't know what law Mr. Smith practised. In

18   fact I do know —

19   A.   I am telling you, you don't.

20   Q.   I do know.

21   THE COURT: Do, Mr. Smith, do you accept that this

22   second paragraph identifies the mortgagees as Mr. Springer

23   and Joyce Griffith?

24   THE WITNESS: Yes, that's correct, Madam, that is

25   correct.

274

1   THE COURT: Yes.

2   THE WITNESS: That is correct.

3   BY MR. NICHOLLS:

4   Q.   So it follows then, Mr. Smith, it follows that

5   Mrs. Watson borrowed money from Michel Springer and Joyce

6   Griffith?

7   A.   It does not follow. With respect it does not

8   follow.

9   Q.   Mr. Smith, you have said to the Court that you

10 accept that Mrs. Watson borrowed money from Michael Springer

11 and Joyce Griffith; is that correct?

12   A.   No, I did not say that.

13   Q.   What did you say?

14   A.   I said that she borrowed money from Mr. Springer

15 to pay Ms. Griffith and Mr. Watson --

16   Q.   Is that document then fictitious?

17   A.   -- not what I said.

18   THE COURT: Is this is a fictitious document then?

19   THE WITNESS: Sorry.

20   THE COURT: Why is Joyce Griffith's name on it --

21   THE WITNESS: Yes, that's correct.

22   THE COURT: -- as a mortgagee?

23   THE WITNESS: That is correct, Madam, and she was a

24 trustee.

25   THE COURT: Well it does not say so on the face of the

NOS. 151 AND 152 OF 2004 COTTLE CATFORD & CO. (a Firm) v.
DELVINA WATSON

1   document.

2   THE WITNESS: But it doesn't have to. You do not have

3   to put that on the deed.

4   BY MR. NICHOLLS:

5   Q.   Mr. Smith?

6   A.   You do not have to put that on the deed.

7   Q.   Mr. Smith, I want to be clear, because consider me

8   an idiot I don't know. I know you do, but consider me an

9   idiot, I give you permission this time. There is a document

10   on record at the land registry which $1,800 in stamp duty

11   was paid in which it says that Michael Springer and Joyce

12   Griffith lent Delvina Watson?

13   A.   It did not say that. It does not say that.

14   Q.   All right. Let me correct myself. Let me correct

15   myself. It said that Delvina Watson charges property for

16   the acknowledgment of $330,000.

17   A.   That's correct.

18   Q.   Right?

19   A.   Does not say by who.

20   Q.   Okay. Okay. Is the Joyce Griffith that took this

21   mortgage and the presumption to a reasonable person would be

22   advanced probably after — the same Joyce Griffith that is a

23   partner of Cottle Catford or was a partner of Cottle

24   Catford?

25   A.   She was a partner of Cottle Catford.

1   Q.   Is it the same person?

2   A.   Sorry.

3   Q.   Is it the same person?

4   THE COURT: The Joyce — you are asking if the Joyce

5 Griffith who is the mortgagee in this document, the same

6 Joyce Griffith who was a partner in Cottle Catford?

7   THE WITNESS: Well, that is correct, the same person.

8 BY MR. NICHOLLS:

9   Q.   Is it the same Joyce Griffith?

10   A.   Yes.

11   Q.   That you are tendering receipts as evidence of

12 receiving a cheque for the amount of money?

13   A.   Yes, that's the same Joyce Griffith.

14   Q.   So Joyce Griffith, in effect lent money to pay

15 herself?

16   A.   No. There is nothing that says that Joyce

17 Griffith lent that money.

18   Q.   So why is her name on the loan?

19   A.   Because she is a trustee.

20   Q.   Of what?

21   THE COURT: And what were her duties as trustee? Where

22 does the document say what her duties were as trustee?

23   THE WITNESS: That is correct.

24   THE COURT: I didn't know that we could create secret

25 trusts in this manner.

NOS. 151 AND 152 OF 2004 COTTLE CATFORD & CO. (a Firm)v.
DELVINA WATSON

1   THE WITNESS: You don't have to. You would not put the

2   trusteeship on the document.

3   MR. NICHOLLS: Ma'am, at this point I think that,

4   sorry. At this point I think that Ms. Griffith should be

5   called because —

6   THE COURT: She hasn't filed anything in the

7   injunction.

8   MR. NICHOLLS: No, no, no. But Griffith, ma'am, and I

9   am saying this has in other issues denied that this loan

0   ever existed. She said it was fictitious. So --

1   THE COURT: So you have sworn evidence to that effect

2   or correspondence?

3   MR. NICHOLLS: I would have to find -- there are court

4   files to that statement.

5   THE COURT: Okay.

6   BY MR. NICHOLLS:

7   Q. Anyhow, but I would move on, ma'am. So Mr. Smith

8   is not accepting this point.

9   Okay, so let's assume that there was no loan to Joyce

0   Griffith. Are you aware, Mr. Smith, that Joyce Griffith and

1   Allan Watson are severely indebted to the Firm of Cottle

2   Catford and Company?

3   A. I am not aware of that.

4   Q. Did you ever?

5   THE COURT: Just a minute, counsel.

1   MR. NICHOLLS: Sorry. Did you — sorry.

2   THE COURT: Just a —

3   MR. NICHOLLS: Sorry.

4   THE COURT: Yes?

5   BY MR. NICHOLLS:

6   Q.   Did you ever investigate them, sorry, represent

7   them in another aspect of recovering money for Cottle

8   Catford?

9   THE COURT: This is Griffith and Watson?

10   MR. NICHOLLS: Yes.

11   THE COURT: Counsel did you ever represent Mr. Griffith

12   and Mr. Watson in the recovery --

13   THE WITNESS: No. I represented Ms. Griffith.

14   BY MR. NICHOLLS:

15   Q.   Not Mr. Watson?

16   A.   In an action brought by Phillip Nicholls.

17   THE COURT: Yes?

18   BY MR. NICHOLLS:

19   Q.   You represented Ms. Griffith?

20   A.   Yes.

21   Q.   Until you accused me of assaulting you and when

22   you --

23   A.   No, no. Until you assaulted me.

24   Q.   I didn't. Was I every charged, sir?

25   THE COURT: Is that relevant?

NOS. 151 AND 152 OF 2004 COTTLE CATFORD & CO. (a Firm)v.
DELVINA WATSON

1   MR. NICHOLLS: No. Well, no, I am, well just ex —

2   A.   I had to withdraw from the case.

3   Q.   Now you accused me of assaulting you.

4   A.   I had to withdraw from the case.

5   Q.   Right. Are you aware of the outcome of that case

6   sir?

7   A.   Sorry.

8   THE COURT: This is the one against Ms. Griffith?

9   THE WITNESS: Of what case?

0   BY MR. NICHOLLS:

1   Q.   Of the outcome of that case?

2   A.   No.

3   Q.   You are not aware? You are not aware that I got a

4   judgment for over, about 500 and that she appealed it and

5   lost; and that she is currently indebted to Cottle Catford?

6   A.   I am not aware of that.

7   Q.   You are not aware of that. Okay. So at the time

8   —

9   THE COURT: But counsel you really want me to refresh.

0   She is not aware that —

1   MR. NICHOLLS: Sorry, ma'am, but —

2   THE COURT: Ms. —

3   MR. NICHOLLS: — it's been so long that I have had to

4   deal with this sort of charade here, sorry, ma'am, my

5   apologies.

280

1   THE COURT: That Mr. Nicholls got judgment.

2   MR. NICHOLLS: You are not aware that I obtained

3 judgments.

4   THE COURT: Against?

5   MR. NICHOLLS: Allan Watson or Joyce Griffith.

6   MR. SPRINGER: May it please, Your Ladyship, I don't

7 understand how the counsel could refer to this as a charade

8 and I take strong objection to it. We either serious or we

9 are not.

10   THE COURT: Who said that word?

11   MR. SPRINGER: He just used that word. I heard that

12 word.

13   THE COURT: Well, I didn't hear, I was busy trying to

14 write.

15   MR. SPRINGER: Well, I heard it.

16   MR. NICHOLLS: Ma'am, I said a charade referencing to

17 the Cottle Catford which has been going on from 2000 in the

18 system, not these proceeding here. If counsel takes offence

19 to it —

20   THE COURT: And that Ms. Griffith is indebted to Cottle

21 Catford in what sum?

22   MR. NICHOLLS: The two of them with interest and costs,

23 right now, I would say $3,000,000 (three million dollars).

24   THE COURT: Thirty what?

1   and costs, it's nearly $3,000,000 between the two of them.

2   BY MR. NICHOLLS:

3   Q.   So, Mr. Smith, you are unaware, so that even if

4   Ms. Griffith was entitled to money then, when you paid the

5   money to her, you were unaware that she was indebted to

6   Cuttle Catford?

7   A.   No, no.

8   Q.   You didn't know that?

9   A.   No, no. I was not interested in that matter.

10   Q.   Of course you didn't -- that is the whole point of

11 --

12   A.   For the simple reason.

13   Q.   You are not interested in it?

14   A.   For the simple reason --

15   Q.   That is the truest thing you said.

16   A.   My position has always been that there was no

17 indebtedness between the partners as the law states --

18   MR. NICHOLLS: Ma'am, this has been the germane problem

19 that's facing us here. Mr. Smith has taken a position. The

20 Court of Appeal has told him he is talking foolishness, and

21 he has gone down the line in trying to -- Mr. Smith is now

22 saying he does not believe that Ms. Griffith borrowed, lent

23 the money to Ms. Watson that was the subject of the receipt

24 that he can't produce a cheque for. If that is so, ma'am, I

25 am asking that we adjourn for Mr. Smith to bring either the

1   receipt, sorry, the cheque, the ledger or —

2   A.   The receipts --

3   Q.   No, no, no, no, no, no.

4   A.   The receipts are here.

5   Q.   Mr. Griffith or Mr. Watson. That receipt is not

6   signed by him and I am not accepting his evidence that is

7   here.

8   A.   The receipts are there with the money was made to

9   Mr. Watson.

10   THE COURT: He has already said that there is no ledger

11 entry and he has already said that he doesn't have the

12 cheque.

13   MR. NICHOLLS: He doesn't have the cheque?

14   THE COURT: So I do not know what I would be making an

15 order for.

16   MR. NICHOLLS: Okay. Well, ma'am, we leave the whole

17 justice to you.

18   THE COURT: But I don't think you should get confused

19 in what would be your submissions.

20 BY MR. NICHOLLS:

21   Q.   So, Mr. Smith, you your evidence is that you gave

22 the cheques or you gave the money to Mr. Watson and

23 Mr. Griffith?

24   A.   I did not pay Mr. Watson or Mr. Griffith I said

25 so.

NOS. 151 AND 152 OF 2004 CUTTLE CATFORD & CO. (a Firm) v.
DELVINA WATSON

1   Q.   You just said that. Who paid the money?

2   A.   Um.

3   Q.   Who paid them, sir?

4   A.   I said Mrs. Watson borrowed money.

5   Q.   So who paid them?

6   THE COURT: He is asking about the actual cheques,

7 tendering of the cheques to them.

8 BY MR. NICHOLLS:

9   Q.   Who paid them?

10   THE COURT: Who tendered the checks to Mr. Watson and

11 Mr. Griffith?

12   THE WITNESS: Mrs. Watson paid them and received a

13 receipt for it.

14 BY MR. NICHOLLS:

15   Q.   Mrs. Watson received a receipt?

16   A.   Was signed by Mrs. Watson.

17   Q.   So she can confirm that? She can confirm that?

18   A.   Mrs. Watson signed these.

19   Q.   Mrs. Watson?

20   A.   Mrs. Watson and Ms -- issued the moneys to them

21 and they gave her the receipt.

22   Q.   Ma'am, I know that I would say without shame,

23 ma'am, I used to call Mr. Smith, Uncle Vernon, I regret the

24 day that name ever came to my name. But I would --

25   THE COURT: There is no need to for personalizing.

NOS. 151 AND 152 OF 2004 CUTTLE CATFORD & CO. (a Firm)v.
DELVINA WATSON

1   MR. NICHOLLS: I would like the Marshal, ma'am, to show

2   Mr. Smith, Mrs. Watson's affidavit here in which she said:

3   "On the 16th day of April, I by my said attorney-at-law paid

4   to Allan Watson the sum of." That's Mrs. Watson's

5   affidavit.

6   THE COURT: What paragraph?

7   MR. NICHOLLS: Paragraph, paragraph seven drawn and

8   prepared by Alvan Babb, dated, and it has a notice saying

9   that the Partnership has ended and that dated the 20th of

10   September, 2007.

11   THE COURT: Paragraph seven.

12   MR. NICHOLLS: Mr. Springer that is what I got to show

13   you.

14   THE COURT: He is showing you paragraph seven.

15   MR. NICHOLLS: Paragraph seven.

16   THE WITNESS: Paragraph?

17 BY MR. NICHOLLS:

18   Q. Paragraph seven. Read paragraph seven. You have

19 just said that you didn't pay her, pay them.

20   A. I did not pay them.

21   Q. But, Mr. Smith?

22   A. I paid you. That's what I said.

23   Q. Can I read — Can you read the paragraph,

24 Mr. Smith, to her lady?

25   A. On the 15th of April I by my said attorney paid to

1   Allan Watson --

2   Q.   Right?

3   A.   -- the sum of that.

4   Q.   I by my said attorney paid to Allan Watson.

5   THE COURT: So in effect, were you the individual who

6   actually tendered the cheques on Mrs. Watson's behalf?

7   THE WITNESS: I would probably -- I would probably have

8   paid them on that. I would probably have tendered her the

9   money.

10   THE COURT: To Ms. Griffith and Mr. Watson?

11   THE WITNESS: Yes. I would have tendered, but as I

12   said Mrs. Watson borrowed those moneys from Mr. Springer.

13   BY MR. NICHOLLS:

14   Q.   And Ms. Griffith.

15   A.   Sorry.

16   Q.   And Ms. Griffith and Ms. Griffith?

17   A.   Yes, those were paid. Those were not paid by me.

18   Q.   They were not paid you?

19   A.   No.

20   Q.   So, Ms. Watson is a liar? Mrs. Watson is a liar?

21   A.   Actually what she say: "I by my attorney at law."

22   She didn't say that I paid the money.

23   Q.   So somebody lying, Mr. Smith?

24   A.   She did not say I paid the money out of my pocket.

25   Q.   I never expected you to pay the money out of your

286

1 pocket, is not what we are saying. The answer is whether

2 the money came through the Firm of Smith and Smith where a

3 cheque can be traced or not?

4   A.   It was not paid --

5   Q.   So, Mrs. Watson is lying?

6   A.   What?

7   Q.   Mrs. Watson is lying?

8   A.   But this is our client.

9   Q.   What is it, stretching the truth?

10   A.   Did she say Smith and Smith paid them?

11   Q.   She just said my attorney Vernon Smith.

12   A.   Did she say the money was a cheque from Vernon

13 Smith or Smith and Smith.

14   Q.   In closing, Mr. Smith, I just want confirmation

15 finally from you that it is your evidence that the total

16 debt of $270,000 was paid by payments to Allan Watson and

17 Joyce Griffith and myself. You admitted that that money

18 didn't go to Cottle Catford? And --

19   THE COURT: You are asking a lot of things.

20 BY MR. NICHOLLS:

21   Q.   Sorry. Is it correct, that it is evidence that it

22 went to Allan Watson, myself and Joyce Griffith?

23   A.   It went to?

24   Q.   Allan Watson, Joyce Griffith and myself?

25   A.   Yes, as partners of Cottle Catford.

1   Q.   As partners in Cuttle Catford.

2   A.   Yes.

3   Q.   And which partnership ended in 2002?

4   A.   That is correct.

5   Q.   And when were those receipts that you said issued

6 were they issued?

7   A.   But they --

8   Q.   What's the date on those receipts?

9   A.   2007.

0   Q.   2007.

1   A.   And the Partnership would have continued until the

2 winding up is completed.

3   Q.   Can I ask you to reconsider. Do you know that

4 there is lawsuit in another matter in which you defended it

5 on the ground that it had nothing to do with them in the law

6 practice?

7   A.   What's that?

8   Q.   In 2006, I have a defence from you and another

9 aspect saying --

0   A.   What, what?

1   Q.   I just drawing --

2   THE COURT: Slowdown, counsel.

3   MR. NICHOLLS: Sorry.

4   THE COURT: Speak slowly.

5

288

1   BY MR. NICHOLLS:

2   Q.   Do you recall in another matter filing a defence

3   stating that Joyce Griffith and Allan Watson in 2004 had

4   nothing to do with Cottle Catford?

5   A.   The Cottle Catford that existed in two thousand

6   and -- that was formed after 2002.

7   Q.   Okay. Now finally Mr. Smith?

8   A.   That had nothing to do —

9   Q.   Finally the 2000 and -- Receipts that you referred

10   to have appeared on the court file and if, ma'am, had the

11   chance she would find them. Can you indicate how they got

12   there?

13   A.   They would have been filed. They would have been

14   sent to the Registry for filing.

15   Q.   There is a letter from Registrar indicating that?

16   A.   I have no letter of the Registrar.

17   Q.   There is letter from the Registrar signed Madam

18   Justice Scott, Maureen Crane-Scott as she then was that they

19   were not through official channels?

20   A.   That they were not?

21   Q.   They were not through official -- They do not bear

22   a court stamp?

23   A.   But they were on the file of the court registry.

24   Q.   So they flew in from Dee-Wee; right? They dropped

25   off from Dee-Wee.

NOS. 151 AND 152 OF 2004 CUTTLE CATFORD & CO. (a Firm)v.
DELVINA WATSON

1   THE COURT: So counsel, can I find out from him whether

2   he is aware whether the receipts were filed.

3   MR. NICHOLLS: That is why I am asking, either how they

4   got there.

5   THE WITNESS: The receipts were filed on the court

6   registry.

7   BY MR. NICHOLLS:

8   Q.   By who?

9   A.   They would have been taken by my office by my

10   clerk.

11   Q.   Do you still have the same clerk that worked with

12   you all these years?

13   A.   No.

14   Q.   Is that clerk still alive?

15   A.   No, well I couldn't tell you.

16   Q.   Oh. You couldn't tell me. Is your clerk still

17   with you?

18   A.   Not that clerk.

19   Q.   How long has your clerk been —

20   A.   -- with me?

21   Q.   Yes.

22   A.   The present clerk was with me only about three or

23   four years.

24   Q.   Okay. And do you remember the name of the clerk?

25   A.   I can't remember.

1   Q.   I can ask around. I have a clerk who has been

2   around 30 years.

3   A.   Those receipts were I am advised were on the file

4   of the court.

5   Q.   But they don't have the court's stamp?

6   A.   Well I couldn't tell you about that. I wouldn't

7   have put them on, because I don't access.

8   Q.   It was beneath your dignity to handle a court

9   file, Smith?

10   THE COURT: Were they served on Cottle Catford? When

11   they were filed in the Registry, were they served? Were

12   copies served on Cottle Catford?

13   THE WITNESS: Served on?

14   THE COURT: Cottle Catford.

15   When they were filed, were copies served on Cottle

16   Catford?

17   THE WITNESS: Could not have been served on Cottle

18   Catford, because they did not exist at that time as an

19   office.

20   THE COURT: But they were. It was filed in a matter

21   Cottle Catford vs somebody.

22   THE WITNESS: It would have been filed in this suit.

23   THE COURT: Yes.

24   MR. NICHOLLS: Right.

25   THE COURT: So was the plaintiff in that suit —

1   THE WITNESS: Yes, Madam.

2   THE COURT: -- served with a copy of the receipts?

3   MR. NICHOLLS: He say they didn't exist. The plaintiff

4   didn't exist.

5   THE WITNESS: It would not have been served on Cottle

6   Catford.

7   BY MR. NICHOLLS:

8   Q. Why is that?

9   Ma'am I have no further questions.

10   A. It would not have been served on Cottle Catford,

11   because Cottle Catford was only exist or continued to exist

12   for the purposes of the winding up. They had no office as

13   such.

14   Q. But you admit addressing letters to Cottle Catford

15   since that date; do you?

16   A. Beg your pardon?

17   Q. Did you -- Do you admit writing letters addressed

18   to the Law Firm of Cottle Catford and Company?

19   A. I wrote?

20   Q. Letters to the Law Firm of Cottle Catford and Co?

21   A. Yes. After 2002, but that was -- that was not the

22   Partnership, that was a Sole Trader.

23   Q. It was a Sole Trader?

24   A. Yes.

25   Q. So why you didn't serve that? Have you ever put

1   this nonsense on record?

2   A.   Beg your pardon?

3   Q.   Have you ever put this nonsensical argument on

4   record?

5   THE COURT: Counsel?

6   MR. NICHOLLS: Sorry.

7   THE COURT: That is not --

8   BY MR. NICHOLLS:

9   Q.   Sorry, ma'am.

10   Have you ever filed these arguments in any matter

11   dealing with Cottle Catford?

12   A.   Yes. We have, we have. I have made submissions

13   to that effect.

14   Q.   And what has happened to them? What has happened

15   to them?

16   A.   As a matter of fact some of the applications I

17   made in respect of the matter caused your thing to be

18   dismissed.

19   Q.   My thing to be dismissed?

20   A.   Your application on the court in respect of them

21   to be dismissed.

22   Q.   Which application is that Mr. Smith, can you show

23   me? Which application has been dismissed?

24   A.   I have, I have about 15, more than — I have at

25   least six different actions that you brought for Cottle

1 Catford.

2   Q.   And you say that with pride Mr. Smith?

3   A.   Yes.

4   Q.   You say it with pride?

5   A.   I can bring them to the Court tomorrow.

6   Q.   But you can't bring the receipts from the office?

7   A.   What?

8   Q.   You can't bring the cheque receipts, you could

9 bring all these other things; you can't bring the cheques?

0   A.   My files are kept you know.

1   Q.   But not your cheque receipts.

2   A.   Not, no.

3   Q.   Okay?

4   A.   Not receipts. What receipts?

5   Q.   Sorry, Mr. Smith.

6   A.   This receipt I have kept.

7   Q.   No, no, no. The cheque. The cheque in which it

8 was paid?

9   A.   I don't deal -- The cheque would be dealt with by

0 the accounting department.

1   Q.   So, the accounting department you are not in

2 charge?

3   A.   No. In fact I am not in charge.

4   Q.   You are not in charge. You signed the cheque?

5   A.   Sorry.

NOS. 151 AND 152 OF 2004 COTTLE CATFORD & CO. (a Firm)v.
DELVINA WATSON

1   Q.   You signed the cheque?

2   A.   I would have signed it for my accountant.

3   Q.   Okay, Mr. Smith?

4   A.   My accountant has --

5   Q.   Ma'am, I have no further questions for you,

6 Mr Smith?

7   A.   -- that signature.

8   MR. NICHOLLS: I honestly believe, Mr. Smith, generally

9 believe so.

10   Ma'am, if you would be minded, I would be very brief

11 with Mrs. Watson.

12   Could she come to the witness stand, she is not a

13 member of Bar.

14   THE COURT: Mrs. Watson?

15   MR. SMITH Q.C: I would like to --

16

17   DELVINA WATSON being duly sworn,

18   testifies as follows:

19   THE COURT: Madam please sit and let the microphone

20 come down.

21   Q.   Your name, please?

22   A.   Delvina Watson.

23   Q.   Address?

24   A.   Long Bay, St. Philip.

25   Q.   Pardon me?

1   Q.   You signed the cheque?

2   A.   I would have signed it for my accountant.

3   Q.   Okay, Mr. Smith?

4   A.   My accountant has --

5   Q.   Ma'am, I have no further questions for you,

6 Mr Smith?

7   A.   -- that signature.

8   MR. NICHOLLS: I honestly believe, Mr. Smith, generally

9 believe so.

0   Ma'am, if you would be minded, I would be very brief

1 with Mrs. Watson.

2   Could she come to the witness stand, she is not a

3 member of Bar.

4   THE COURT: Mrs. Watson?

5   MR. SMITH Q.C: I would like to --

6

7   DELVINA WATSON being duly sworn,

8   testifies as follows:

9   THE COURT: Madam please sit and let the microphone

0 come down.

1   Q.   Your name, please?

2   A.   Delvina Watson.

3   Q.   Address?

4   A.   Long Bay, St. Philip.

5   Q.   Pardon me?

1   A.   Long Bay, St. Philip.

2   THE COURT: Mr. Babb or counsel do you wish to lead

3   her?

4   MR. BABB: Yes, ma'am.

5   EXAMINATION-IN-CHIEF BY MR. BABB:

6   BY MR. BABB:

7   Q.   Mrs. Watson?

8   A.   Yes.

9   Q.   Now, is it true to say that the reason you are

10   here is as a result of proceedings being brought against

11   you?

12   A.   Yes sir. Yes, ma'am.

13   Q.   Now, those court proceedings are styled Cottle

14   Catford and Delvina Watson, that's just for the record of

15   the Court?

16   A.   Yes, ma'am.

17   Q.   But?

18   THE COURT: Mr. Babb?

19   BY MR. BABB:

20   Q.   Do you understand that?

21   A.   Yes, ma'am.

22   THE COURT: Mr. Babb, pull the microphone down. Yes,

23   thank you.

24   BY MR. BABB:

25   Q.   Now, in those court proceedings, is it true to say

1   that you were brought before the court for debt owed to

2   Cottle Catford?

3   A.   Yes, ma'am.

4   Q.   And is it true to say that you acknowledged that

5   you owed a debt to Cottle Catford?

6   A.   Yes, ma'am.

7   Q.   Now, is it true to say that the Cottle Catford

8   that you acknowledged that you owed the debt to, do you know

9   who the partners of Cottle Catford were?

10   A.   Yes, ma'am.

11   Q.   Can you tell the Court?

12   A.   Allan Watson, Joyce Griffith and Phillip Nicholls

13   to my knowledge.

14   Q.   Do you recall when, exactly when this debt that

15   you acknowledged was accrued to Cottle Catford?

16   A.   No, I do not recall.

17   Q.   Right. Was it the before the 31st of December,

18   2002?

19   A.   To my knowledge.

20   THE COURT: Pardon me?

21   MR. BABB: Pardon?

22   THE COURT: I didn't hear what you said, ma'am.

23   THE WITNESS: To my knowledge.

24   BY MR. BABB:

25   Q.   Yes. You said, you are saying to your knowledge

1   the debt was accrued before the 31st of December, 2002?

2   A.   Yes, ma'am.

3   Q.   And it would be fair to say that the -- at the

4   time that the debt was accrued, it was owed to Cottle

5   Catford as you know it with partners being Joyce Griffith,

6   Phillip Nicholls and Allan Watson?

7   A.   Yes, ma'am.

8   Q.   Do you know what happened to that Cottle Catford

9   as you know it?

10   A.   No, sir. No, ma'am.

11   Q.   Are you aware that that Cottle Catford as you know

12   it was dissolved on the 31st of December, 2002?

13   A.   No, ma'am.

14   Q.   Right?

15   A.   I don't recall.

16   Q.   Now, the debt that you acknowledged owing to

17   Cottle Catford, did you have an attorney at the time in

18   respect of that matter?

19   A.   Could you repeat?

20   Q.   At the time of you acknowledging the debt owed to

21   Cottle Catford, who was your attorney? Are you hearing me

22   Mr. Watson?

23   A.   I am hearing you, but I don't remember. I don't

24   recall.

25   Q.   Right. Do you recall the amount of money that you

1   acknowledged owing to Cottle Catford?

2   A.   I know it was three hundred and plus thousand.

3   Q.   Did you have a mortgage at any time in respect of

4   that amount owed?

5   A.   Yes, I did.

6   THE COURT: Yes.

7   BY MR. NASH:

8   Q.   Can you recall who were the persons holding the

9   mortgage?

10   A.   No, I don't recall.

11   Q.   The moneys that you acknowledged were owed to

12 Cottle Catford, did you pay them or give instructions for

13 them to be paid at any time?

14   A.   I gave instructions for the whole matter to the

15 handled.

16   Q.   And to the best of your knowledge were those

17 moneys paid?

18   A.   To the best of my knowledge, yes.

19   Q.   Now, when you gave instructions for them to be

20 paid, would it be fair to say that you would have given

21 those instructions to an attorney-at-law?

22   A.   Yes, I did.

23   Q.   And did that attorney-at-law in your conversations

24 subsequent to your instructions, advised you that your debt

25 was liquidated in full?

1   A.   Yes, sir.

2   Q.   Now, in your dealings with Cottle Catford as you

3 referred to earlier having partners of Joyce Griffith, Allan

4 Watson and Phillip Nicholls, did you have any dealings, any

5 transactions or any business with any Cottle Catford that

6 did not include those three persons as partners?

7   A.   No, sir.

8   Q.   No, ma'am.

9   A.   No, ma'am.

10   Q.   I am asking the questions, but you are answering

11 the Court?

12   A.   Thank you.

13   Q.   So the judgment which you acknowledged, it will be

14 fair to say then that that judgment was judgment in respect

15 of Cottle Catford as you know it with those three persons

16 mentioned before as partners?

17   A.   Yes, ma'am.

18   Q.   Ms. Watson, are you aware that moneys were

19 advanced on your behalf for payment?

20   A.   Yes, ma'am.

21   MR. NICHOLLS: I didn't hear the question, ma'am.

22 Moneys were advanced to do what?

23   MR. BABB: On her behalf for payment.

24   THE COURT: Madam, don't bend down like that in here,

25 please. You doing it again. You need to pull up the thing

NOS. 151 AND 152 OF 2004 CUTTLE CATFORD & CO. (a Firm) v.
DELVINA WATSON

1   a little higher.

2   THE WITNESS: Certainly.

3   MR. BABB: That is all, ma'am.

4   THE COURT: Mr. Nicholls?

5   <u>CROSS-EXAMINATION BY MR. NICHOLLS</u>:

6   MR. NICHOLLS: Yes. With your permission I would like

7   to ask the Marshal show Mrs. Watson some cheques that are in

8   evidence, ma'am.

9   MR. BABB: Ma'am --

10   MR. SMITH Q.C: But we have to see them.

11   MR. BABB: -- before -- if the witness can be shown

12   anything I think --

13   MR. SMITH Q.C: We have to see them, please.

14   MR. BABB: -- counsel will have to see it first and

15   counsel would have to --

16   MR. SMITH Q.C: We have to see it.

17   MR. BABB: -- acknowledge to the Court or set a

18   foundation as to what it is that he needs to show her.

19   MR. NICHOLLS: Ma'am, the cheques have been an

20   affidavit served on the other side already.

21   MR. BABB: That does not matter.

22   MR. SMITH Q.C: We have to see those documents.

23   MR. NICHOLLS: If you want to see the cheques, ma'am, I

24   have no problem with them seeing the cheques.

25   THE COURT: How many are there?

302

NOS. 151 AND 152 OF 2004 COTTLE CATFORD & CO. (a Firm)v.
DELVINA WATSON

1   MR. NICHOLLS: There are five cheques, ma'am.

2   THE COURT: Please give --

3   THE WITNESS: I can't read them I am sorry. Can my

4   counsel read them for me, cause I do not read them without

5   magnifying glass, I am sorry.

6   BY MR. NICHOLLS:

7   Q.   You have glasses in here?

8   A.   No, I don't have my magnifying glass, I am sorry.

9   THE COURT: She needs a magnifying glass?

10   BY MR. NICHOLLS:

11   Q.   Mrs. Watson, you indicated that you dealt with

12   Cottle Catford and Company when they were three partners

13   Phillip Nicholls, Allan Watson and Joyce Griffith. Do you

14   recall the name of the attorney you dealt with at Cottle

15   Catford?

16   A.   Could you repeat that?

17   Q.   Do you recall the name of the attorney-at-law who

18   worked for you at Cottle Catford?

19   A.   Allan Watson, ma'am.

20   Q.   Allan Watson. Is Allan Watson related to you?

21   A.   Allan is my must husband.

22   Q.   Pardon?

23   A.   Yes. Yes, ma'am.

24   THE COURT: I can't hear you ma'am.

25   THE WITNESS: Yes, ma'am.

NOS. 151 AND 152 OF 2004 CUTTLE CATFORD & CO. (a Firm) v.
DELVINA WATSON

1   THE COURT: Are you related to him?

2   THE WITNESS: He is my husband I said, ma'am.

3   THE COURT: Thank you.

4   Yes?

5   BY MR. NICHOLLS:

6   Q. And your husband was also your attorney?

7   A. Yes, ma'am.

8   Q. I cannot hear you.

9   A. Yes, ma'am, at that time.

10   Q. Did he ever charge you fees.

11   A. Not to my knowledge.

12   THE COURT: Pardon?

13   THE WITNESS: Not to my knowledge, ma'am.

14 BY MR. NICHOLLS:

15   Q. So the relationship between you and Allan Watson

16 was not one of client and attorney?

17   A. He was my attorney. He was my husband.

18   Q. He was your attorney. He was your husband, but he

19 charged you no fees.

20   MR. BASS: I think that is a decision for the attorney

21 to make, but he is not here right now.

22   MR. NICHOLLS: Ma'am.

23   THE COURT: And therein lies the rub.

24   MR. BASS: Pardon, ma'am.

25   THE COURT: And therein lies the rub.

NOS. 151 AND 152 OF 2004 CUTTLE CATFORD & CO. (a Firm) v.
DELVINA WATSON

1   BY MR. NICHOLLS:

2   Q.   Mrs. Watson?

3   A.   Yes.

4   Q.   Do you know the whereabouts of your husband,

5   attorney?

6   MR. DANE: Ma'am, how is that important, ma'am?

7   THE WITNESS: I understand I am here to answer for my

8   debt.

9   MR. DANE: Ma'am, that is not relevant to the

10 proceedings.

11   MR. SMITH Q.C: That is not relevant.

12   MR. NICHOLLS: Ma'am, she has made certain allegations

13 that I would like to substantiate from the person. Asking

14 if she knows the whereabouts of the person so that I may

15 contact them.

16   MR. DANE: Ma'am, that's not relevant.

17   MR. SMITH Q.C: That is not relevant. That is not

18 relevant. That is not relevant to the proceedings, ma'am.

19   THE COURT: Proceed counsel, moving on.

20 BY MR. NICHOLLS:

21   Q.   Mrs. Watson, you indicated you were indebted to

22 Cuttle Catford; is that correct?

23   A.   Yes, ma'am.

24   Q.   Do you recall when?

25   MR. DANE: Ma'am, I think the witness has already

NOS. 151 AND 152 OF 2004 COTTLE CATFORD & CO. (a Firm)v.
DELVINA WATSON

1   answered that question. She said she do not recall exactly

2   when, but she was sure it was before December 31, 2002. She

3   said that in her evidence-in-chief.

4   BY MR. NICHOLLS:

5   Q.   Will counsel stipulate that the affidavit that I

6   have filed listing the ledger accounts from Cottle Catford

7   along with the cheques written in the name of Mrs. Watson

8   and other persons totaling over 6270,000 and ending I

9   believe at June or July 2001 is correct?

10   THE COURT: But you have already got — have you not

11 already got judgment in that amount?

12   MR. NICHOLLS: Well, this is whole, ma'am. So, okay.

13   THE COURT: Move on.

14 BY MR. NICHOLLS:

15   Q.   Now, Mrs. Watson, while your attorney your husband

16 at Cottle Catford, did your attorney or husband write you

17 cheques on the Clients' Account to Cottle Catford?

18   MR. WATTS: Ma'am, that is an unfair question to the

19 witness. The witness cannot say where the money came from.

20 Her attorney whether he wrote cheques or not, that's all the

21 I think the witness can say. I think it is unfair to ask

22 the witness about the internal machinations of Cottle

23 Catford.

24   THE COURT: Machinations might not be an appropriate

25 word.

1   MR. BASS: Internal workings, ma'am.

2   THE COURT: Machinations give you — internal workings

3   yes, but machinations have a connotation to it, plots and

4   you know.

5   MR. BASS: Ma'am, whatever connotation it may have, My

6   Lady, may be relative. But I am saying, ma'am, that it's a

7   question that the witness cannot be properly expected to

8   answer.

9   THE COURT: Whether are not she received cheques, yes.

10   MR. BASS: Simple.

11   BY MR. NICHOLLS:

12   Q. Ma'am, do you ever recall receiving cheques from

13   Cottle Catford?

14   A. No, ma'am, not to my recollection.

15   Q. Can you see?

16   THE COURT: Just a minute. Not to your knowledge that

17   you received cheques from Cottle Catford.

18   BY MR. NICHOLLS:

19   Q. Ma'am, I don't know in the circumstances can the

20   Marshal read these cheques to Mrs. Watson? She is saying

21   she can't see them.

22   THE COURT: Well you can refer to them.

23   BY MR. NICHOLLS:

24   Q. Right. I hold in my hand, ma'am, cheques dated

25   15th of February, 2001, 11th of April, 2001, October 27th

1   2000, May 16th, 2000; all drawn in favour of Delvina Watson

2   in the handwriting and under the signature of Allan Watson

3   and totaling about 658,000. Do you recall ever receiving

4   any of those cheques, ma'am?

5   A.   No, ma'am.

6   Q.   You don't?

7   A.   No, ma'am.

8   Q.   Your signature isn't on the back of these cheques;

9   you don't recall that?

10   A.   Ma'am.

11   MR. BABB: Ma'am if she said she don't recall receiving

12   the cheques, how could he further question her about the

13   cheques, ma'am. She is not saying she didn't receive them.

14   MR. NICHOLLS: She doesn't recall.

15   MR. BABB: She is not saying that she paid. She is

16   saying she cannot recall receiving them.

17   BY MR. NICHOLLS:

18   Q.   But you recall that you are indebted to Cottle

19   Catford?

20   MR. BABB: She already said that.

21   BY MR. NICHOLLS:

22   Q.   Before, excuse me I am asking this not you.

23   MR. SMITH Q.C: Madam.

24   BY MR. NICHOLLS:

25   Q.   Before 2002; is that correct?

308

1   A.   Yes, ma'am.

2   Q.   You said, ma'am, that you do not recall when the

3 Partnership ended; is that correct?

4   A.   That's correct.

5   Q.   Are you still married to Allan Watson?

6   MR. DABE: Ma'am, what's the relevance of this, ma'am.

7   MR. SMITH Q.C: But what, Madam.

8   MR. NICHOLLS: Ma'am, the evidence here. Ma'am, the

9 evidence here is that the Partnership ended in December

10 2002.

11   MR. DABE: So what does her being married to Mr. Watson

12 has to do with that?

13   MR. SMITH Q.C: So what does that have to do?

14 BY MR. NICHOLLS:

15   Q.   Ma'am, it is her evidence that Allan is her

16 husband not me.

17   MR. DABE: So what.

18   MR. NICHOLLS: Her evidence is Allan Watson is her

19 husband. If their evidence is that the Partnership has

20 ended in 2002, I am just trying to establish if they were

21 still married the same time. I can question her about that.

22   MR. DABE: Ma'am, but what is the relevance of being

23 married to Mr. Watson has to do with it?

24   Mr. Watson has a personal capacity as being married and

25 then he has an official capacity as being a former partner.

1   In the same way, ma'am, that Joyce Griffith has a capacity

2   in a personal capacity --

3   THE COURT: Just a minute, please.

4   MR. BAGG: -- and she may have a personal capacity, a

5   professional capacity as being partner.

6   THE COURT: Just a minute, please. Even if you could

7   establish that they were still married at the time you

8   cannot impute certain knowledge.

9   MR. NICHOLLS: I am not imputing knowledge, ma'am. I

10   am simply asking Mrs. Watson in her capacity as the wife of

11   Allan Watson whether she was aware Mr. Watson no longer went

12   to work --

13   MR. BAGG: Ma'am, that is not relevant. It has nothing

14   to do with proceedings.

15   MR. SMITH Q.C: What does that have to do with her

16   debts?

17   THE COURT: What's the relevance counsel?

18   MR. NICHOLLS: Ma'am, there is a lot of argument here

19   that Mrs. Watson gave instructions to pay Mr. Watson and

20   Mr. Watson received the money as a partner in Cottle

21   Catford. Mrs. Watson is aware that Mr. Watson was no longer

22   a partner of Cottle Catford at the time. It is my argument

23   also --

24   THE COURT: So you have to frame your question

25   differently. If when -- You would have to establish from

310

1   her she said whether those payments were tendered on her

2   behalf or whether she tendered them herself. When you get

3   past that hurdle at the time they were tendered, was she

4   still married to Mr. Watson?

5   MR. NICHOLLS: That's what I just asked her.

6   THE COURT: No, but you didn't ask the base like that,

7   the basis like that.

8   MR. NICHOLLS: Mrs. Watson following Her Ladyship's

9   guide.

10   THE COURT: Which she graciously accept.

11 BY MR. NICHOLLS:

12   Q. Which I graciously accept. Were you still married

13 to Mr. Allan Watson when the debt from Cottle Catford was

14 occurring?

15   A. To my knowledge, yes.

16   Q. To your knowledge?

17   THE COURT: We are not telling secrets in here. You

18 will need to speak a little more loudly.

19   THE WITNESS: I said to my knowledge.

20   MR. SMITH Q.C: It is implied she was married.

21   MR. BASS: That is common sense.

22 BY MR. NICHOLLS:

23   Q. Are you still married to Allan Watson?

24   A. Yes, ma'am.

25   Q. You indicated to counsel that you instructed

1   counsel to settle the debt due to Cottle Catford in 2000,

2   well you didn't say when; is that correct?

3   A.   Could you repeat.

4   Q.   You indicated that you had instructed counsel --

5   THE COURT: Just a minute.

6   Mr. Royce, can I borrow a pen please, both of mine have

7   gone one time.

8   BY MR. NICHOLLS:

9   Q.   You had instructed counsel, sorry, to settle the

10 debt of Cottle Catford?

11   A.   Correct.

12   Q.   Do you recognise any persons who you dealt with

13 sitting in this court?

14   A.   Yes.

15   Q.   Pardon me?

16   A.   Yes, ma'am.

17   Q.   Who is the person that you instructed.

18   A.   Mr. Watson, Mr. Smith.

19   Q.   So, am I to understand that when you gave the

20 instructions to Mr. Smith your husband was with you?

21   MR. BASS: Pardon me.   I didn't hear the question.

22   THE WITNESS: I don't recall.

23   MR. NICHOLLS: Ma'am, the witness just said that she

24 instructed Mr. Watson and Mr. Smith with respect to the

25 debt.

NOS. 151 AND 152 OF 2004 COTTLE CATFORD & CO. (a Firm) v.
DELVINA WATSON

1   MR. DASH: All right. And your question?

2   MR. NICHOLLS: Mr. Watson was her attorney.

3   MR. DASH: And your question?

4   BY MR. NICHOLLS:

5   Q. My question to her was when these instructions

6   were given, were they given to jointly to Mr. Smith and

7   Mr. Watson?

8   A. I did not recall.

9   Q. Who then?

10   THE COURT: Just a minute.

11   MR. NICHOLLS: Sorry. You do not recall. Who then if

12   Mr. Watson and Mr. Smith --

13   THE COURT: Counsel.

14   MR. NICHOLLS: Sorry, sorry.

15   THE COURT: You have this habit. I say to you just a

16   minute.

17   MR. NICHOLLS: Sorry.

18   THE COURT: And as soon you stop you go again, just

19   pause.

20   Yes?

21   BY MR. NICHOLLS:

22   Q. Who between Mr. Watson and Mr. Smith did you

23   consider your attorney at this time or were both your

24   attorneys?

25   MR. SMITH Q.C: My lady, that's an improper question.

1   That is an improper question.

2   THE COURT: He is not asking about the nature of the

3   conversations. He is not asking any thing about law client

4   privilege.

5   MR. SMITH Q.C: No, this, this.

6   THE COURT: He is just asking who at the time —

7   MR. NICHOLLS: Did you consider?

8   MR. SMITH Q.C: Well, Madam.

9   THE COURT: -- of the debt she said she was given

10   instructions by -- she give instructions to Mr. Smith and

11   Mr. Watson. She does not recall if she gave instructions to

12   them jointly, so who did she consider at that time to be her

13   attorney.

14   MR. SMITH Q.C: In what matter?

15   THE COURT: We are dealing with the matter of the debt.

16   MR. SMITH Q.C: In what matter?

17   MR. NICHOLLS: We are dealing with the matter of the

18   debt, ma'am.

19   THE COURT: And the giving instructions.

20   MR. NICHOLLS: And the giving instructions. I am

21   asking --

22   THE COURT: That's how I understand it.

23   BY MR. NICHOLLS:

24   Q.   -- who did Mrs. Watson consider to be her

25   attorney?

1   A.   Both, ma'am.

2   Q.   Who she said?

3   THE COURT: Both.

4   MR. SPRINGER: Both.

5 BY MR. NICHOLLS:

6   Q.   Both were your attorney.

7   Did you in giving instructions to both your attorneys,

8 pay or issue or instruct that a cheque be issued to settle

9 the debt?

10   MR. DASS: Ma'am, I think that question has some

11 connotation. It needs clarity, ma'am, I myself can't

12 understand it.

13   THE COURT: She has sworn an affidavit in here.

14   MR. DASS: Yes, ma'am.

15   THE COURT: We just read, was it paragraph seven of

16 that same affidavit.

17   MR. DASS: But the question is ambiguous, ma'am.

18   THE COURT: So the question is did she give

19 instructions --

20   MR. DASS: To settle the debt?

21   MR. NICHOLLS: To settle the debt?

22   THE COURT: -- to settle the debt. Simple.

23   MR. DASS: Ma'am, if that's the case, ma'am, it's

24 already answered in affidavit.

25   MR. NICHOLLS: No, no, no, no.

315

1   MR. SMITH Q.C: She has answered it.

2   BY MR. NICHOLLS:

3   Q.   She is only about to say.

4   Did you instruct Mr. Smith to settle the debt?

5   MR. DASH: Ma'am, she already said that.

6   MR. SMITH Q.C: That is not —

7   THE COURT: Did you instruct Mr. Smith to settle the

8   debt?

9   THE WITNESS: I instructed my attorneys to settle the

10   debt.

11   THE COURT: Your attorneys meaning Mr. Smith and

12   Mr. Watson?

13   THE WITNESS: Correct.

14   MR. SMITH Q.C: Yes.

15   BY MR. NICHOLLS:

16   Q.   Did you borrow money to settle the debt?

17   A.   Yes, ma'am.

18   Q.   Who did you borrow it from?

19   A.   The first set I borrowed from the Royal Bank of

20   Canada on hearing of the debt.

21   THE COURT: You borrowed from Royal Bank of Canada?

22   THE WITNESS: And also my husband.

23   THE COURT: Yes?

24   THE WITNESS: Secured the funds.

25   THE COURT: Pardon me?

1   THE WITNESS: My husband secured the funds.

2   THE COURT: Your husband secured the funds?

3   THE WITNESS: Yes.

4   THE COURT: Yes?

5   BY MR. NICHOLLS:

6   Q.   These funds were used to repay who, ma'am?

7   A.   I instructed my attorneys to make all payments.

8   THE COURT: To who?

9   THE WITNESS: To all payments to who the debt was owed.

10 BY MR. NICHOLLS:

11   Q.   So I —

12 THE COURT: Just a minute counsel.

13 MR. NICHOLLS: Sorry.

14   Q.   I have acknowledged receiving funds, Mrs. Watson.

15 So your evidence is that you secured a loan from Royal Bank

16 of Canada; in addition, your husband secured a loan and

17 therefore according to the previous —

18 THE COURT: No. I borrowed from Royal Bank of Canada

19 and also my husband --

20 MR. NICHOLLS: Secured the funds?

21 THE COURT: -- and my husband secured the funds.

22 BY MR. NICHOLLS:

23   Q.   Mr. Smith has indicated that he advanced the

24 payment to me, so is it correct to say that the loan you got

25 as well as the funds received from your husband were used to

1   repay him and Joyce Griffith?

2   A.   Not to my knowledge. We did not utilise the Royal

3   Bank loan.

4   THE COURT: You did not utilise the Royal Bank loan?

5   THE WITNESS: No.

6   THE COURT: I borrowed money to settle the debt. I

7   borrowed from Royal Bank of Canada and also my husband, and

8   no we did not utilise the Royal Bank loan. I am confused.

9   BY MR. NICHOLLS:

10   Q.   Mrs. Watson, do you want to explain? Are you --

11   Do you remember where the money came from?

12   A.   As in your first court appearance with me before

13   Justice Cornelius I supplied when it was stated that I

14   refused to pay the debt. I submitted a letter to Justice

15   Cornelius which stated that I had in fact gotten a loan to

16   pay the loan, but we did not use that loan afterwards. You

17   were there too.

18   THE COURT: So the question still is where did the

19   money come from to pay the debt.

20   THE WITNESS: My husband was able to secure another

21   loan, a loan that paid the debt finally.

22   BY MR. NICHOLLS:

23   Q.   Which debt was this, ma'am?

24   A.   The debt that you brought against me in the Court.

25   Q.   I brought against you?

NOS. 151 AND 152 OF 2004 COTTLE CATFORD & CO. (a Firm)v.
DELVINA WATSON

1   A.   Cottle Catford.

2   Q.   Cottle Catford? So —

3   THE COURT: To repay the debt to Cottle Catford?

4   MR. NICHOLLS: To Cottle Catford.

5   THE WITNESS: Correct.

6 BY MR. NICHOLLS:

7   Q.   And the argument is that Cottle Catford consisted

8 of myself your husband and Joyce Griffith. So you borrowed

9 money with the assistance of your husband to repay?

10   A.   That is correct, ma'am.

11   Q.   Pardon?

12   THE COURT: She said it's correct.

13 BY MR. NICHOLLS:

14   Q.   You borrowed money to repay your husband from him.

15 That is for I to find Mr. Smith.

16   THE COURT: Does she know where her husband secured

17 this other loan from?

18 BY MR. NICHOLLS:

19   Q.   Are you aware where your husband got this money

20 from?

21   A.   I do not recall.

22   THE COURT: Pardon me? You do not recall where he got

23 the money from?

24   THE WITNESS: I do not recall.

25

1   BY MR. NICHOLLS:

2   Q.   Do you recall signing a mortgage in favour of

3   Michael Springer and Joyce Griffith?

4   A.   Yes, I recall.

5   Q.   The amount of money in the mortgage is $330,000,

6   did you receive that money?

7   A.   I don't recall the figure, but I recall the

8   transaction.

9   THE COURT: That's not what he asked you.

10   BY MR. NICHOLLS:

11   Q.   Did you receive the amount of money stated in the

12   mortgage?

13   A.   My attorneys would have handled everything.

14   THE COURT: No, Madam.   No, Madam.   No, Madam.   That

15   will not do.   You recall signing a mortgage to Ms. Griffith

16   and Mr. Springer.   Did you receive the moneys that that

17   document says were loaned to you, some three and something

18   thousand dollars.   Did you receive the $300,000 from

19   Mr. Springer and Ms. Griffith?

20   A.   It was -- Did I actually receive it in my hand?

21   Well --

22   THE COURT: Or did you actually receive it in an

23   account in your name?   Did you receive that money?

24   A.   I don't recall receiving the cheque in my hands,

25   ma'am.

1   BY MR. NICHOLLS:

2   Q.   Do you recall making a payment of money to Smith

3   and Smith and or Allan Watson to settle any debt?

4   MR. BABB: Ma'am, I think the witness --

5   THE WITNESS: I don't re --

6   MR. BABB: -- has already said that she put the matter

7   in her attorneys hand to be dealt with.

8   THE COURT: Mr. Babb, with respect.

9   MR. BABB: Yes, ma'am.

10   THE COURT: There is an issue as how this was executed,

11 okay.   There is evidence of a loan.   There is this document.

12   MR. SMITH Q.C: That's correct.

13   THE COURT: This document refers to a loan, so it is

14 not unfair or unusual for counsel to be asking for

15 particulars with respect to the loan.

16   MR. BABB: I do agree with you.

17   THE COURT: The moneys going to her and the year is

18 2007, seven years ago.

19   MR. BABB: I do agree, ma'am.

20   THE COURT: There is no evidence of Alzheimer's.   It is

21 a fair question.

22   MR. BABB: I do agree, ma'am, but at the same time the

23 witness obviously is having difficulty recalling.

24   THE COURT: Well let her say that.

25   MR. BABB: And she has already.   Very well.

1   THE COURT: She is able to say that.

2   MR. BAER: But she has already made it clear, ma'am,

3   that she put the matters in the hands of her attorneys.

4   THE COURT: And there is no dispute about that, so we

5   need to know what is she saying, that the money was paid to

6   her attorneys for the business to the transacted, because we

7   have evidence of a loan. We have evidence of the payment of

8   a loan. We have according to evidence of instructions. I

9   am not disputing that.

10   MR. BAER: Very well, My Lady.

11   THE COURT: But the mechanics. I believe that is what

12   counsel is going after.

13   Proceed please, Mr. Nicholls.

14   BY MR. NICHOLLS:

15   Q. Mrs. Watson, can you -- your evidence is that you

16   put it in your attorney's hand and you left him with all the

17   instructions as to how the debt will be paid?

18   A. Yes.

19   THE COURT: But the evidence is her attorneys.

20   MR. NICHOLLS: Her attorneys.

21   THE COURT: So, I am assuming it is both Mr. Watson and

22   --

23   BY MR. NICHOLLS:

24   Q. It's Mr. Watson --

25   THE COURT: -- and Mr. Smith.

1   Q.   -- the other attorney you referred to?

2   A.   Yes, ma'am, my attorneys, I left it in the hands

3   of my attorneys to settle up.

4   Q.   Now, Mrs. Watson, you indicated that you borrowed

5   money from Mr. Springer and Ms. Griffith, has that loan been

6   repaid?

7   A.   Again, I left this matter entirely in my

8   attorneys' hands to clear up everything, ma'am.

9   THE COURT: So, Madam, do you know whether or not --

10   THE WITNESS: To my knowledge I was told and I

11   understand everything has been paid.   Everything has been

12   paid.   Everyone has been paid.

13   BY MR. NICHOLLS:

14   Q.   Including your husband?

15   A.   I cannot.

16   Q.   So, Mrs. Watson, as far as you are concerned, you

17   obtained a loan of over $270,000 to repay everybody at

18   Cottle Catford, and that loan was paid by one third to me,

19   one third to your husband and one third to Joyce Griffith;

20   is that your evidence?

21   A.   I did not participate in the payments, I left it

22   entirely to my attorneys as I said.

23   Q.   That's not the evidence?

24   THE COURT: But you received the money for the

25   payments?

NOS. 151 AND 152 OF 2004 CUTTLE CATFORD & CO. (a Firm)v.
DELVINA WATSON

THE WITNESS: I am sorry.

THE COURT: Did you receive the money in order to have

your attorney make the payments?

THE WITNESS: No, it went through my attorneys and I

asked that the matter be handled.

THE COURT: So the money went through your attorneys?

THE WITNESS: Correct.

MR. NICHOLLS: Ma'am, that's not the evidence of

Mr. Smith.

MR. GARE: That's her evidence though.

MR. NICHOLLS: With all respect, you want the case and

eat it. Mr. Smith under oath said here that he did not make

any payments directly to Joyce Griffith and Allan Watson, so

am I --

MR. GARE: But she hasn't said that either.

BY MR. NICHOLLS:

Q.   So is it then that Allan Watson and Joyce Griffith

were never paid?

MR. GARE: Ma'am, I think the witness has already said

she left it in the hands of her attorneys and told them to

settle the matter. Her attorneys corresponded with her and

told her.

THE COURT: She never said they corresponded with her.

Where did that evidence come from?

MR. GARE: Well, correspond — Ma'am, she said in her

1   evidence-in-chief that she learned from her attorneys —

2   THE WITNESS: Informed.

3   MR. BABB: -- and she just said it not even two minutes

4   ago. She learned from her attorneys that the debt was

5   settled. So to come and ask the witness about whether or

6   not A was settled in person or B was settled in person is an

7   improper question.

8   MR. NICHOLLS: But, ma'am.

9   THE COURT: No.

10   MR. BABB: Ma'am, the witness has already said, I am --

11   THE COURT: Saying that you've left something to your

12 attorneys, it does not necessarily follow that you do not

13 know what they have done on your behalf.

14   MR. BABB: Ma'am, but she has said that her attorneys

15 as far as she knows from her attorneys, the debt was settled

16 in full. She never gave evidence as to how she knew it, so

17 he took -- Mr. Nicholls asked her what the attorneys did is

18 an improper question. Mr. Nicholls will have to ask the

19 attorneys what they did on before of Mrs. Watson.

20   THE COURT: No. She may know. If she doesn't, well,

21 she will say she doesn't know.

22   MR. BABB: Ma'am, but --

23   MR. NICHOLLS: Ma'am, with all due respect Mr. Babb is

24 misleading the Court. Mr. Smith stated here that he had

25 nothing to do with the payment to Ms. Griffith and

1   Mr. Watson. He was very clear on that, on more than one

2   occasion he said he paid me.

3   MR. SMITH Q.C: I said.

4   MR. NICHOLLS: He was very clear on that.

5   MR. SMITH Q.C: I said that —

6   MR. NICHOLLS: And Mrs. Watson here is saying that —

7   MR. SMITH Q.C: — the debt.

8   THE COURT: Just a minute counsel.

9   MR. NICHOLLS: Mrs. Watson here is saying, ma'am, that

10   she left it to her attorneys.

11   MR. BARR: Simple.

12   MR. SMITH Q.C: And that is correct.

13   MR. NICHOLLS: Therefore I used the words spirited, not

14   in an offensive terms, a jackass would see that they haven't

15   been paid 'cause she said she didn't pay them. He said he

16   didn't pay them. So —

17   MR. BARR: The witness never said she didn't pay

18   anybody, she said she left it to her attorneys.

19   MR. SMITH Q.C: I also said that she borrowed money

20   from Mr. Springer.

21   MR. BARR: That was the evidence. So if you want to

22   make it up as you go long.

23   THE COURT: But she is also saying that she can't

24   remember.

25   MR. BARR: Ma'am, this is almost ten years ago.

326

NOS. 151 AND 152 OF 2004 COTTLE CATFORD & CO. (a Firm)v.
DELVINA WATSON

1   MR. NICHOLLS: Ma'am, we are talking —

2   THE COURT: Tell me something and almost ten years ago

3   and you borrowed nearly $300,000 and you -- ten years and

4   you can't remember it.

5   MR. BASS: Ma'am, but if the debt was settled and the

6   witness has said that as far as she know, her attorneys told

7   her the debt was settled. Ma'am, she has a right to take it

8   off her mind.

9   MR. NICHOLLS: But, ma'am, Mr. Babb --

10 THE COURT: And which attorneys would have told her

11 interesting, which attorneys would have told her they were

12 settled.

13 MR. NICHOLLS: Mr. Babb here, ma'am, is putting

14 Mr. Smith in grave doubt. Mr. Smith said he did not settle

15 the debt. Mr. Smith said so.

16 THE COURT: Well.

17 MR. NICHOLLS: So if --

18 MR. SMITH Q.C: That.

19 MR. BASS: Where he hear this, ma'am?

20 THE COURT: That would be for you. That would be for

21 you --

22 MR. BASS: Where did Mr. Nicholls here this?

23 MR. NICHOLLS: Mr. Smith said so in evidence. Were you

24 here?

1   money and moneys were paid to Mr. Watson and thing from

2   moneys borrowed from Mr. Springer.

3   MR. NICHOLLS: By whom?

4   MR. SMITH Q.C: By whom?

5   MR. NICHOLLS: Who paid the money?

6   MR. SMITH Q.C: Sorry.

7   MR. NICHOLLS: Who paid the money?   You said you did

8   not pay it and she said —

9   MR. SMITH Q.C: The money that was paid on her behalf.

10   MR. BASS: That was the evidence.

11   MR. NICHOLLS: But you said you did not pay it.   Who

12 paid the money?

13   THE COURT: Accuse me.   We have a witness here.

14   MR. NICHOLLS: Mrs. Watson, you are confirming that you

15 left everything in your attorneys' hands?

16   MR. BASS: Simple.

17   A.   That is correct.

18   THE COURT: Can I find out who were the attorneys then

19 who would have done the —

20   MR. NICHOLLS: -- the payments.

21   THE COURT: -- repayments of the debt, if it is still

22 the same two?

23 BY MR. NICHOLLS:

24   Q.   Yes.   It is the same two attorneys, ma'am,

25 Mrs. Watson?

NOS. 151 AND 152 OF 2004 CUTTLE CATFORD & CO. (a Firm)v.
DELVINA WATSON.

1   A.   I am sorry what did you say?

2   THE COURT: When the debt was repaid you said you

3 learnt from your attorneys that the debt had been repaid,

4 who are those attorneys?

5   THE WITNESS: I learnt that from the attorneys, yes.

6   THE COURT: Who are these, those attorneys?

7   THE WITNESS: The two attorneys that I said, Allan

8 Watson and Mr. Smith.

9   THE COURT: I am speaking in relation to the debt on

10 the mortgage to Mr. Springer and Ms. Griffith, that's what I

11 am speaking about let me be clear. Did you also learn from

12 them two that the debt to —

13   THE WITNESS: That is —

14   THE COURT: — Ms. Griffith and Mr. Springer —

15   THE WITNESS: — that is correct.

16   THE COURT: — had been repaid?

17 BY MR. NICHOLAS:

18   Q.   Are you clear on that Mrs. Watson, you are taking

19 about different debt? The debt that you borrowed to repay

20 Mr. Springer and Ms. Griffith from Mr. Springer and

21 Ms. Griffith has been cleared?

22   A.   To my knowledge that is what I said I was doing.

23   Q.   Who told that that?

24   A.   My attorneys.

25   Q.   Mr. Smith?

329

1   A.   And to my knowledge the last time we were at court

2   I remember receipts came up, so why should I doubt it.

3   Q.   When did Mr. Smith become your attorney, do you

4   recall?

5   A.   Mr. Smith was our -- was my husband and my

6   attorney from way back.

7   Q.   Way back. When did you fire him?

8   MR. DASS: Ma'am.

9   A.   Am I answering to the debt, Madam.

10 BY MR. NICHOLLS:

11   Q.   Did you every dismiss Mr. Smith?

12   MR. DASS: Oh that is a proper question.

13 BY MR. NICHOLLS:

14   Q.   Did you ever dismiss Mr. Smith from working for

15 you?

16   A.   Ma'am, this is connected with my debt that was

17 paid?

18   THE COURT: Is reasonable question.

19 BY MR. NICHOLLS:

20   Q.   Did you ever dismiss Mr. Smith?

21   A.   Pardon.

22   THE COURT: Did you ever dismiss Mr. Smith, ma'am?

23   THE WITNESS: No, ma'am.

24 BY MR. NICHOLLS:

25   Q.   Did Mr. Smith ever write you and informed you he

330

1   was no longer your attorney?

2   A.   Not that I can recall at this moment.

3   Q.   Is Mr. Allan Watson still your attorney?

4   A.   No, sir.

5   Q.   When did Mr. Watson cease being your attorney?

6   A.   I don't recall.

7   THE COURT: How much longer? The cafeteria closes at

8   2:00? Otherwise I would be --

9   MR. NICHOLLS: I am -- would say that nothing more --

10 anything more useful can't get from the witness.

11   THE COURT: Thank you.

12   Any re-ex Mr. Babb?

13   MR. BABB: Ma'am, just a few questions, ma'am.

14 <u>RE-EXAMINATION BY MR. BABB:</u>

15 BY MR. BABB:

16   Q.   Just a few questions, ma'am.

17   Mrs. Watson, you said under cross-examination that your

18 husband also secured funds to assist with the payoffs.

19   A.   Yes.

20   Q.   Do you recall how those funds were secured?

21   MR. NICHOLLS: Ma'am, I object to that.

22   THE COURT: She said RBC and then they did not use

23 them. You mean the second set of funds?

24   MR. BABB: Ma'am she said -- She said I borrowed money

25 from RBC and also my husband secured funds. That is the

NOS. 151 AND 152 OF 2004 COTTLE CATFORD & CO. (a Firm) v.
DELVINA WATSON

1   answer that I have.

2   MR. NICHOLLS: Yes, yes. Ma'am, she cannot give —

3   Look we know what's going on in here Mr. Watson is a

4   fugitive from this Island she cannot give evidence of what

5   Mr. Watson did. If they want to secure that evidence here

6   bring him.

7   THE COURT: If she knows. If she knows.

8   MR. DABB: Ma'am, but he has just established that

9   Mr. Watson is her husband.

10   MR. NICHOLLS: Uh huh.

11   THE COURT: When you were objecting.

12   MR. NICHOLLS: When you objected.

13   MR. DABB: But it went through.

14   MR. NICHOLLS: In the end you objected.

15   MR. DABB: It went through, so he can't eat his cake

16   and have it too. If he can put it in for one reason, ma'am,

17   he must take it for the other.

18   THE COURT: There is no need to be shouting please.

19   MR. NICHOLLS: No, ma'am, I am saying —

20   MR. DABB: Ma'am, I am not shouting at all my voice is

21   loud.

22   MR. NICHOLLS: — that the proper person to direct that

23   question to is Mr. Watson.

24   THE COURT: But if he can ask her if she has knowledge,

25   either she does or she does not.

1   MR. BARR: Right.

2 BY MR. BARR:

3   Q. Do you know where he secured the funds from?

4   A. Yes sir. Yes, ma'am.

5   MR. NICHOLLS: Where?

6   MR. BARR: It's me asking the questions not you.

7   THE COURT: But if you don't ask it I will.

8   MR. BARR: Very well, ma'am.

9   THE COURT: Where did he secure it from Mrs. Watson?

10   THE WITNESS: To my knowledge from Mr. Michael Springer

11 and --

12   MR. BARR: Very well.

13   THE COURT: Excuse me.

14   MR. BARR: Sorry, sorry.

15   THE COURT: That is as big a hint as they ever come.

16   MR. BARR: No, ma'am, I was not referring to

17 Mrs. Watson at all. Sorry, ma'am, I shall spoken to

18 Mr. Springer you had asked a question.

19   THE COURT: Speak to your junior counsel for me,

20 please.

21   MR. BARR: Ma'am, ma'am, I spoke to Mr. springer.

22   THE COURT: Shh.

23   MR. BARR: And I was just --

24   THE COURT: I am asking the question, shh.

25   MR. BARR: Very well, ma'am, I was not referring to the

NOS. 151 AND 152 OF 2004 CUTTLE CATFORD & CO. (a Firm)v.
DELVINA WATSON
1   conversation --

2   THE COURT: Shh.

3   MR. BABB: -- between yourself and the witness.

4   THE COURT: Shh.

5   MR. NICHOLLS: The judge is asking a question.

6   THE COURT: You were saying Mrs. Watson, where did your

7   husband secure the money from?

8   THE WITNESS: Mr. Michael Springer to my knowledge and

9   Ms. Joyce Griffith.

10   THE COURT: And Ms. Joyce Griffith.

11   MR. BABB: I didn't hear the answer. I didn't hear her

12 answer.

13   THE COURT: Yes, Mr. Babb you were re-examining.

14   MR. BABB: Ma'am, yes I only had one question, ma'am,

15 and that's it.

16   THE COURT: Oh, I thought you said you had a few

17 questions.

18   MR. NICHOLLS: He done with that.

19   MR. BABB: Ma'am, I was going to ask the witness the

20 question you asked the witness that, Your Ladyship, asked

21 the witness.

22   THE COURT: Thank you very much. Mrs. Watson, you can

23 come back down.

24   So now we will have to adjourn for a date convenient

25 for the submissions then?

1   MR. DABB: Right.

2   BY MR. DABB:

3   Q.   Do you know where he secured the funds from?

4   A.   Yes sir.   Yes, ma'am.

5   MR. NICHOLLS: Where?

6   MR. DABB: It's me asking the questions not you.

7   THE COURT: But if you don't ask it I will.

8   MR. DABB: Very well, ma'am.

9   THE COURT: Where did he secure it from Mrs. Watson?

10   THE WITNESS: To my knowledge from Mr. Michael Springer

11   and --

12   MR. DABB: Very well.

13   THE COURT: Excuse me.

14   MR. DABB: Sorry, sorry.

15   THE COURT: That is as big a hint as they ever come.

16   MR. DABB: No, ma'am, I was not referring to

17   Mrs. Watson at all.   Sorry, ma'am, I shall spoken to

18   Mr. Springer you had asked a question.

19   THE COURT: Speak to your junior counsel for me,

20   please.

21   MR. DABB: Ma'am, ma'am, I spoke to Mr. Springer.

22   THE COURT: Shh.

23   MR. DABB: And I was just --

24   THE COURT: I am asking the question, sth.

25   MR. DABB: Very well, ma'am, I was not referring to the

1   conversation --

2   THE COURT: Shh.

3   MR. RABB: -- between yourself and the witness.

4   THE COURT: Shh.

5   MR. NICHOLLS: The judge is asking a question.

6   THE COURT: You were saying Mrs. Watson, where did your

7   husband secure the money from?

8   THE WITNESS: Mr. Michael Springer to my knowledge and

9   Mr. Joyce Griffith.

10   THE COURT: And Mr. Joyce Griffith.

11   MR. RABB: I didn't hear the answer. I didn't hear her

12 answer.

13   THE COURT: Yes, Mr. Rabb you were re-examining.

14   MR. RABB: Ma'am, yes I only had one question, ma'am,

15 and that's it.

16   THE COURT: Oh, I thought you said you had a few

17 questions.

18   MR. NICHOLLS: He done with that.

19   MR. RABB: Ma'am, I was going to ask the witness the

20 question you asked the witness that, Your Ladyship, asked

21 the witness.

22   THE COURT: Thank you very much. Mrs. Watson, you can

23 come back down.

24   So now we will have to adjourn for a date convenient

25 for the submissions then?

About the Author

PHILIP VERNON NICHOLLS was born on October 6th 1960, the first of three boys of Neville and Yvonne Nicholls. Stephen is a financial analyst and Christopher an oncologist, while Philip followed in the footsteps of his father in becoming an attorney-at-law. His mother was a teacher for many years at the former Girls Foundation and Queens College, and was on staff at the University of the West Indies when Philip also joined the Faculty of Law there as an Associate Tutor ,something he did for over 20 years.

His early education was at the Merrivale Preparatory School, also known as Mrs. Carrington's school, where his two brothers were all schooled before the three of them entered Harrison College. After Harrison College he entered the Faculty of Law at the University of the West Indies, Cave Hill Campus from where he graduated with an Upper Second Class Degree in Law before completing his professional Legal Education Certificate at the Norman Manley Law School in Jamaica in 1985. From there he read and obtained a Master's in International Business Law from the Victoria University of Manchester in 1987. He was called to the Bar in Barbados in 1986 and joined the firm of Cottle Catford in January of 1987 as an associate attorney-at-law.

He was admitted as a partner of the firm from January 1st 1992 and remained as a partner of the firm until he closed it on October 30th 2009.

He is a former president of Pickwick Cricket Club, and served on the board of the Barbados Cricket Association between 1988 and 2005, the last five as honourary secretary. He has also sat on several other boards in the island, and was the last president of the Canada Barbados Business Association. He has served as chairman of the Disciplinary Committee of the Bar Association and the Barbados Hockey Federation, and currently sits on the Complaints Committee and Rules Committee of the Barbados Cricket Association.

He has three daughters, Carissa and twins named Anya and Edaynah, but is no longer married to his former wife Beverley, who is also an attorney-at-law.

Printed in Great Britain
by Amazon

65689510R00200